NATIONS
REMEMBERED

NATIONS REMEMBERED

An Oral History of the Cherokees, Chickasaws, Choctaws, Creeks, and Seminoles in Oklahoma, 1865–1907

THEDA PERDUE

University of Oklahoma Press
Norman and London

For Charles Hudson

Library of Congress Cataloging-in-Publication Date

Nations remembered: an oral history of the Cherokees,
   Chickasaws, Choctaws, Creeks, and Seminoles in
   Oklahoma, 1865-1907 / [selected by] Theda Perdue.
      p. cm.
   Includes bibliographical references and index.
   ISBN 0-8061-2523-3 (pbk.)
   1. Indians of North America—Indian Territory—History.
   2. Indians of North America—Indian Territory—History--
   Sources.
   I. Perdue, Theda, 1949-
   [E78.I5N317   1993]   92-50726
   970.004'97--dc20   CIP

Originally published in hard cover as *Nations Remembered:
An Oral History of the Five Civilized Tribes, 1865–1907*, by
Theda Perdue, the first in the Contributions in Ethnic Stud-
ies series by Greenwood Press, an imprint of Greenwood
Publishing Group, Inc., Westport, CT. Copyright © 1980 by
Theda Perdue except for the Preface to the Paperback Edi-
tion, copyright © 1993 by Theda Perdue. This paperback
edition is published by the University of Oklahoma Press,
Norman, Publishing Division of the University, with per-
mission of the author and Greenwood Publishing Group,
Inc. All rights reserved. Manufactured in the U.S.A.

1   2   3   4   5   6   7   8   9   10

Contents

Illustrations

Preface to the Paperback Edition

Much has happened since publication of the first edition of *Nations Remembered* in 1980. First of all, I have abandoned use of the phrase "Five Civilized Tribes," which appeared in the subtitle of the earlier edition. For well over a century, writers have applied the term to the Native peoples whom the United States forced from the Southeast to what is today eastern Oklahoma in the 1820s and 1830s. "Civilized" referred to their receptivity to the federal government's "civilization" program, which entailed commercial agriculture, republican government, Christianity, and fluency in English. To early observers, the Cherokees, Chickasaws, Choctaws, Creeks, and Seminoles seemed particularly adept at this cultural transformation while other Native peoples lagged behind. My own subsequent research in the Southeast, as well as that of other scholars, suggests that culture change was neither as rapid nor as complete as earlier observers and writers had thought. The individual responses within a particular population varied dramatically, and the process generally involved careful selection and adaptation rather than wholesale adoption of Anglo-American culture.[1] Furthermore, the term separates southern Indians from other Native peoples. While each people has its own history and particular set of relations with the federal government, the dominant themes, especially in terms of policy, link them. To set southern Indians apart is misleading. For example, although the Dawes Act originally exempted the five southern nations from allotment, within a decade Congress had extended allotment to them and the process was well underway. Finally, "civilized" connotes superiority and entails a value judgment that scholars should avoid. Consequently, I have chosen to retitle the second edition. Since the appearance of the first edition, scholars increasingly have used oral history in order to reconstruct the lives and experiences of people who did not leave more traditional historical sources. Charles Joyner, for example, relied heavily on interviews to analyze slave culture on coastal Carolina rice plantations, and a massive oral history project enabled Jacquelyn Dowd Hall and her coauthors to write the history of southern cotton-mill workers.[2] These studies and others demonstrate where scholars must go next with oral history. Simply presenting the interviews with annotation, as I have done here, is merely a first step. I hope that this volume not only serves to introduce students and casual readers to the southern Indians in Oklahoma, but also to challenge scholars to take the next step. The Indian-Pioneer History of Oklahoma is an enormously rich collection that scholars need to exploit in writing the ethnohistory of southern Indians. Perhaps the paperback edition of *Nations Remembered* can serve as a reminder of the collection's importance and as a rallying cry for a new history of Native people in Oklahoma.

Theda Perdue
Lexington, Kentucky

Notes

1. For example, see Michael D. Green, *The Politics of Indian Removal: Creek Government and Society in Crisis* (Lincoln: University of Nebraska Press, 1982); William G. McLoughlin, *Cherokee Renascence in the New Republic* (Princeton: Princeton University Press, 1986); James H. Merrell, *The Indians' New World: Catawbas and Their Neighbors from European Contact through the Era of Removal* (Chapel Hill: University of North Carolina Press, 1989); Daniel H. Usner, Jr., *Indians, Settlers and Slaves in a Frontier Exchange Economy: The Lower Mississippi Valley Before 1783* (Chapel Hill: University of North Carolina Press, 1992).

2. Charles Joyner, *Down By the Riverside: A South Carolina Slave Community* (Urbana: University of Illinois Press, 1984); Jacquelyn Dowd Hall, James Leloudis, Robert Korstad, Mary Murphy, Lu Ann Jones, and Christopher B. Daly, *Like a Family: The Making of a Southern Cotton Mill World* (Chapel Hill: University of North Carolina Press, 1987).

Preface to the First Edition

My introduction to the interviews conducted in the 1930s under the auspices of the Works Progress Administration came while I was doing research on *Slavery and the Evolution of Cherokee Society, 1540–1866* (Knoxville, Tenn., 1979). I used many reminiscences of slaves and masters in order to reconstruct the social institutions and experiences of these two groups in antebellum Cherokee society. Often I became so absorbed in the interviews that I read straight through entire volumes without stopping to consider whether the people were Cherokee or even had anything to do with slavery.

I decided that a volume of excerpts from the interviews would prove useful to scholars as well as interesting to the general public. Working within the guidelines established by the Oklahoma Historical Society (that no interview could be used in its entirety and that the identity of the narrator should be concealed if possible), I went through the collection of interviews in the summer of 1978 and selected those I considered most informative and revealing. Starting from almost one thousand pages copied in Oklahoma, I have narrowed the selections even further and have attempted to ascertain the validity of factual remarks. I have corrected punctuation and occasionally added conjunctions to make the narratives more readable. Following each excerpt I have noted the tribal affiliation of the subject and the volume and page of the Indian-Pioneer papers from which the excerpt was taken. In the annotations, I have corrected mistakes, provided supplemental information, and indicated

sources for material on the particular subject being discussed. I also
have given the genera for plants mentioned in the interviews; I have
omitted species because these are often uncertain.

Throughout this work, I have used the term "progressive" to refer
to those Indians who favored adoption of Anglo-American culture
and ultimate assimilation into the dominant white society. By
"traditionalist" or "conservative," I mean those Indians who wanted
to preserve traditional practices and values and to maintain their
cultural integrity. These terms often appear in historical sources and
in contemporary works; they do not represent a value judgement
on the part of the author.

Theda Perdue
Cullowhee, North Carolina

Acknowledgments

I would like to thank a number of individuals and institutions for their assistance. John Bell, John Finger, and Charles Hudson read the manuscript and offered many helpful suggestions. Gary White drew the maps, and James H. Horton provided the genera for plants mentioned in the interviews. Pelham Thomas and J. H. Perdue described obsolete farm implements, and Joyce Moore supplied information on natural dyes.

George Frizell assisted with bibliography. Katie Bark, David Griffith, and Jerome Williams performed many tedious tasks, such as verifying notes and proofreading. Sheila Anders, Kelly Hamrick, Karen Hensley, Trina Sims, Carolyn Wiggins, and Mildred Wilson typed the manuscript. My colleagues, the departmental secretary Joe Ginn and chairman Ellerd Hulbert, and my husband Lee Kennett offered support and encouragement.

A grant from the American Philosophical Society made the research possible. Vice Chancellor Robert E. Stoltz and Dean John McCrone of Western Carolina University provided financial assistance for typing and copying.

Above all, Martha Blaine, Manon Atkins, and the entire staff of the Oklahoma Historical Society were knowledgeable and cooperative. It is a genuine pleasure to do research at the Oklahoma Historical Society, and I always look forward to returning.

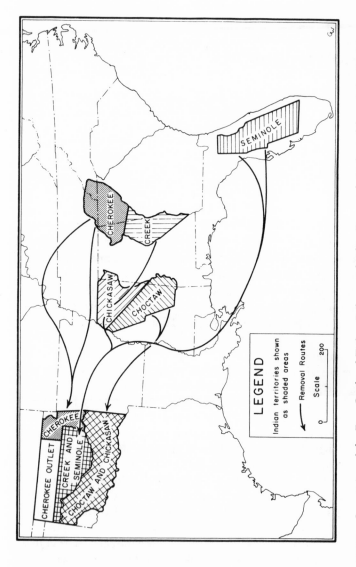

MAP 1. Locations of the Five Civilized Tribes Before and After Removal. (Adapted from John W. Morris, Charles R. Goins, and Edwin C. McReynolds, *Historical Atlas of Oklahoma*, 2d ed., Norman: University of Oklahoma Press, 1976. Used by permission of the University of Oklahoma Press.)

Introduction

The use of oral history as a specific methodological approach to the study of the past is relatively recent. Interest in this approach arises both from technological innovations, which make interviewing easier and recording more accurate, and from a desire to know about the everyday lives of former generations, the experiences of "plain folks," and the histories of people who for some reason, such as illiteracy or poverty, did not leave written records. Nostalgia for a supposedly simpler and more satisfying way of life has encouraged the recording of oral history. Teachers of literature, history, and the social sciences have capitalized on this nostalgia in order to interest their students in subjects which somehow have managed to acquire reputations for dullness. *The Foxfire Book* (ed. Eliot Wigginton, New York, 1972), containing interviews conducted in the southern Appalachians by students at Rabun Gap School in northern Georgia, represents one of the most successful efforts in this direction.[1] More importantly, however, the impetus to compile oral histories has come from a commitment on the part of many historians to people the past with individuals who never led armies, never served in Congress, never invented the cotton gin or steamboat, and never wrote a great book as well as with people who did. Thus, oral history represents the democratization of a discipline which too often has been elitist.

Historians who seek to broaden our understanding of the past in this way have found a treasure trove in the interviews conducted and compiled during the 1930s by the Writers' Project of the Works Progress Administration, a federally funded program designed to employ people on relief rolls. Many of these interviews are housed in the National Archives in Washington, D.C.; others are in state and university archives throughout the United States. Of the thousands of interviews, those given by former slaves are the most widely available. Norman Yetman selected and published what he considered to be the best of the interviews in *Life Under the Peculiar Institution: Selections from the Slave Narrative Collection* (New York, 1970), while Benjamin A. Botkin excerpted them in *Lay My Burden Down: A Folk History of Slavery* (Chicago, 1968). George P. Rawick drew heavily from the narratives in *From Sundown to Sunup: The Making of the Black Community*, the introductory volume to a published compilation of the interviews entitled *The American Slave: A Composite Autobiography*, 18 vols. (Westport, Conn., 1972). In *Such as Us: Southern Voices of the Thirties* (Chapel Hill, N.C., 1978), Tom E. Terrill and Jerrold Hirsch edited interviews with rural Southerners about the difficulties they experienced. In all cases, these collections of interviews filled a void in traditional history, and patterns emerged in the lives of people who wore linsey-woolsey instead of silk, ate collard greens and hog jowl instead of pheasant under glass, and worried about the Klan, the boll weevil, and the mortgage rather than alliances, elections, strategies, and soirées.

This particular work contains excerpts from interviews conducted in Oklahoma with Indians whose ancestors lived in the southeastern United States and, through the interviews, presents a collective autobiography of southeastern Indians from the Civil War to Oklahoma statehood. While these tribes speak different languages and have separate political organizations, their cultural traditions are remarkably similar. Apparently, this similarity does not stem from the United States government's Indian policy, which lumped together the "five civilized tribes," but from a common dependence on agriculture which began over a thousand years before their initial contacts with Europeans. Treated as a distinct group by early eighteenth-century writers such as James Adair,[2] by the British colonial and early American governments which administratively divided northern and southern tribes at the Ohio River,[3] and by modern cultural anthropologists,[4] the southeastern Indians suffered a common fate in the early nineteenth century when the United States determined to move them west of the Mississippi River and open their lands to white occupation.

The removal of the southeastern Indians from their ancestral homeland and their resettlement west of the Mississippi River is a tragic, unsavory chapter in American history but one for which the United States could find numerous precedents. From the first European incursions in North America, territorial acquisition was an essential component of the American dream, and colonizers relentlessly denied the right of native inhabitants to the land. The rapid acculturation of the southeastern Indians in the first three decades of the nineteenth century weakened old justifications for dispossessing "savages," so states whose chartered boundaries contained Indian land began to insist that tribal governments threatened their sovereignty. State legislatures extended laws over Indian residents while denying them the equal protection of state courts. Whites invaded tribal land and through purchase, fraud, or seizure, forced Indians from their homes. The refusal by Andrew Jackson's administration to intervene further emboldened the states, and the passage of the Indian Removal Act by Congress in 1830 firmly committed the federal government to negotiating the cession of Indian land and the removal of five major Indian tribes from the southeastern United States.

The removal crisis magnified cultural and economic divisions within each Indian nation, particularly the Creek, Choctaw, and Cherokee nations. Progressive Indians, who largely had abandoned traditional values and life-styles, tended to favor removal since white aggression and political turmoil jeopardized their wealth and property as well as their positions of leadership. For reasons rarely understood by progressives, the conservatives clung tenaciously to their land in the face of even the most audacious attacks on them by state governments, militia, intruders, and vigilantes. Through a variety of duplicitous means ranging from bribery to capture and circumvention of the chiefs, federal treaty commissioners formulated agreements with the tribes which led to the forced migration of the vast majority of Indians from the Southeast to what is now the State of Oklahoma. Because of the tremendous hardships and many casualties suffered by the exiles, the episode came to be known as the "Trail of Tears."[5]

After removal, the southeastern Indians were largely forgotten by white Americans. Upstaged perhaps by the "wild" Indians of the Plains, the five "civilized" tribes no longer commanded the attention of the United States government. Furthermore, the great war chiefs of the Plains captured the imagination of the American public, and the memory of even such illustrious southern warriors as the Seminole, Osceola, to say nothing of such highly acculturated leaders as the Cherokee, John Ross, began to fade. Whites became conscious of southern Indians only when their alliances appeared desirable during the Civil War, their land essential for railroad right of ways, and their natural resources available for exploitation. Even then, transactions between southern Indians and white Americans rarely aroused the excitement of the Ghost Dance, the vindictiveness of Custer's Last Stand, or the sympathy of the Nez Perce flight, and so the transplanted Indian nations from the Southeast retreated into the historical shadows.

The details of the internal dynamics of these Indian societies after removal might have been lost forever to the historical record had white America not experienced the Great Depression in the 1930s. In conjunction with the University of Oklahoma and the Oklahoma Historical Society, the Works Progress Administration employed between eighty and one hundred individuals to send questionnaires to and conduct interviews with Oklahoma citizens who were knowledgeable about the days before statehood. Grant Foreman, the well-known Oklahoma historian, supervised the collection and compilation of the information, which ultimately filled 112 volumes.[6] One copy of this "Indian-Pioneer History" is housed in the library of the University of Oklahoma; a second copy as well as an index to the material is located in the Oklahoma Historical Society in Oklahoma City.

The recollections contained in this work are from the "Indian-Pioneer History." These specific excerpts were selected to present a broad spectrum of perspectives, experiences, attitudes, and lifestyles. Nevertheless, since the societies of southeastern Indians were exceedingly complex, a limited collection of brief excerpts from the interviews cannot present a perfectly balanced view of their lives. In addition, the complete collection of interviews is not entirely representative of the population of Indian Territory. In particular, the vast majority of Indians interviewed spoke English. Fortunately, however, a few interviewers were bilgual Indians; so some translations of interviews with conservatives who knew only their native tongue could be included.[7]

Generally omitted from this particular work are mere chronicles of political events and controversies. Adequate factual accounts of treaty negotiations, elections, and tribal legislation can be found elsewhere, as the reader will see in the notes following relevant chapters. Furthermore, the presentation of a comprehensive history of the southeasterrn Indian nations is not the intent of this book. For general surveys, the reader should consult Grace Woodward, *The Cherokees* (Norman, Okla., 1963), or Peter Collier, *When Shall They Rest? The Cherokees' Long Struggle with America* (New York, 1973); Arrell M. Gibson, *The Chickasaws* (Norman, Okla., 1971); Angie Debo, *The Rise and Fall of the Choctaw Republic* (Norman, Okla., 1934); Angie Debo's study of the Creeks, *The Road to Disappearance* (Norman, Okla., 1941); and Edwin C. McReynolds, *The Seminoles* (Norman, Okla., 1957). These works should satisfy any reader's wish for background information lacking in the interviews, introductions, or annotations.

In using the interviews as historical sources, one must consider that the subjects were usually elderly and that sometimes age had dimmed their memories. Consequently, factual errors (which have been corrected in the notes) occasionally appear in the reminiscences, but these do not detract from the interviews' primary value, particularly to the social historian or the ethnologist. In fact, these interviews reveal many things that more conventional historical sources do not: they record how southeastern Indians lived on a day-to-day basis, how they viewed the tremendous changes that occurred between the Civil War and Oklahoma statehood, and how they remembered their own history. Through these recollections, the forgotten nations and their citizens can be restored to our historical consciousness.

Notes

1. *The Foxfire Book* was followed by *Foxfire 2* (1973), *Foxfire 3* (1975), and *Foxfire 4* (1977).

2. Samuel Cole Williams, ed., *Adair's History of the American Indians* (Johnson City, Tenn., 1930).

3. Francis Paul Prucha, *American Indian Policy in the Formative Years: The Indian Trade and Intercourse Acts, 1790–1834* (Lincoln, Neb., 1962).

4. Charles Hudson, *The Southeastern Indians* (Knoxville, Tenn., 1976); John R. Swanton, *The Indians of the Southeastern United States* (Washington, D.C., 1946).

5. Many books have been written on Indian removal. Among the best are: Arthur H. DeRosier, Jr., *The Removal of the Choctaw Indians* (Knoxville, Tenn., 1970); Grant Foreman, *Indian Removal: The Emigration of the Five Civilized Tribes of Indians* (Norman, Okla., 1932); Arrell M. Gibson, ed., *America's Exiles: Indian Colonization in Oklahoma* (Oklahoma City, 1976); John K. Mahon, *History of the Second Seminole War, 1835–1842* (Gainesville, Fla., 1967); Thurman Wilkins, *Cherokee Tragedy: The Story of the Ridge Family and the Decimation of a People* (New York, 1970); Mary E. Young, *Redskins, Ruffleshirts, and Rednecks: Indian Allotments in Alabama and Mississippi* (Norman, Okla., 1961).

6. Volume 45 does not exist, and therefore the final volume bears the number 113.

7. Readers who do not realize the extent to which the southeastern Indian languages are spoken and cultural traditions maintained should consult Albert L. Wahrhaftig, "The Tribal Cherokee Population of Oklahoma," *Current Anthropology* 9 (1968): 510–18.

NATIONS
REMEMBERED

Chapter 1 · War and Its Aftermath

THE END OF THE CIVIL WAR FOUND THE SOUTHERN INDIANS IN A
distressing situation. The conflict had engulfed their nations, and they
had suffered greatly as a result. When war began, both North and
South looked to Indian Territory as a source of grain and livestock and
as an invasion route into enemy territory. Pro-Southern agents encouraged the Indians to ally with the Confederacy, whose government offered to assume the treaty obligations of the federal government as well as to permit Indian representation in Congress. Apparently willing to surrender this buffer between Kansas and Texas
to the South, the Union withdrew troops from Indian Territory.
Consequently, the five southern Indian nations formed alliances
with the Confederate States and promptly became embroiled in
their own civil wars.

Although their national governments signed treaties with the
Confederacy, the majority of Cherokees, Creeks, and Seminoles
seems to have favored the Union cause. Many fled to Kansas where
they sought protection and support from the United States. Others
remained in Indian Territory and carried on a guerilla campaign
against the Confederate force that occupied their territory as well
as against Southern sympathizers. When Union troops invaded
Indian Territory and, after a series of military engagements, reestablished their position in the area, many Confederate partisans
took refuge in the Choctaw and Chickasaw nations or in northern
Texas. Once again, those who remained conducted raids against the

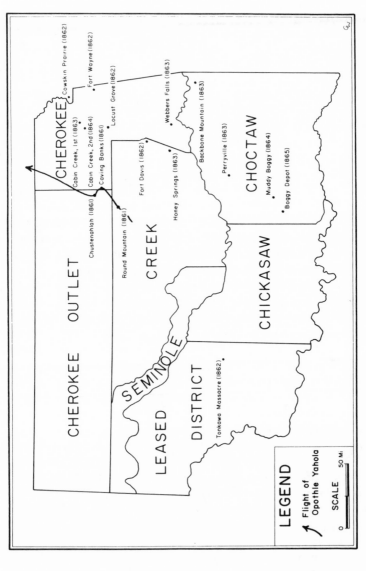

MAP 2. The Civil War in Indian Territory. (Adapted from John W. Morris, Charles R. Goins, and Edwin C. McReynolds, *Historical Atlas of Oklahoma*, 2d ed., Norman: University of Oklahoma Press, 1976. Used by permission of the University of Oklahoma Press.)

occupying force and sought retribution against Unionists. This inter-necine struggle coupled with actual battles devastated these three nations and forced most residents to depend on government rations for subsistence.

The Chickasaws and Choctaws were more united in their support of the Confederacy, although several hundred did flee to Kansas in the first year of the war. The absence of a strong pro-Union citizenry and the geographical location of these nations spared them some of the destruction suffered by more northerly nations. Never-theless, the theft of livestock, particularly cattle, and other property and the inability of constituted authorities to deal effectively with crime led to a depletion of their economic resources. Furthermore, the material demands that refugees from the Cherokee, Creek, and Seminole nations placed on the Choctaws and Chickasaws quickly reduced the latter tribes to the status of government wards as well.

When the South surrendered, most Indian refugees hesitated to return home, in part because of the devastation that awaited them but also because they feared their opponents' vengeance. So ap-prehensive were Southern sympathizers among the Cherokees, Creeks, and Seminoles that they sought a division of their nations. For a while the federal government, which had just fought a war for union, seemed ready to partition the nations. The negotiators finally agreed to permit the nations to remain intact, but the terms of the treaties forced the five tribes to grant citizenship to former slaves and cede territory to the federal government for the settlement of Plains Indians. Those who had fought on the side of the United States protested the harsh terms of the treaties, but to no avail.

The following accounts reveal the attitudes of some southern Indians (in this case, Cherokee and Creek) toward the great Amer-ican conflict, describe the deprivations and dangers suffered in the course of the war, and indicate how the southern Indians faced the challenge of rebuilding their nations and their lives.

Civil War in the Cherokee Nation: Unionists

My first knowledge of Uncle Spencer Stephens was his marriage to Sarah R. Hicks at or near Park Hill, Cherokee Nation. My grandfather, Reverend Samuel A. Worcester, so long a mis-sionary, educator, and minister to the Cherokees (first at Brainerd,

Tennessee, and later at Park Hill where he built a mission school, created a printing office, and there printed the Bible, Hymns, and tracts) also taught the pupils in the school as well as classes in every district of the Cherokee Nation to sing by note.[1] Grandpa Worcester died in April 1859, at Park Hill. Shortly before his death he sold the mission building to my father, Abijah Hicks, who with his wife, Hannah (Worcester), took care of him during his declining years and moved from our home a mile away to come for Grandfather.[2]

Afterwards, we moved from the "Burnet Place," so called, because while Uncle Spencer and Aunt Sarah were living in our house, the "Pin Indians"[3] set fire to the place and burned it down, thinking Uncle Spencer was a Southern sympathizer and that he owned the house instead of my *father*. But that, too, was a terrible mistake since Uncle Spencer and Aunt Sarah went to Baxter Springs, Kansas, with a refugee train out from Fort Gibson just before the breaking out of hostilities in the Cherokee Nation.[4] [The train was led by] Colonel William A. Phillips of Salina, Kansas, who afterwards mustered his regiment of the "flower" of the Cherokee Nation *first* families into the Indian Home Guards stationed at Fort Gibson during the war. Uncle Spencer was an officer, either Lieutenant or Captain, in Colonel Phillips' regiment and was thus entitled to burial in the National Cemetery at this place in the "Officers circle" under the Stars and Stripes.[5]

While they lived in Kansas, the tragedy of their young married life happened in the death of their little daughter, Delia, from strychnine administered by a drunken doctor. Also, an infant son, Chester, died there. Upon returning to the Nation,[6] Aunt Sarah and Aunt Nan lived at the mission at Park Hill while Uncle Spencer was training for war duty. He was given quarters in the stone barracks[7] on Garrison Hill in Fort Gibson where my sister Emma and I spent the night with Aunt Sarah . . . having come from Park Hill with "Swiss Frank," as we called him, who had come along and stopped with another for a season until he found a way to get out of the fighting territory. . . . We had to come to Fort Gibson by ox team to get provisions as all stores, churches, schools and homes were abandoned at that time.

Soldiers met us out at the site of the National Cemetery where orderlies were grazing the horses and mules from the Garrison and told us to hurry in as the "Sesech" were making a raid from Fort Davis across the Arkansas River to drive off the stock. We galloped the tired oxen into the fort instantly and escaped the conflict. (Cherokee, 1: 306–7)

Civil War in the Cherokee Nation:
Confederates

In the year of 1861, the Civil War broke out. I was only eight years old at the time, and my two brothers were younger than I. At the very beginning of the war, all the settlers of the country were forced to leave and seek safety for themselves and families. Some went North seeking protection from the Northern armies, and others fled to the South.

My father was neutral and did not want to go away; he did not believe in fighting. Also, he did not believe in slavery, and long before the war he freed the one Negro slave whom he had inherited from his father's estate.[8]

In 1861, a company of Southern soldiers led by Captain Charley Holt came to our place. Captain Holt called to father and said, "Get ready, Watt, and let's go. You will have to fight." Consequently, father was forced into the Southern Army.

At the time they took father away, there were no other families left in the country. We had three horses, and mother got on one of them and took my youngest brother (who was only about three years old), and my other brother took our feather bed and quilts on another pony. I was on the third one, loaded with all the pots, pans, and cooking utensils I could carry. We started out and for several days we just scouted around, up and down the Canadian River, trying to stay as near to father as we could. We could get plenty to eat anywhere. Everyone had gone, leaving chickens, cattle, and everything to run wild, and there was lots of corn in the little fields; but in a short time the war became so fierce that mother realized that we must get out of the country or be killed so we headed south and kept going until we reached the Red River. We were not able to cross the river, and upon scouting around we found that this was Choctaw country and that the Choctaws were not being molested by the war so we decided to stay there and did stay for the duration of the war.[9]

Father continued in the service of the Southern Army, serving under General Stand Watie[10] until 1865, when he died of sickness right at the close of the war. He was buried at a little place that was called Jackson in an Indian cemetery.

As soon as the war was over, we came home. The Arkansas River was a line between the North and the South,[11] and those who had gone north were afraid to cross to the south side of the river, and those who had gone south were afraid to cross to the north side. When we returned to our old home, we found one chair which was made of hickory by the famous Sequoyah, writer of the Cherokee alphabet,[12] in the potato cellar under the house. I still have the old chair. We also found our old black mottled-face milk cow who had escaped being eaten by the soldiers. She was almost wild but soon grew gentle again. That is all we had to start our home on again. (Cherokee, 10: 485–87)

The Creek Civil War

The beginning of the Civil War found the Creek Indians in a very comfortable condition. Many white and colored people had married into the tribe and became citizens of the tribe.[13] All the Creeks having come from the South and many being slave owners at the time of the removal naturally pursued the same lines in their new lands. Slavery led to the outbreak of the Civil War between the states of the North and the states of the South, but the Creeks preferred to not take sides with either, remembering well how they lived and strived in the years past to climb to the top to acquire what they possessed and the peace that reigned among them. The government of the Confederacy and that of the Union sought to make treaties with the Creeks to fight either on this side or that. The Creeks did not and absolutely was not persuaded. They wanted to have nothing to do with it, but as time passed on, some of them yielded one way or the other. Most of the Chiefs or Agents of the tribe were southern men and through Albert Pike,[14] Confederate Commissioner, made a treaty with one faction of the Creeks to fight with the South.[15]

My father was one of this faction to join the Southern Army, and my folks moved to Fort Washita, where I was born. There was another faction of the Creeks under the leadership of an old Creek Chief named Opothle Yahola who refused to be bound by the treaty and started to take refuge in Kansas. This very much angered Albert Pike and the Confederacy because they thought it was this faction's intentions to join the Union Army, but in fact they did not really want to fight for either side. These Creeks got all their earthly possessions together, it was along in the late fall of the year, I believe it was in November 1861, and they started their journey to Kansas. They did not have weapons to defend themselves in anything like comparison with those of the soldiers. They followed the old buffalo trail a few miles west of the present towns of Eufaula, Checotah, Muskogee, Wagoner, and Pryor, Oklahoma, into Coffeeville, Kansas.[16] Confederate Colonels D. H. Cooper and J. M. McIntosh pursued and attacked them.[17] They suffered loss untold and finished their trip into Kansas in the dead of the winter in a terrible storm, sick, dying, and destitute. After reaching there, they had to join the Union Army, and they were willing, for they were much angered at the Confederacy because they attacked them.[18] Some of my people were among these Creeks, and that explains why some of my relatives of today are Republican and some are Democrat.

In 1862, in July, some of the Creeks joined the Union Army, and regiments were formed under General James Blunt[19] and occupied Fort Gibson, and they remained under the Union troops throughout the War. Likewise, some of the Creeks, and most of them for that matter, were with the Confederate. Regiments were organized and stationed at Fort Washita along with other troops of whites out of Texas, and other forts in the Choctaw and Chickasaw Nation. Raiding parties from both sides scoured the country, burning houses and cabins, driving off horses and cattle, and in fact destroying and demolishing everything they could find.

There were only a few battles fought in the Indian Territory that was in the Creek Nation. Near the present town of Wainwright, Oklahoma, on Elk Creek, was camped the Confederate Army. I would say it was about half-way between Wainwright and Oktaha, Oklahoma. The Union Army stationed at Fort Gibson sent spies and located them. Rube Childers was the principal one of the spies, and he returned to Fort Gibson and gave the information to General Blunt, and the Union Army proceeded to close in on them. The Confederate Army was under General William Steele and General

Doug Cooper. The Union Army had maneuvered to within range of the attack, and on that July morning General Blunt mounted on his fiery steed, at the break of day, viewed the two armies now arrayed in position for battle. It was a clear bracing day, mellow with the richness of mid-summer. All at once a smoke arose, a thunder shook the ground, and a chorus of shouts and groans yelled along in the twilight air. Thus it was all day long wherever General Blunt went there followed victory, and at last toward the setting of the sun the crisis of the conflict came, the two armies, that of the Union and that of the Confederates, gave their very all to crush their opponents. The Confederates were forced to retreat southward across the Canadian River into the darkness of the wilderness, thus a victory for General Blunt commanding the Union Army.[20]

Later on during the war, the Confederates surprised a Union Army wagon train of supplies on the military trail out of Kansas near Grand River at about the present town of Pensacola, Oklahoma. They captured the wagon train of over three hundred wagons and a large number of prisoners. This surprise attack was pulled by General Stand Watie of the Confederate Army.[21]

There was a Confederate fort called Fort Davis west of Fort Gibson on the north bank of the Arkansas River. Generals Stand Watie, Cooper, and Gano[22] occupied this fort.

I don't recall much that I have been told about Fort Davis, but I believe it was in the summer of 1862, it was burned by General Blunt's army of the Union forces. You see that was another encounter in the Creek Nation. It seems that the Creek Nation had all the battles and naturally suffered greater losses than did the other nations.[23]

I do recall my father telling me that on account of unsanitary conditions, both armies suffered immensely from diseases of small-pox, cholera, and other epidemics.

The Civil War was one in which the Creek Indians and I guess the other tribes would have not participated, for they were not concerned but were subjects of persuasion. It was disastrous to them from start to finish, for their property was destroyed and many of them lost their lives and in the end much of their land was taken from them. Their slaves were set free,[24] which was of little loss compared with the other losses I have told you about.

The closing of the war found the Creek Nation in a more pitiable condition than the rest of the nations of the five tribes[25] due, as I have said, to the most activities of the war being centered in the Creek Nation. Homes destroyed, horses, oxen, and cattle killed or driven off, and besides adjusting differences with the Cherokee and Seminoles, a peace conference was held at Fort Smith, Arkansas, in the fall of 1865. I believe it was in September that year. All tribes were present, and they finally agreed with the government that unused lands that had been theirs would be made into reservations for Indians of Kansas, Nebraska, and other places and that the Negro slaves should be citizens of the tribes, right-of-ways granted for railroads, and tribal governments set up under the United States' supervision. When the lands were given to other Indians it naturally reduced the acreage. The Negro also acquired ownership in the land as much as the Creeks themselves and enjoyed part of the tribal funds. Each tribe had certain understandings as to what the slave Negro would get. After the Fort Smith meeting it was taken to Washington and was discussed pro and con for a long time before it was all thrashed out.

For ten years or more after the war, people were very busy building cabins and reestablishing themselves. Railroads started building, and the people as a whole were beginning to recuperate from the losses sustained by the Civil War. (Creek, 9: 353–58)

Notes

1. Samuel Austin Worcester (1798–1859) was a missionary of the interdenominational American Board of Commissioners for Foreign Missions. He began his work among the Cherokees at Brainerd Mission, within the limits of present-day Chattanooga, Tennessee, in 1825. When the Cherokee Nation established a newspaper, Worcester moved to the capital, New Echota, near present-day Calhoun, Georgia, where he assisted the first editor, Elias Boudinot, obtain a press and type and begin the printing operations. When the State of Georgia passed a law requiring all whites living within the Cherokee Nation to take an oath of allegiance to the state, Worcester refused to comply with the terms of this affront to Cherokee sovereignty. He was convicted and sentenced to the penitentiary. When the U.S. Supreme Court ruled that Georgia had no authority over residents of the Cherokee Nation, the state ignored the decision, and President

Andrew Jackson declined to enforce it. When Worcester was finally released, he moved west and reestablished the printing press, first at Union Mission and later at Park Hill near Tahlequah, the town which became capital of the Cherokee Nation after removal. In the years preceding the Civil War, Worcester became embroiled in a controversy between the antislavery administrators of the American Board in Boston and the missionaries in the field over the admission of slaveholders, who often were the most avid Christians, to the church. The issue was resolved with the closing of American Board missions at Worcester's death. For information on Worcester, see Althea Bass, *Cherokee Messenger: The Life of Samuel Austin Worcester* (Norman, Okla., 1936). Robert Lewit examines the controversy over slavery in "Indian Missions and Antislavery Sentiments: A Conflict of Evangelical and Humanitarian Ideals," *Mississippi Valley Historical Review* 50 (1963–64): 39–55.

2. During the Civil War, Union sympathizers assassinated Abijah Hicks, whom they mistakenly believed to be a Confederate partisan. His wife, Hannah, struggled to care for their young children in the face of raids by Confederates and Unionists alike. She recorded her experiences, which have been published in "The Diary of Hannah Hicks," *The American Scene* 13 (1972): 2–24.

3. The "Pin Indians" were Union sympathizers who wore crossed pins on or under their lapels as identifying insignia.   Individuals usually referred to as "Pin Indians" were associated with the Keetoowah Society, ostensibly a cultural revitalization movement but one in which Evan and John Jones, two abolitionist Baptist missionaries, were active.

4. By April 1861, federal troops had withdrawn from Indian Territory. Some Unionists promptly took refuge in Kansas. After hostilities began in the winter of 1861–1862, these early arrivals were joined by a steady stream of other Indians as well as runaway slaves. Many of the refugees enlisted in the Union Army and participated in the federal invasions of Indian Territory. See Dean Banks, "Civil War Refugees from Indian Territory in the North, 1861–1864," *Chronicles of Oklahoma* 41 (1963-64): 286–98; Wiley Britton, *The Union Indian Brigade in the Civil War* (Kansas City, Mo., 1922).

5. The National Cemetery is at Fort Gibson.

6. After invasions and withdrawals in 1862 and 1863, federal troops permanently reoccupied the Cherokee Nation in the spring of 1864, and returned the refugees in Kansas to their homes.

7. The stone barracks, built in 1845, are still standing.

8. Some southern Indians had owned African slaves since the eighteenth century. By the mid-nineteenth century, a number of wealthy Indians were

operating large plantations with slave labor, while many others owned one or two slaves. According to the U.S. census of 1860, which accidentally included Indian Territory, 8,376 slaves lived in the territory and comprised 14 percent of the total population. See Annie Heloise Abel, *The American Indian as Slave Holder and Secessionist* (Cleveland, 1915); Michael F. Doran, "Negro Slaves of the Five Civilized Tribes," *Annals of the Association of American Geographers* 68 (1978): 335–50; Rudi Halliburton, Jr., *Red Over Black: Black Slavery Among the Cherokee Indians* (Westport, Conn., 1977); Daniel F. Littlefield, Jr., *Africans and Seminoles: From Removal to Emancipation* (Westport, Conn., 1976); Daniel F. Littlefield, Jr., *Africans and Creeks: From the Colonial Period to the Civil War* (Westport, Conn., 1979); William G. McLoughlin, "Red Indians, Black Slavery, and White Racism: America's Slaveholding Indians," *American Quarterly* 26 (1974): 367–85; Theda Perdue, *Slavery and the Evolution of Cherokee Society, 1540-1866* (Knoxville, Tenn., 1979).

9. Many Confederate partisans fled to the Choctaw Nation or crossed the Red River and took refuge in northeastern Texas. See Angie Debo, "Southern Refugees of the Cherokee Nation," *Southwestern Historical Quarterly* 35 (1932): 255–66.

10. Stand Watie was a political opponent of Cherokee Principal Chief John Ross. He had favored removal from the Southeast and narrowly escaped assassination in 1839, when his brother Elias Boudinot, uncle Major Ridge, and cousin John Ridge were killed for signing the removal treaty. After a period of civil war, Watie and Ross reconciled, at least publicly, in 1846. When the Civil War threatened, Watie proclaimed his allegiance to the Confederacy and began recruiting Cherokees for the Southern Army in defiance of Ross's neutrality proclamation. This action was probably one of the factors that prompted Ross to sign a treaty with the Confederacy in October 1861, and to commission John Drew to raise a regiment. Since the Confederate command doubted the loyalty of the Drew regiment (and with good reason, since many of them ultimately deserted), Watie's regiment, composed of the "true southern party," remained separate. When federal troops captured, or rescued, Ross in 1862, the Confederate Cherokees elected Watie Principal Chief, while the Union Cherokees gave their allegiance to Acting Principal Chief Thomas Pegg. By the end of the war, Watie had attained the rank of brigadier general, and he holds the distinction of being the last Confederate general to surrender. See Mabel Washbourne Anderson, *Life of General Stand Watie* (Pryor, Okla., 1915); Frank Cunningham, *General Stand Watie's Confederate Indians* (San Antonio, Tex., 1959); Edward Everett Dale and Gaston Litton, eds., *Cherokee Cavaliers: Forty Years of Cherokee History as Told in the Correspondence of the Ridge-*

Watie-Boudinot Family (Norman, Okla., 1939); Kenny Franks, *Stand Watie and the Agony of the Cherokee Nation* (Memphis, Tenn., 1979); Gary E. Moulton, *John Ross, Cherokee Chief* (Athens, Ga., 1978).

11. The Cherokee Reconstruction Treaty of 1866 provided that any Southern sympathizers who desired could move south of the Arkansas River into the Canadian District and elect their own officials. See Charles J. Kappler, ed., *Indian Affairs, Laws and Treaties*, 2 vols. (Washington, D.C., 1904), 2: 943–94; Hanna Warren, "Reconstruction in the Cherokee Nation," *Chronicles of Oklahoma* 45 (1967): 180–89.

12. In 1821, Sequoyah, an unlettered Cherokee, developed an eighty-six-symbol syllabary which the Cherokees rapidly adopted for their newspaper, laws, translations of the Bible, hymns and religious tracts, personal correspondence, sacred formulas, and so forth. See Grant Foreman, *Sequoyah* (Norman, Okla., 1938).

13. In the two decades before the Civil War, the Creeks passed a series of laws governing the relationships between Indians and blacks and between masters and slaves. One of these laws prohibited intermarriage between the races, but the law possibly was not enforced. Angie Debo, *The Road to Disappearance* (Norman, Okla., 1941), pp. 126–27.

14. Born in Massachusetts, Albert Pike practiced law in Arkansas for a number of years before the Civil War. In the 1850s, he successfully represented the Choctaws in a suit against the United States in which the tribe collected almost $3 million. Consequently, Pike acquired a reputation of fairness in his dealings with the Indians which helped him successfully negotiate Confederate treaties with the five tribes. See Robert Lipscomb Duncan, *Reluctant General: The Life and Times of Albert Pike* (New York, 1961).

15. At the beginning of the Civil War, only about one-half of the Creeks were loyal to the Confederacy. In the course of the war, even that support eroded. Debo, *Road to Disappearance*, pp. 149–50.

16. The route described is about fifty miles east of the actual route, which took Opothle Yahola and his followers from west of Tulsa northeast, near present Skiatook, and then into Kansas. Confederate forces attacked the loyal Creeks at Round Mountain on November 19, and then engaged them in the Battle of Caving Banks on December 9, and the Battle of Chustenahlah on December 26. Edwin C. Bearss recounts this desperate trek in "The Civil War Comes to Indian Territory, 1861: The Flight of Opothleyoholo," *Journal of the West* 11 (1972): 9–42. Accounts of specific battles can be found in Muriel H. Wright, "Colonel Cooper's Civil War Report on the Battle of Round Mountain, 1861," *Chronicles of Oklahoma* 27 (1949): 187–206; and LeRoy Fischer and Kenny Franks, "Confederate Victory at Chusto-Talasah," *Chronicles of Oklahoma* 49 (1971–72): 452–76.

17. Douglas H. Cooper, the former U.S. agent to the Choctaws and Chickasaws, had switched his allegiance to the Confederacy. Daniel N. McIntosh, a Creek who favored the Southern alliance, commanded a regiment of his tribesmen.

18. By the summer of 1862, approximately eight hundred Creeks had joined the Union Army.

19. James G. Blunt commanded the Kansas Division.

20. The Battle of Honey Springs was fought near the site where the Texas Road crossed Elk Creek on July 17, 1863. The Union Army routed the Confederates, who had intended to capture Fort Gibson.

21. On September 18, 1864, Watie captured a federal supply train worth $1.5 million at Cabin Creek, just north of Grand River in present-day Mayes County.

22. Richard Gano commanded the Texas Brigade, which participated in the capture of the supply train at Cabin Creek.

23. In reality, the Creek Nation had few of the battles fought in Indian Territory during the Civil War. Hostilities centered in the Cherokee Nation, where, as a matter of fact, the Battle of Cabin Creek took place. The major primary source for the military history of the Civil War in Indian Territory is *The War of the Rebellion: A Compilation of the Official Records of the Union and Confederate Armies*, 70 vols. (Washington, D.C., 1880–1901), series 1, vol. 3. Among the many works written on the Civil War in the West, the following are particularly pertinent: Annie Heloise Abel, *The American Indian as a Participant in the Civil War* (Cleveland, 1919); Leroy Fischer, *The Civil War in Indian Territory* (Los Angeles, 1974).

24. Although the loyalists among the southern Indians accepted emancipation of slaves before the Civil War ended, most slaves, of course, were in the possession of Confederates. However, the treaties negotiated between the United States and the Indian nations and signed in 1866 provided for the abolition of slavery and the extension of citizenship to former slaves. The literature on reconstruction in Indian Territory includes Annie Heloise Abel, *The American Indian Under Reconstruction* (Cleveland, 1925); Thomas F. Andrews, "Freedmen in Indian Territory: A Post-Civil War Dilemma," *Journal of the West* 4 (1965): 367–76; M. Thomas Bailey, *Reconstruction in Indian Territory: A Story of Avarice, Discrimination, and Opportunism* (Port Washington, N.Y., 1972); Lewis Kensall, "Reconstruction in the Choctaw Nation," *Chronicles of Oklahoma* 47 (1969): 138–53; Daniel F. Littlefield, Jr., *The Cherokee Freedmen: From Reconstruction to American Citizenship* (Westport, Conn., 1978); Ohland Morton, "Reconstruction in the Creek Nation," *Chronicles of Oklahoma* 9 (1931): 171–79.

25. Since most battles occurred in the Cherokees' territory, that nation suffered the greatest—indeed, almost total—destruction.

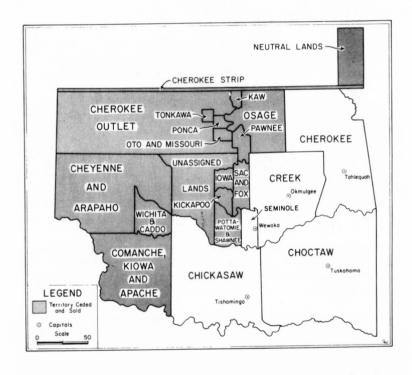

MAP 3.　Lands Ceded and Sold by the Five Civilized Tribes Between the Civil War and Allotment. (Adapted from John W. Morris, Charles R. Goins, and Edwin C. McReynolds, *Historical Atlas of Oklahoma*, 2d ed., Norman: University of Oklahoma Press, 1976. Used by permission of the University of Oklahoma Press.)

Chapter 2 · Law and Disorder

FOLLOWING THE CIVIL WAR, THE SOUTHERN INDIANS BEGAN THE task of rebuilding their nations. Although many individuals had remained loyal during the Civil War, the United States insisted that the official alliances tribal governments had made with the Confederacy justified their treatment as vanquished foes. The terms of the Reconstruction treaties signed in 1866 demanded the abolition of slavery, the extension of citizenship to freedmen, the granting of rights of way to railroads, and the cession of land. In exchange for small cash payments, the Choctaws and Chickasaws ceded their leased district and the Creeks their western territory. The Seminoles relinquished all their land for fifteen cents an acre and purchased land from the Creeks for $1.25 an acre. The Cherokees agreed to sell the Cherokee Strip and neutral lands in Kansas and to permit settlement of other tribes on the outlet.

Except for the Seminoles, who had southern and northern chiefs until 1877, the "civilized" tribes quickly reestablished a united government within each nation. Although the degree of centralization varied, all five tribes had national political institutions by the Reconstruction period. The Cherokees established a bicameral legislature called the National Council. Each electoral district sent two members to the upper house, or Senate, while representation in the lower house, or Council, was apportioned on the basis of population. The principal chief headed the executive branch of government,

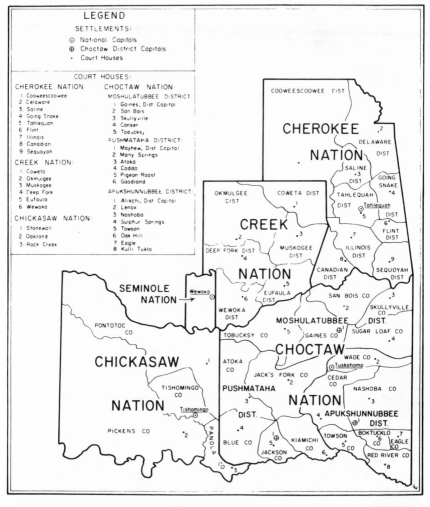

LEGEND

SETTLEMENTS:
⊙ National Capitals
⊕ Choctaw District Capitals
· Court Houses

COURT HOUSES:

CHEROKEE NATION:
1 Cooweescoowee
2 Delaware
3. Saline
4 Going Snake
5 Tahlequah
6 Flint
7 Illinois
8 Canadian
9 Sequoyah

CREEK NATION:
1 Coweta
2 Okmulgee
3 Muskogee
4 Deep Fork
5 Eufaula
6 Wewoka

CHICKASAW NATION:
1 Stonewall
2 Oakland
3 Rock Creek

CHOCTAW NATION:
MOSHULATUBBEE DISTRICT
1 Gaines, Dist Capital
2 San Bois
3 Skullyville
4 Conser
5 Tobucks

PUSHMATAHA DISTRICT:
1 Mayhew, Dist Capital
2 Many Springs
3 Atoka
4 Caddo
5 Pigeon Roost
6 Goodland

APUKSHUNNUBBEE DISTRICT:
1 Alikchi, Dist Capital
2 Lenox
3 Nashoba
4 Sulphur Springs
5 Towson
6 Oak Hill
7 Eagle
8 Kulli Tuklo

MAP 4.   Political Divisions of the Southern Indian Nations. (Adapted from John W. Morris, Charles R. Goins, and Edwin C. McReynolds, *Historical Atlas of Oklahoma*, 2d ed., Norman: University of Oklahoma Press, 1976. Used by permission of the University of Oklahoma Press.)

and the judicial branch consisted of a supreme court as well as district courts. The Chickasaw Nation, which was divided into three counties, was governed by a legislature composed of a Senate and a House of Representatives and a governor. The Choctaw Nation was also divided into counties, which were then grouped into districts. Although each district had a chief and each county a court, the Choctaws also had a bicameral National Council, a principal chief, and a supreme court. The Creeks used their traditional towns, membership in which derived from birth rather than residence, as the basic elective and administrative unit. Each town elected one member of the upper legislative house, the House of Kings, and as many delegates as their population justified to the House of Warriors. The Creeks also had a principal chief, and each of the six districts in the Nation had a court, a district attorney, and a police force. The Seminoles exceeded the Creeks in placing responsibility for government on the traditional towns. Each Seminole town elected a chief, or *tustenuggee*, who met in council with the principal chief to make and enforce laws.

In the period between the Civil War and Oklahoma statehood, the southern Indians relied heavily on these national political institutions to meet the challenge of maintaining order in Indian Territory. The Civil War had bequeathed a legacy of rampant crime and violence with which the republican governments of the five tribes tried desperately to cope. In part, the violence resulted from political factionalism. Removal from the Southeast to Indian Territory had provoked bitter controversy and, in some cases, virtual civil war. These deep-seated antagonisms surfaced in times of stress and, coupled with hatreds kindled during the American Civil War, lingered long after peace had been officially restored. Furthermore, the devastation of war produced poverty which in turn bred crime, as Indians struggled to survive, recoup their losses, and exact vengeance from those whom they believed responsible for their suffering.

The relocation in Indian Territory of Plains tribes, who had not developed the sophisticated political, legal, and judicial institutions of the southern Indian nations, contributed to the postwar chaos. Compounding the problem of cultural disparity, the economic situation of these new arrivals was probably worse than that of the southern Indians. Unable to follow freely the buffalo herds upon which they had been economically dependent, these Indians turned to raiding the livestock of their neighbors. Most vulnerable of the five tribes were the Chickasaws, whose nation adjoined the lands of the Kiowas, Apaches, and Comanches. When confronted with incursions, the Chickasaws organized a militia to protect the borders of their nation and conduct forays into the reservations of the Plains Indians in search of stolen livestock. The United States War Department, which possessed the only legitimate authority to police the Plains tribes, did not object to the vigilante tactics some-times employed by the militia because the Chickasaw Nation bore the expense for the recovery of livestock, an expense which might otherwise have fallen upon the federal government.

The Chickasaw militia's quasi-legal raids into the Plains Indians' reservation is only one example of the confusion over jurisdiction that reigned in Indian Territory between the Civil War and Oklahoma statehood. Other problems stemmed from the plethora of courts in Indian Territory. Treaties guaranteed that Indians would be tried in their own courts, and a United States Court was established in Fort Smith, Arkansas, to adjudicate matters involving whites. The United States court antagonized Indian nations by forcing marshals, whose income depended on a fee system, into Indian Territory to arrest suspects, and occasionally the tension erupted into violence. At other times, white residents of Indian Territory as well as Indians did not wait for courts to act and took the law into their own hands. Further problems arose when a citizen of one nation committed a crime in another. The Seminoles and Creeks, in particular, had difficulties in this respect because the two nations adjoined and the Seminoles enforced their often harsh laws ruthlessly and quickly.

This confusion over jurisdiction made Indian Territory an ideal haven for people who preferred to live beyond the reach of the law. Many notorious outlaws began their careers as rustlers in Indian Territory. They soon graduated to the illegal transportation and sale of whiskey and then to armed robbery and murder. Bootleggers, gunslingers, posses, rustlers, public hangings, and vigilantes projected an image of Indian Territory as the "Wild West." Nevertheless, as one of the following interviews suggests, some Indians romanticized outlaws and regarded them as victims of unfair treatment or unprovoked harassment. Apparently, considerable popular support existed for people like Ned Christie, whose seven years on the lam represented to some Cherokees a struggle against encroachments by the United States government.

The violence that plagued postwar Indian Territory occasionally extended beyond outlaws and desperadoes and into the political arena. Generally politics were conducted peacefully. However, sometimes opponents bitterly contested elections, and these elections seem to have been the ones most vividly recalled. Since public balloting made neutrality or secrecy impossible, candidates openly employed coercion to influence the outcome. Unsuccessful office seekers occasionally resorted to arms rather than accept the final tally, and then guards had to protect victorious candidates from assault.

Political sentiments reached this feverish pitch in the period between the Civil War and Oklahoma statehood because the issues that southern Indians confronted at the polls involved their fundamental values, beliefs, and world views. In many respects, philosophical and cultural as well as economic and political lines separated Unionists from Confederates, supporters of tribal governments from proponents of statehood, defenders of communal land from advocates of private property, and conservatives from progressives. Thus, political factionalism and even crime gave formal expression to extremely deep divisions within the southern Indian nations. Consequently, the chaos and violence of the postwar period indicate not only greed, disrespect for constituted authorities, and general lawlessness but also perhaps a disaffection by many southern Indians with the policy of the United States government, with tribal acquiescence to American economic expansion, and at times with their own political leadership.

Comanche Raids

We had lots of trouble with the Comanches.[1] The people in the neighborhood had a lot of horses, and the Comanches liked to steal horses. I remember one night when the Comanches were on a raid, my father rounded up all of our horses and put them in the lot to keep the Comanches from stealing them. The next morning they had driven off all of the horses except one small colt which was not big enough to jump the fence. They made another raid one night when there was a big snow on the ground. All of the settlers for miles around gathered at the Edmon Pickens home. After the raid the men, eighteen in number, started out after the Comanches. There was also one Negro in the crowd. There were somewhere between two and three hundred Comanches in the raid.

The Chickasaws caught up with the Comanches at about where McMillan is now located. They were so badly outnumbered it was impossible to get the horses back. Part of the Comanches would go ahead with the horses while the others stopped to fight. The Negro, William Henry, was riding a mule. The Comanches got after him. He got so excited he fell from his mule. He had on a large overcoat, and he pulled it over his head and started running. The Comanches got both his gun and coat. One of the men let the Negro ride back with him to the Pickens home.

One of the Comanches got after Dave Pickens. Pickens shot him, but the other Comanches carried him away. After the battle, it was discovered that Dave Pickens had an arrow sticking in the back of his saddle and through into his overcoat. Every one started to help remove the arrow since it would have been impossible for him to have gotten out of the saddle without being hurt by the arrow. They all got excited or something, but anyway the arrow cut Pickens in the side just a small place. The arrow was poisoned and Pickens lived only a few days. He died just as soon as the poison went through his system.

On another raid the Comanches entered a home and were about to cut a woman's finger off to get her ring. She offered a jug of molasses if they would give her time to remove the ring herself. One of the Indians knocked her down with the jug and took his hatchet and cut her finger off.

They also made a raid near Baum. On this raid they ran into two girls on horseback. One girl jumped from her horse and yelled at her sister to do the same, but the girl was so badly frightened that she stayed with her horse. The Comanches ran her into her own yard, killed her, and took the horse.

A year or two after these raids the United States government gave the Chickasaws permission to go into the Comanche country and look for their horses.[2] They went and found horses in large numbers but none of their own. A few years later I went on a visit to Lawton and met a real old Comanche. I asked him why it was that we never found any of our horses. I said, "Remember anything about Comanche used to steal horses?" He said, "No, me from Texas, steal horse in Texas bring over here, steal horse over here take him to Texas." That was the whole story. The horses that were stolen from the Chickasaws were carried to Texas, and the horses that were stolen in Texas were carried to Lawton. (Chickasaw, 6: 319-20)

The Beck and Proctor Fight

On a picturesque little stream called Flint Creek stands a historical mill called the Hilderbrand Mill, where once lived the Widow Hilderbrand. However, at the time of this story, Mrs. Hilderbrand had married again, this time to a man named Jim Kesterman.[3] It was at this milll that a great tragedy occurred which later developed into what is known as the "Proctor Fight."

At the time of the tragedy I was a boy of fourteen years, but the details are as fresh in my mind as though it happened only yesterday.

Mrs. Kesterman, or "Aunt Polly," as she was usually called by those who knew her best, was a half-breed Cherokee Indian, and Kesterman was a white man. They were considered law-abiding citizens. White Sut Beck, Black Sut Beck, and Sam and Bill Beck also were half-breed Cherokees and nephews of Mrs. Kesterman.

During the Civil War the Becks and Zeke Proctor served in the army but under different flags. Proctor served in the Federal Army and the Becks in the Confederate Army. Nevertheless, they were good friends until the trouble started which I will write about. . . .

It was sometime during the month of February 1872, that Proctor and Kesterman began having trouble over some stock. Proctor lived about ten miles from the Hilderbrand Mill. One morning he saddled his horse and rode over to the mill to talk the matter over with Kesterman. He bade them the time of day, and the talk drifted to the trouble about the stock. Finally, they got into a heated argument, and it would be impossible to tell all that was said, as I am only telling it as I heard it told. Proctor, seeing Kesterman reach for his gun, drew his gun and fired. Mrs. Kesterman, thinking that she might save her husband, ran in between the two men and the bullet intended for Kesterman hit her, killing her instantly. Kesterman then ran up the steps to a second story of the mill. Proctor fired two more shots at his retreating figure, shooting two holes in the latter's coat. Proctor then mounted his horse and rode away.

Arriving at his home, he told what he had done. He then sent a man to tell Jack Wright, who was sheriff of Goingsnake District, of the affair. Jack Wright lived about five miles east of Baron Creek Station. When the man delivered the Proctor message to him, he went over and arrested Proctor, placed a guard over him, and reported the case to the prosecuting attorney.

Cornick Sixkiller[4] was appointed special judge to try the case. On April 1872, the case was called. Proctor was arraigned for trial, and, while the lawyers were arguing, up rode a posse of men headed by Deputy U.S. Marshal Owens accompanied by White Sut Beck, a nephew of Mrs. Kesterman, the other Becks already being there on the ground and heavily armed back in a grove where stood the little log school house that is known as the Whitmire School,[5] which was being used on this special occasion as a court house. . . .

White Sut Beck seemed to be leading the marshal's forces and with his crowd made for the court house. Sut Beck leveled a double-barreled shotgun on Zeke Proctor. Then Johnson Proctor, a brother to Zeke, grabbed the gun and received the full charge of shot in his breast, the other load striking Zeke in the knee. The battle was then on, and it would be impossible to describe the horrible and bloody scene that followed. The firing of guns got so rapid that the bullets rained like hail in every direction. For a moment it seemed like a duel to the death on both sides, but finally the posse fled before the bullets from Proctor's side.

When the smoke of the battle had cleared away, the ground in front of the little log school house was covered with the dead and the wounded. Proctor had his men, what was left of them, and stood victor over the scene. Nine men were killed and two mortally wounded.[6]

About an hour later, my mother who was a widow had us boys to hitch a span of mules to the wagon, drive to the scene of battle, and with the assistance of Proctor and his men, the dead and wounded were loaded into the wagon and taken to our house. The wounded were carried into the house, which was converted into a temporary hospital, until the relatives came and took them away. The nine dead men were laid on our big porch. . . .

My eldest brother, Steve Whitmire, and the school teacher, whose name was Mack, saw the whole affair from start to finish. The teacher had dismissed school, and he and my brother had stayed at court.

When the excitement had somewhat died down, the sheriff took Proctor over to the old Scraper home where he was guarded until the next day. He was then tried by a jury of twelve men and found "not guilty."

After the events above described, society was thrown into a turmoil from which it took a long time to recover and to discuss the terrible battle, which was destined to leave a lasting impression on the minds of so many people.[7] (Cherokee, 11: 371–76)

Ned Christie

This old family place is known today as the old Ned Christie place and is the place where the notorious outlaw, Ned Christie, fought single-handed the United States government for four or five years.[8] I wonder if anyone has ever told how peculiar this battle was that raged between the government officers and this lone Indian citizen? He was a man that certainly loved his family because he never did leave home to escape the officers. He was an honorable Cherokee citizen, a member of the Cherokee Council, and he really thought he was only defending himself from an intruder on his personal rights when he beat an officer to the draw here in Tahlequah.

He had been in session with the Cherokee Council, and at the end of the week he had been in the habit of acquiring a pint of good whiskey and starting home. This time he had probably taken a little too much to drink, and no doubt it showed in his walk before mounting his steed and during his short walk to mount his steed. This officer thought it smart for him to hail an Indian Councilman and embarrass him by hailing him before a court. Christie thought this man was an intruder or a hold-up man instead of an officer. He just drew his own gun that he always carried for self-protection, as it was during the days when self-protection was a common law. He thought himself lucky when his opponent fell, but on further examination he found he had slain an officer of the law. At that, Christie became excited and just rode home to his family. He really did not know what he should do in a case of this nature. He stated to me that after he had time to realize that he would be charged with murder, he thought it no benefit to try to beat the murder case under the existing Cherokee laws. He just decided to die at home fighting.

After he had been fighting the officers about a year he came up to our place which was located about a mile and a half north of his place. He wanted to buy our forty-four caliber Winchester, and we sold it to him. He left our home stating he was certainly glad to get the new gun and believed he would be able to live a little longer with his family by being able to kill a few more of those marshals. He said that he always just had to kill one or two men or seriously wound one or two and the rest always made that an excuse to leave. They would say they had to carry the wounded back to hospitals for medical attention. He said he would peep through some hole in his log house and watch them loading the injured men into wagons to haul them away. He said nearly every time they were loading the dead people in that they always got rather careless about staying behind trees, and that he could have killed two or three more of them easily. He always felt sorry for those men and just contented himself by letting them go back home once more to see their wives and children. When these men would leave, my brothers and I could always tell they were gone because the shooting would cease. We would go a running down there to see the battle ground and pick up empty cartridge shells and to see how many men Ned had killed or wounded. By the time we could get down there Ned would be outside looking about the place seeing what needed to be done. He would see if the cows needed to be milked or the horses needed to be watered. After he finished his chores, he would play marbles with us boys with a great deal of delight and often laughed very heartily.

A lot of his neighbors always came to visit him and express their joy that he had come through safe once more. You see Ned was a nice neighbor and a very intelligent man to talk with. Very few people ever knew that his son, Arch Christie, always stayed hid in the house so as to be ready to help his father fight when the United States marshals came again to fight his father.

I want you to say in this story that the government never did ask him to give up to the authorities after the first time. They always tried to slip up on him and kill him while he was about his work around the little farm. The mystery of all this slipping up business was they always failed to slip up on him. He had very wise and reliable Indian fortunetellers at his command, and he always told his family to leave the house about an hour before the marshals were to be there. He and his son, Arch, ate their meal the last thing and brought in plenty of drinking water. Then they examined their guns and put the ammunition in pouches and hung them on their persons. Then they put their guns in the portholes ready for action.

The United States agents once shot Ned right at the upper end of his nose with a forty-four caliber Winchester bullet, and the bullet stopped at the back of his head just inside the outer skin. You could feel the bullet rolling around loose inside of the skin. Ned told us boys at that time that when the bullet entered his head he turned blind and fell right back on his back on the floor of the upstairs. That is where he was when a man shot him just as he peeped through a hole.

He could hear the officers keep shooting at the house and the thing that worried him most he was afraid they would notice that he had quit shooting. Then they would come rushing in and pick him up while he was unable to speak. His son kept firing often enough to keep them believing he was up yet and that perhaps he was playing his usual trick on them. This trick was that he would often quit firing for a while and they would think he was probably dead. They would begin to walk up toward the house, and when they got out in the open, he would open up with the best sharpshooting and mow down a bunch. Then away they would scatter into the woods, falling over each other as they went. This time they had shot him through the head and Arch, his son, had kept up a pretty good stall for him so that after about an hour he began to see a spot of light about the size of a pin head. It got larger and larger very slowly, and after so long he could see everything. All this time his mind was perfectly clear, but he was unable to speak or see. After several hours his son, Arch, got a couple of fellows squarely down on the ground dead, and the gang loaded them up and left.

This group of officers numbered about thirty men, and there were six wagons and teams. After they left his neighbors came in and doctored him, and they immediately began to build him a stone fort on a mountain just west of his place. He stayed on that mountain for two months, night and day, and after that he was able to be up and do some more fighting.[9] (Cherokee, 50: 181–86)

The Leard Murder

The Leards[10]—Mrs. Leard was the victim—lived in the Seminole country three miles east of the present site of Maud. The line that separated "old" Oklahoma from the Indian Territory ran north and south through the neighborhood where Maud is now located. On the immediate east side of the line was located the Seminole country and to the immediate west "old" Oklahoma. . . .[11]

The Leard home consisted of two one-room houses built in the fashion of that day. One house was made of logs daubed with red mud. The other one-room house was made of boards with a porch. The Leards had four children, the oldest of whom was Frankie, age seven. Mr. Julius Leard was away at the time of the murder of his wife; the children were the only eyewitnesses to the actual crime. It was up to Frankie to identify the murderers.

The Leard hired hand had been away from the Leard household for several hours, and on his return a horrible sight met his eyes. In the yard lay the body of Mrs. Leard with swine feeding on her body. The Leard hired hand notified the neighbors. Just on the inside of the door of the board room house lay Mrs. Leard's nine-weeks-old baby almost dead. It was quite evident that the baby was dying from a fall. Under a pile of newly washed clothes one of the other children was found. Frankie, aged seven, was found wandering about in the nearby woods. The neighbors questioned him, and from his answers the manner in which the crime was committed took shape.

Some time during the early part of the morning, Frankie related, Lincoln McKeesy and Palmar Sampson,[12] both of whom he knew by face and name, came up to his mother who was washing clothes at the board room house. The two Seminole Indians wanted to borrow Mr. Leard's saddle. Mrs. Leard informed them that her husband was away and that he had the saddle with him. The Seminoles left only to return about three o'clock in the afternoon of the same day. It is more than likely their departure that morning had been in anger. When Mrs. Leard saw them returning, she rushed into the house and grabbed up a shot gun. When the two men came to the door, she tried to shoot them, but luck was aginst her. The gun jammed. She threw it to the floor, grabbed up her baby, and ran out into the yard. The two Indians gave pursuit. Lincoln caught up with Mrs. Leard and, with the stock of the shot gun which she had thrown down, knocked her senseless. Lincoln then jerked the baby free of her arms and threw it up over the porch in through the doorway of the room where it was found dying. Lincoln walked over to the porch on which Frankie was standing. The criminal held up a booted foot and asked Frankie if he recognized the boots. Frankie didn't recognize them. It is an act of Providence that he failed to recognize them. By recognizing them he would have more than likely been killed because the boots belonged to his father and had been stolen by Lincoln McKeesy while the outlaws headed farther back into the Seminole country. Frankie tried to drag the body of his mother into the house. Such was the manner of the crime.

Word was gotten to Mr. Leard, who was over in the Chickasaw Nation at the time. Sixty men—sympathizers from the Chickasaw Nation—came with him to his house, and several posses were organized. The Pottawatomie Indians joined the white men and Chickasaw Indian posses. One such posse headed by Mr. Leard and of which my uncle, Russ Guin, was a member gave chase in the Seminole country after two Seminoles on horseback who appeared overanxious to get away. My uncle shot the horse out from under one of them, and the other Seminole made his escape. The posse asked the captured Indian where Lincoln McKeesy could be found. The sulky Seminole wouldn't talk. However, the posse had a remedy for that. They hanged him by the neck. Nevertheless, before he would become senseless they would let him to the ground to give him an opportunity to talk. He talked. He said Lincoln McKeesy could be found at a nearby Indian mission.

The posse found Lincoln boldly walking about the mission. The collar of his shirt was open and blood could still be seen on his underclothing. The posse threw their guns on him and made him mount. They took him to my grandfather's house to which place the Leard children had been taken. Frankie identified McKeesy as one of the murderers. The criminal was chained in the loft of Grandpap Guin's house.

The next day another posse caught Palmar Sampson near Eufaula. The moment the two (Lincoln and Palmar) were brought face to face, they started quarreling. Palmar, who spoke better English than did McKeesy, was asked what they were quarreling about. Palmar said Lincoln was accusing him of killing Mrs. Leard.

By the next day the excitement was at a feverish heat. The women wanted to burn the Indians at the stake. The men wouldn't let them. However, on the third day after the crime, the men took the two Seminoles to a nearby Stomp Ground. There, with a chain several feet in length, they shackled the two Seminoles to two trees. Brush was taken from an arbor and piled about them. Mrs. Leard's father, Mr. Martin, was privileged to set fire to the brush. The moment the brush around Lincoln McKeesy burst into flame, he leaped into it, but Palmar pulled away as long as he could. Some of the spectators shot their guns into the air; many of them turned their backs to the grim spectacle, and several tried to leave, but there were men to make them remain.

Almost at the instant the fire was lit, six United States laws from Muskogee rode up. They had been sent by Governor Barnes[13] who in turn had been notified by an Indian preacher of the pending tragedy. The laws were disarmed and detained, but as soon as the burning was over, they were given their guns and permitted to return to Muskogee. However, several days later they came back with warrants for the arrest of all who had taken part in the burning.

I remember one United States Marshal, Heck Thomas by name, coming to our house in search of Papa. Papa would always be hidden in the loft of our house or elsewhere. However, three of my uncles were not so lucky. They served jail sentences. As far as I know, only one man, Mont Ballard, received a prison sentence.[14]

Through the summer and up into late November rumors came into "old" Oklahoma that the Seminoles, angered by the fate of two of their number, were preparing for the warpath. But so were the white men, with the Pottawatomie Indians as their aids. All the guns and ammunition was gotten ready for use. The men stayed in groups at various houses. However, for the most part, they slept on the outside, the women and children occupying the indoors. I remember one November night of that year a light snow fell on those of us who were sleeping in the yard. That month of November, signs of border warfare reached their climax. Reports had it that six or seven hundred Seminoles stood equipped for battle. However, before they could swing into action, John Brown, the Seminole-Creek Chieftain, from his home at Seminole came to the Indian encampment west of Wewoka. He didn't say much, but what he did say was to the point. In effect it was, "If you go over there into Oklahoma, you'll be killed by the whites. If any of you come back alive, I'll see that you are killed. Take your choice; it's death either way if you strike." The Indians disbanded. (Creek, 80: 220-27)

Bootlegging

On another occasion, while riding on a passenger train on the Rock Island—then the Choctaw—railroad, [Sweeney Folsom of the Indian Police] was "tipped off" that a casket in the express car and consigned to Krebs contained not a body, as it was made to appear, but a quantity of whiskey.[15] On the arrival of the train at Krebs, the casket was unloaded from the express car, with all the silence and reverence which usually is stressed in the presence of death. In the meantime, Mr. Folsom had arranged with the conductor to hold the train pending an investigation of the matter. He then demanded of the express agent that the casket be again placed aboard the train so that it could be turned over to the United States deputy marshal at McAlester. To this demand, the agent demurred, but upon being presented with the credentials of Mr. Folsom as an officer of the law he finally complied with the demand, and the train proceeded on its way to McAlester, where the casket was turned over to the proper authorities and, upon being opened, was found to contain the contraband whiskey just as it had been reported to Mr. Folsom.

The Indian Police[16] were kept quite busy preventing the introduction of whiskey into the counties bordering on the State of Arkansas and would, especially in holiday season, such as Christmas and the Fourth of July, station themselves on roads or trails leading into the Territory, in order to intercept and search parties having a suspicious appearance. On one of these occasions, Mr. Folsom had secured the assistance of a cowboy in watching his station. After a time, they discovered that a lone horseman had taken "roundings" on them and could be seen at some distance within the territorial line urging his horse to the utmost. The cowboy immediately gave chase, and, after an exciting run of six miles, he captured the supposed culprit on whose person he found a lone pint of alcohol and which the offender insisted he was taking home for his grandmother who was very sick. The cowboy refused to be dissuaded from the faithful performance of his official duties and returned the devoted grandson to the state line so that Mr. Folsom could be given an opportunity to dispose of the weighty matter. Following an eloquent appeal on the part of the offender, Mr. Folsom accepted his statement concerning his grandmother as being the truth and, therefore, permitted him to proceed to his home and admonished him to be sure that the liquor was used only by his sick grandmother. (Choctaw, 24: 413–15)

Punishment

Each nation of the five civilized tribes was a little domain within itself. They had their own tribal laws,[17] and their domains were divided into districts, and each district had its separate and distinct trial judge, prosecuting attorney, sheriff, and deputies.

I will tell you particularly of the Cherokee Nation, as that is one in which most of my activities centered. The Cherokee Nation was divided into nine districts, viz: Flint, Goingsnake, Delaware, Saline, Tahlequah, Illinois, Canadian, Sequoyah, Coo-wee-coo-wee, or Claremore District. . . .

In each district of the Nation was a court house and a whipping post. If someone committed an offense, the sheriff would arrest them and bring them into court. The sheriff was entirely responsible for the prisoner after the arrest was made, and, if there were no jails, the prisoner would be chained and locked to prevent his escape. Often times the prisoner would be chained to the sheriff's bed while he and the sheriff slept.[18]

The prisoners would be tried by a jury and if found guilty would be sentenced by the judge to be whipped at the whipping post. For the first offense, and I will use for example, say, stealing a pony, he would get twenty-five lashes with a hickory stick. The second offense would mean fifty lashes, the third offense a hundred lashes, and the fourth offense he would be hung. They would not hang him to a tree but had an improvised scaffold. They would carry the prisoner to the top of the scaffold. They stood him on a trap door, and, at the signal of the sheriff, the deputy sheriff would pull the trigger on the trap door and let him fall, breaking his neck. To make sure that his neck was broken as he dangled from the rope, the Sheriff would grab him by his feet and give him a good yank to make sure that his neck was broken and that he was dead. As a boy I used to be around the whipping post and the court a great deal. The whipping post was a forked tree, the fork being about five and one-half or six feet from the ground. The prisoner's hands were tied together and pulled over through the fork and tied to the other side around the tree. His feet were tied to the tree so that he could do nothing but flinch and hallow. Each prisoner was stripped to his waist. Where second and third offenders required so many lashes, he would be released from the tree, take him down to the spring, and bathe his back together with his stomach where he had rubbed the hide off of same against tree. They continued to do this with the prisoner until he had meted out his sentence.

Yes, I can remember any number of whippings that took place at Goingsnake court and post. I particularly remember, as if it were yesterday, when they whipped the Maynard boys and the Post boys, and the Wolf boy was hung.[19] (Cherokee, 7: 254–56)

*   *   *

The early Muskogee-Creek tribal laws were very strict and were carried out fully within the law. Many a guilty man or woman are said to have received lashings for punishments. Those lashings were done with stout hickory switches upon a person who was stripped of his clothes to his waist. The lashes were laid so hard and of such long durations that most often blood would come upon the back.

I had tried to escape coming within the laws of my tribe, but somehow the law was smarter than I was for I was caught for some crime, and the law, as usual, carried out their duty. I have come under and experienced the penalty of the guilty. I was stretched up to the limb of a tree, hands tied securely and feet bound and a pole inserted between my two feet, while a member of the lighthorse-men[20] stood on the pole to keep my body steady and keep it from swinging. Such was the way in which I was inflicted with the punishment from the law, and I know when I felt the lashes received from the hickory, and I remember the name of the man who did the whipping and his name was No-kus-e-le of the Tulsa tribal town. He was a very large man as I also remember.

I didn't know I had committed a crime so much as to be sentenced to be whipped when I had only stolen a hog. At the time I was arrested I happened to be over at the Quasady settlement, which was then about one and one-half miles south of the present Cromwell, Oklahoma, but the whipping was done near the present vicinity of Weleetka, Oklahoma. Cowee Harjo, a member of the Wewoka lighthorsemen, arrested me, and I was sentenced in the Wewoka district.

I was a young man at the time so that I don't very well remember who the judge was then. I have always believed that I was the last Indian that was punished by lashings under the old Indian tribal laws because it was not long after I received the punishment that the Indian tribal laws were abolished.[21] (Creek, 47: 100–1)

Politics

Tahlequah, the seat of the Cherokee government, was active during my life there. The Cherokees occupied offices there in the Cherokee capitol building, and the Cherokee Council met at regular intervals. I remember some very exciting times during the political conventions there. There were two major parties there, the National party and the Downing party.[22] Each party had a candidate for chief, their candidates being nominated at these conventions, and sometimes, especially when drunk, they would cause a lot of trouble.

During one of these conventions my uncle, Eli Wofford, who was chief of police, got killed and another uncle, Leonard Williams, was wounded in the same fight. They were arresting a drunk Indian when some of this Indian's political allies took up the matter, and a free-for-all fight followed with the above-mentioned result.

There was always a big celebration when a new chief was sworn in. My father acted as interpreter during these times and interpreted the new chief's address to the Indians who could not understand

English. The chief usually spoke in English. My father was well educated for a man of his time.

We children surely enjoyed these inaugural ceremonies. Crowds of Indians came to town bringing whole families and spent two or three days. There would be dancing at night. My mother used to board the councilmen when they were in town attending the meeting of that body. Fireworks would be shot off at night, including the shooting of the anvils. My father added quite a lot of noise to the celebration one night when he shot off a stick of dynamite. The old printing shop of my father, a brick building, now stands near the old capitol building there in Tahlequah.

I remember when they had public hangings there. Indians would come in from miles around to witness these executions. However, I never saw a public hanging as my parents never attended one and always saw to it that we children were kept safely at home during these executions. For lesser crimes, whipping was administered, the criminal being tied to a tree and the lashing given him while thus tied.

It was also a practice among the Cherokees to tie up drunken men when they became troublesome. My uncle, Than T. Wofford, was United States marshal for quite a long time for Tahlequah and that district. The time my Uncle Eli Wofford was killed was to be the last convention held by the National and Downing parties.[23] (Cherokee, 106: 456–58)

Elections

Political affairs were always at fever heat. The voting places in the Creek Nation was at Tallahassee, Coweta, Okmulgee, and Eufaula.

The usual method of voting for a long time would be that all who were around the voting place would line up for the party whom they wished to vote. The clerk would count the number in each line and make a record of same. Later on they would go into the clerk, give him their name, and tell him for whom they wished to vote, and he would make a record of that. Should a young man become of lawful age, which was twenty-one years, there would have to be a number of citizens of the tribe who would vouch for his being of age before he was allowed to vote. The first vote cast would be for the Chief of the tribe, second vote Vice Chief, third vote Treasurer, fourth for the Clerk, fifth vote for Supreme Judge, sixth vote for the Town King, seventh vote for the Legislature, and the eighth vote was for the House of Warriors. (Creek, 1: 395)

*   *   *

Once, when an election was being held for the electing of a Principal Chief of the Choctaw Nation, a blacksmith and another man got into a fight over it, the blacksmith stabbed the other man. He mounted his horse, rode a mile, got his gun, and returned to town and literally shot up the town looking for this blacksmith. Shot into his home, shop, and every other house where he suspected he might be hiding until he fell exhausted from the loss of blood at our door. My husband dressed his wound and took him home in a buggy. He soon recovered, and he and the blacksmith were apparently friends after that. It was just "a friendly argument" over an election.

It was right exciting on election day. There would always be lots of fights. On that day, mentioned above, I saw a Negro man just slap a white man down as fast as he would get up, slapped him with the side of his pistol on the side of the head. Doctors were kept busy on election days. Nobody was arrested or punished for these "free-for-all" fights, and sometimes they killed a few of the crowd. (White resident of the Choctaw Nation, 1: 237)

The Green Peach War

I remember the Green Peach War as if it were yesterday. Some say that the reason they called it the Green Peach War was because some of the people could not say Isparhechar but would say Green Peachie, and others would say that it was at the time of the year that there was green peaches on the trees.[24] Isparhechar's party was what we could call today the Republican party, and the Checotah party was what we would the Democrat party.[25] An election was held in 1882, and the result of that election was that the Checotah party had beaten the Isparhechar party, and the Isparhechar party claimed that it was a crooked election and would not consent to Sam Checotah taking office.[26] I had been over to what is now Beggs, Oklahoma, to get a little money that was due me on the Severs pay-off.[27] I only had four dollars and eighty cents coming to me, and on my way back I took sick and stopped in at Mr. Severs' home, and Mrs. Severs had my dinner fixed for me. While I was eating dinner, a line of men at least a mile long was marching by headed by Isparhechar going to Pecan Creek to enlist all of the colored people that he could to join him. Mrs. Severs said to me, "Jake we are going to have a war just as sure as the world." After I ate my dinner I mounted my horse and went to my Uncle John Harrison's, who lived over at Choski post, which was about two or three miles east of the present town of Haskell, Oklahoma. When I came to what was later known as the Gentry Ferry, a number of people was there building rafts of logs to get their household goods and women folks across the river. I swam my horse across the river and on to my uncle's. I stayed there until the next day, and it was necessary for me to go to Muskogee on a business errand. I traveled back across the river and thence southeast, coming to the road on which the stage traveled at Pecan Creek, and there was five or six hundred of Isparhechar men camped there. I was rather in favor of Isparhechar for I felt that they had been robbed of the election. They were talking as to whether or not that they should surrender and let Checotah take office or die, and they decided that they would rather die. I came on to Sugar Creek, that was down near the present town of Taft, and I ran on to the Checotah army, but I did not tarry there nor did they bother me, and I finished my trip to Muskogee. The Isparhechar and Checotah armies had a battle on Sugar Creek, and after this battle they came out on the prairie east of what we called Billie Grimmet's place and had another skirmish. Scouts were sent back to Cloud River on Jake Brown's place and made arrangements or at least came to the conclusion that the Isparhechar army would move into the territory of the Checotah stronghold at the Creek Agency and proceeded to surround Agency Hill and were not more than two or three miles apart from each other after they arrived there. They picked me up then (that is, the Isparhechar army) and sent me as a scout to where the Veteran's Hospital[28] is now, and I got a letter and carried it back to Isparhechar, and the letter instructed them that they should disband and scatter or the troops of the United States government would be called in to handle them. Lee Perryman with the Isparhechar army finally took an oath in behalf of Isparhechar to not rebel. Henry Reed, who was the judge at Lee, took a number of the men and sentenced them to the whipping post, giving them fifty lashes apiece, and with this the thing died down considerable, but, in the late winter of 1882, Isparhechar went to Okmulgee and met Sleeping Rabbit,[29] and they again reorganized the Isparhechar army, and they met the Checotah army of about seven or eight hundred men southwest of Okmulgee and killed seventeen of Checotah's men, but Checotah captured Sleeping Rabbit and killed him. In December of 1882, the Isparhechar army retreated to the Sac and Fox country with about twelve hundred men under what they called General Will Robinson.[30] They were followed by the Checotah army, but the Sac and Fox would not permit them to fight in their territory, and at this point the Isparhechar army retreated to the Cheyenne country and stayed there until April.[31] The U.S. Government stepped in and took charge, captured Isparhechar and his men, and moved them into Fort Gibson in April 1883, and kept them as prisoners of war. Isparhechar finally gave up and signed a treaty with the government that he would cease such activities.[32] Sam Checotah was finally seated as Chief of the Creek Tribe and remained chief until the next election, which was in 1884.[33] (Creek, 9: 389–93)

Notes

1. In *The Comanches: Lords of the South Plains* (Norman, Okla., 1952), Ernest Wallace and Adamson Hoebel present an ethnohistory of the powerful Plains tribe. Studies of other Plains Indians include the following: Virginia Cole Trenholm, *The Arapahoes, Our People* (Norman, Okla., 1970); Mildred P. Mayhall, *The Kiowas* (Norman, Okla., 1962); and Donald J. Berthrong, *The Southern Cheyennes* (Norman, Okla., 1963). Among the works which deal with the relocation of Plains Indians in Oklahoma and their confinement to reservations are Ralph K. Andrist, *The Long Death: The Last Days of the Plains Indian* (New York, 1964), and Wilbur Sturdevant Nye, *Carbine and Lance: The Story of Old Fort Sill* (Norman, Okla., 1969).

2. In 1868, Governor Cyrus Harris of the Chickasaws requested permission to organize a force of sixty rangers to protect his nation from the Comanches, and the United States War Department approved his proposal. Apparently, the rangers were fairly successful in deterring Comanche raids, and by about 1870, the Plains tribes seem to have transferred most of their cattle-rustling activities to northern Texas. Nye, *Carbine and Lance*, pp. 41, 47, 112–15.

3. The author has maintained the spelling of the victim's surname that appears in "Indian-Pioneer History." However, the name is sometimes spelled "Kesterson" or "Chesterton." Kent Ruth, comp., *Oklahoma: A Guide to the Sooner State*, rev. ed. (Norman, Okla., 1957), pp. 293–94.

4. Ruth identifies the judge as Blackhawk Sixkiller. *Oklahoma: A Guide to the Sooner State*, p. 293.

5. The Whitmire School was near present-day Westville.

6. Kesterman had filed charges against Ezekiel Proctor in the U.S. District Court at Fort Smith, Arkansas, and the posse was attempting to arrest him to stand trial on those charges. This action was clearly in violation of treaties between the Cherokees and the United States guaranteeing Cherokee courts jurisdiction in cases involving Cherokee citizens. Thus the "Proctor fight" was more than a feud; it was in part a battle between the United States and the Cherokee Nation. This event caused great bitterness on the part of many Cherokees and helps explain their attitude toward people like Ned Christie who defied the U.S. marshals.

7. In the aftermath of the massacre at the schoolhouse, the United States Court returned twenty indictments against Cherokee citizens. Ultimately these were dismissed. Proctor was later elected sheriff of the Flint District and a member of the Council.

8. This event occurred near Wauhilla, east of present Tahlequah, in the early 1890s.

9. United States marshals pursued Ned Christie for seven years, during which time he reportedly killed eleven people. Finally, sixteen men under the command of U.S. Marshals Heck Thomas and Paden Tolbert attacked his log fort in the Spavinaw Hills with thirty shells from an army cannon, two thousand rifle bullets, and dynamite. Even after a blast destroyed one wall of his fort, Christie refused to surrender, and he was killed with his Winchester in his hands. Joseph G. Rosa and Robin May, *Gun Law: A Study of Violence in the Wild West* (Chicago, 1977), p. 55. For other studies of outlaws in Indian Territory, see Richard A. Graves, *Oklahoma Outlaws* (Oklahoma City, 1915), and Paul Trachtman, *The Gunfighters* (New York, 1974). For studies of their nemeses, see Homer Croy, *He Hanged Them High* (New York, 1952), which deals with Isaac Parker, the "Hanging Judge" of the U.S. Court in Fort Smith, and C. G. McKennon, *Iron Men: A Saga of the Deputy United States Marshals Who Rode the Indian Territory* (Garden City, N.J., 1967).

10. The surname actually is spelled "Laird."

11. In 1889, the United States government opened the Unassigned Lands, which remained from the Creek and Seminole cessions of 1866, to white settlement. In 1890, the Oklahoma Territory was organized to provide

government for the residents of this tract of land. The Pottawatomie Reservation, which adjoined the Seminole Nation, was opened for white settlement in 1891, and was incorporated into the Oklahoma Territory. The Laird murder occurred six years later within the Seminole Nation and near the border with Oklahoma. Julius Laird, a white man, had leased land from Thomas McGeisey, a Seminole citizen.

12. Once again, names are misspelled. The individuals accused of the crime were Lincoln McGeisey and Palmer Sampson.

13. Cassius M. Barnes was Territorial Governor of Oklahoma.

14. A number of errors exist in this account. Lincoln McGeisey was the son of Thomas McGeisey, superintendent of schools in the Seminole Nation and the person from whom Laird, a white man, leased land. Because he came from a prominent family, McGeisey was probably educated. Palmer Sampson, on the other hand, understood no English. Neither man was identified as a participant in the murder by little Frankie Laird, who presumably knew McGeisey fairly well. Palmer Sampson was no doubt innocent since he had an alibi for the time of the murder. The heirs of the two men sued for damages in the United States Court and collected $5,000 for each death. Furthermore, other Seminoles who had been tortured by the mob were awarded damages. The grand jury returned indictments against sixty-nine persons for involvement in the burning of Sampson and McGeisey, and a number of them received sentences ranging from three to twenty-one years. The narrator probably remembered Mont Ballard because, when he was released from prison, his hometown of Maud accorded him honors for his "defense of American womanhood." The historian, Edwin C. McReynolds, interprets the "executions" as manifestations of white racism and hostility toward tribal government in which McGeisey's father participated. In addition, the mob violence indicates some hostility between the Chickasaws and Creeks, some of whom were involved, and the Seminoles. Edwin C. McReynolds, *The Seminoles* (Norman, Okla., 1957), pp. 336–41; Geraldine Smith, "The Mont Ballard Case" (M.A. thesis, University of Oklahoma, 1957).

15. The Rock Island Railroad was finished in 1887 so this episode must have occurred some time after that date.

16. In 1880, an Indian Police Force was appointed for the five southern tribes. Headquartered at the Union Agency in Muskogee, the Indian Police removed intruders and enforced the Federal Intercourse Laws prohibiting the sale of alcohol in Indian Territory. The members of the force were Indian, and offenders were tried in the U.S. Court at Fort Smith.

17. The most accessible collection of the legislation of the five tribes is *Constitutions and Laws of the American Indian Tribes*, series 1, 20 vols.

(Wilmington, Del., 1973), series 2, 33 vols. (Wilmington, Del., 1975). In series 1, Chickasaw legislation can be found in volumes 1 and 2, Cherokee in 5 through 10, Choctaw in 11 through 17, and Creek in 18 through 20. Volumes 1 through 7 of series 2 contain Cherokee laws, 8 through 12 Chickasaw, 13 through 26 Choctaw, and 27 through 30 Creek.

18. The Cherokees built a national jail in Tahlequah in the 1870s. However, no district jails were constructed, and prisoners often spent considerable time in the personal custody of the sheriffs, as described by the narrator. An excellent study of the transformation of Cherokee attitudes toward punishment can be found in Rennard Strickland, *Fire and the Spirits: Cherokee Law from Clan to Court* (Norman, Okla., 1975), pp. 169–74.

19. This concept of law and punishment differs markedly from the aboriginal system of retribution and vengeance. Traditionally, if a man stole from another, he was expected to return or replace the goods taken. If a man killed another, the clan (or kin group) of the slain man avenged his death by killing either the murderer or one of the murderer's kinsmen. John P. Reid, *A Law of Blood: The Primitive Law of the Cherokee Nation* (New York, 1970).

20. The national police forces of the southern Indians were called the Light-Horse Guard. The members of the guard both apprehended criminals and administered punishments. Carolyn Thomas Foreman, "The Light-Horse in Indian Territory," *Chronicles of Oklahoma* 34 (1956): 17–43.

21. The Curtis Act of 1898 abolished all tribal laws and courts and replaced them with United States laws and district courts.

22. The Downing party emerged after the Civil War as a coalition of people who were unhappy with the leadership of William P. Ross, who had succeeded his uncle John Ross as Principal Chief, and those who had supported the Confederacy in the Civil War. The National party was composed of the remainder of the old Ross party. The Downing party appealed primarily to progressives, while the National party drew its strength from traditionalists.

23. The best political history of post-removal Cherokees is Morris L. Wardell, *A Political History of the Cherokee Nation, 1838–1907* (Norman, Okla., 1938).

24. The latter explanation is the most widely accepted. Isparhecher is pronounced "Spi-e-che." Angie Debo, *The Road to Disappearance* (Norman, Okla., 1941), p. 246.

25. The most widely used spellings are "Isparhecher" and "Checote."

26. The contested election that originally set the stage for the Green Peach War was in 1879. Three parties nominated candidates: the Muskogee party put forth Ward Coachman, the National Constitutional party Samuel

Checote, and the Loyal Creeks Isparhecher. Many irregularities, including failure to close rolls before voting commenced and refusal to seal returns after polls closed, occurred during the election. Checote was finally seated. In addition to being a personal triumph for Checote, the outcome of the election also represented a victory for a national constitutional government as opposed to government by practically autonomous traditional towns, which Isparhecher favored. After the election, Creek conservatives, led by Isparhecher, began to hold councils at the Nuyaka Square Ground where they were joined by various other disaffected Creeks, including freedmen who had become Creek citizens and criminals who sought to avoid punishment under the national law. Debo, *The Road to Disappearance*, pp. 268–79.

27. The narrator is probably referring to the $4 per capita distribution of funds resulting from the sale of land to the Seminoles, a transaction of which Isparhecher strongly disapproved.

28. Agency Hill and the Veteran's Hospital are in Muskogee.

29. Sleeping Rabbit was the leader of a group of Creeks who lived in the Cherokee Nation.

30. William Robinson, who had served in the Confederate Army, actually led the Checote forces which were pursuing Isparhecher.

31. The followers of Isparhecher took refuge among the Seminoles and Cherokees as well as among the Sac and Fox.

32. Isparhecher agreed to a constitutional convention, which reaffirmed the unified national political system he had opposed.

33. The election of 1884 was also disputed. Joseph M. Perryman took the oath of office, but one week later the Council ruled that Isparhecher had won. The old rebel served over two months before another decision gave the election back to Perryman. Remunerated for his brief term, Isparhecher left office quietly. Debo, *The Road to Disappearance*, pp. 280–84.

Chapter 3 · **Subsistence**

POLITICAL FACTIONALISM WAS NOT THE ONLY MANIFESTATION OF divergent Indian values. Dramatically different ways of life also reflected deep divisions within the nations. Even in the late nineteenth century many Indians subscribed to traditional values, which emphasized living in harmony with the natural world and acquiring no more than could be used immediately. This value system constrained the majority of southeastern Indians to live near the subsistence level, but a few, such as Robert Jones, a Choctaw who adopted the capitalistic values of white Americans, accumulated considerable wealth, and exhibited a far more opulent life-style.

Many Indian fortunes had their genesis in the eighteenth-century deerskin trade. The depletion of game and the cession of hunting grounds forced descendants of traders and hunters to invest their capital in other ventures, particularly in African slaves as labor for plantations, ranches, salines, and similar enterprises. After the Civil War and the abolition of slavery, these entrepreneurs diversified their interests further and participated in various aspects of economic development, including railroads, commerce, mining, and ranching (see Chapter 7).

The majority of southern Indians possessed neither the ability nor perhaps the desire to live like the elite. Most citizens of the five nations clearly existed at the subsistence level, barely producing enough from the soil to survive and usually supplementing crops

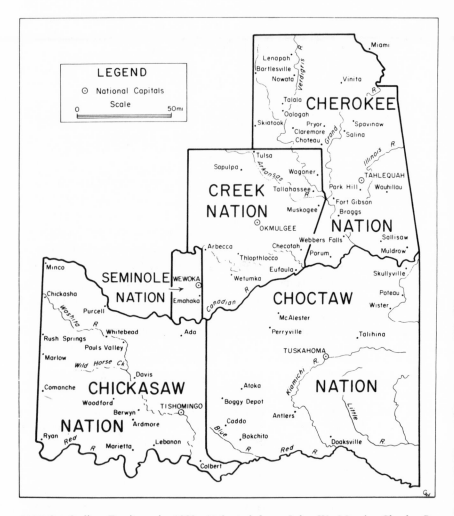

MAP 5. Indian Territory in 1889. (Adapted from John W. Morris, Charles R. Goins, and Edwin C. McReynolds, *Historical Atlas of Oklahoma*, 2d ed., Norman: University of Oklahoma Press, 1976. Used by permission of the University of Oklahoma Press.)

with wild foods, game, and fish. They lived in crude log houses and wore simple homemade clothing. By statehood some of them, no doubt, had begun to envy the splendid life-styles of people like the Joneses, but many southern Indians still seem to have preferred their own way of life and perhaps the satisfaction and contentment it brought over the aggressive and competitive life of the elite.

Life at the Top

Robert Jones was a half-blood Choctaw Indian and a graduate of the Old Choctaw Academy, Scott County, Kentucky.[1] He owned farms all up and down Red River, thousands of acres in each farm, with stores and gins on each farm. It has been said that he was the first operator of "chain stores." He owned about twenty-eight stores in all and had white men to operate them. The overseers on his farms were usually white men. One farm of about ten thousand acres southwest of Idabel was called Rocy Comfort; another south of Idabel was Shawneetown, seven thousand acres; Lake West farm is nine miles south of Boswell, comprising about six thousand acres; the Hog Wallow farm of about five thousand acres is south of Bennington.[2]

Because these farms were so near the river, his wife could seem to have no good health so he told her to select a place for a home and he'd build there. She selected a place four miles southeast of the present town of Hugo, Oklahoma—a hill profusely covered with wild roses—and on this hill he built a perfect mansion and he named it "Rose Hill."

My mother, Mary Floyd, was housekeeper at Rose Hill for several years. She probably came with them from Mississippi. She was what was considered an old maid in those days. She was about thirty years old when she met and married my father, Shelton Tucker, who was a machinist and had come to Rose Hill to operate the steam gin on that farm. I understand that some of the gins and grist mills on the other farms were operated by horse power. Oh yes, there were grist mills on each farm. Solomon Hotema was the minister who married my parents in 1875.

I can see Rose Hill in my mind's eye. It was a large two-story frame house with tall, ridged columns supporting the porch, which extended all along the front of the house, and they had the first transoms over the door that I ever saw.

Mother said that some of the material in the house was imported from France. Just what this material was, I do not recall now. We visited there frequently. I remember the house faced the south. A walk of native stone, lined on either side by cedar trees which are standing today, led the way to the native stone steps. To the south of the house was as fine an orchard as I ever saw. [It had] the most delicious fruit, and all from seedling trees.

A wide hall, a room within itself, divided the two large front rooms. At each end of the house were large chimneys of native stone. Immediately back of the hall extended to the north [were] two rooms. A stack chimney of native stone afforded fireplaces for both rooms above and below stairs, as did also the chimneys at either end of the house.

Once when I was twenty-two years old, I went up in the attic and saw lots and lots of old records that I wish had been preserved for history's sake. One was a bill of lading for $3,500 worth of cotton that Mr. Jones had shipped to New Orleans.

He owned two steamboats, and, aside from the large amount of commodities produced on his own farms, he bought all the surplus salt, leather, cotton, hides, etc. from all over the country and shipped it to New Orleans. He had a large store and warehouse down on the river, from which point the steamers started, and no doubt had them all along the river adjoining his farms. (White resident of Choctaw Nation, 11: 32–34)

Farming

After the Civil War they did not have cross-cut saws, but they had axes, wedges, and mauls which they used to build their houses, barns, and fences. They built their homes in the bottom lands of creeks and rivers.[3] The neighbors would get together and make rails to fence small fields for their corn and gardens.[4] After the rails were all cut for each family's field, they would all be notified on a certain day of the month, in the light of the moon, to lay what they called the worm rail, which was first on the ground.

The men, women, and children would help to lay the first rail at each home. After this was done, they could take their time in building up the rest of the fence, but the bottom rail had to be layed at a certain time in the light of the moon or the rail would rot in a year.

They had about the same principle in clearing the timber for their fields. In the month of August, when the moon was at a certain stage, they would take their ax and cut a ring around each tree, which would kill them instantly, roots and all.[5] They would let them stand until the following year. At a certain time, they would push the trees over and roots would come out of the ground. Then they would cut and drag the trees off the land. This made them plenty of dry wood for several winters. White men cut trees any time, not look at moon, and plow around stump, and break their plows for years.

On their return from Texas[6] to the Indian Territory, they had no matches to start their community log fire, which kept burning all the time. In this way they would carry hot coals to their place of cooking. One method they had to start their log pile burning was with a muzzle-loading shotgun. They would load with powder and cotton instead of shot. He would shoot the cotton into the brush at the log pile, which soon started a blaze.

The Cherokee Indians had two reasons for planting their fruit trees in the corners of their rail fences on the inside of the fields. One was the trees would not be injured by the team or plows in cultivating the field. The other was a fine protection to the rail fence and crop in the field. As the fruit would ripen and fall on the outside of the fence, the native hogs would smell the ripe fruit and they would come up and eat the fruit, root up the ground, and lay under the shade of the trees, waiting for more fruit to fall. In this way they kept the vegetation down all around the field for quite a space.[7]

They would build a pen out of dry logs, say, ten feet by ten feet and eight feet high. They would build one outside pen about thirteen feet by thirteen feet and eight feet high, then haul limestone and fill in the space between the two pens. They would haul dry brush and pile up on the walls of the pen and set it on fire. In this way they made lime for their community. One Indian for many years used a bottle of Syman's liniment for a spirit level on foundations, buildings, and dams. Out on the prairie, they would build a dam across a ravine for water for the stock.

Before the white man began grazing cattle in the Indian country, the Indians did not worry about feed for their stock in the winter. A weed grew in the creek and river bottoms that had a small pod of peas on it. They called this weed beggar's lice. The horses, cattle, and deer would stay fat all winter on this and on cane breaks,[8] which were plentiful before grazing cattle by white men.

The hogs would live on the nuts and acorns in the woods all the year, and the wolves and coyotes did not bother the pigs. As the native hogs were of wild nature and were ready for a fight at the crack of brush, all the hogs in the wood would help the mother sow to protect her young. But after the white man imported better breeds of hogs from the North and turned them loose among the native hogs, it was not many years until the wolves would steal the young pigs. They were not ready to fight for their young as the wild hogs were. (Cherokee, 1: 445–50)

*   *   *

All the Indians loved to hunt and fish. There were lots of wild game, such as wild pigeons, turkeys, quail, prairie chickens, deer, opossum, raccoon, fox, coyotes, mink, muskrat, squirrel, rabbits, etc. All the streams were full of fish.

We raised corn and some wheat as well as cattle, hogs, and sheep. There were lots of wild hogs, too. . . .

We cut our wheat with an old scythe and cradle attached, bundled it, and tied it with straw. We threshed it by tramping it out with horses, and this job of riding the horses fell to us kids. They would pile the wheat down on a wagon sheet, floor, or ground, and then by riding the horses over it they would tramp out the grain. Then we would pick up the straw after it was well tramped, shake it out good, and then gather up the grain. We would wait until there was a strong windy day and then by pouring the wheat from one vessel to another or by just picking it up and pouring the wheat back in another pile, the wind would blow out the dirt and chaff.

Later on there was an old water mill over on Flint Creek run by a Mr. Hilderbrand. Everyone knew this mill from Siloam Springs, Arkansas, to Pryor and Choteau, Indian Territory, as the Hilderbrand Mill. This mill was located at what would now be the junction of highway number ten from Siloam Springs, Arkansas, to Tahlequah, Oklahoma. Mr. Hilderbrand also run a sawmill at this location. It usually took about a week from where we lived to go to the mill, as we would have to cross the old Markham Prairie, which was east of Choteau and Pryor and then on east across Rose Prairie. . . .

We tilled our soil with a homemade bull tongue[9] and planted the corn by hand. We would broadcast our wheat. We had no harrows, cultivators, etc. We leveled our ground by rolling a log over it and sometimes just dragging it with a brush. (Cherokee, 6: 510-13)

*   *   *

We would plant our corn with a big-eyed hoe.[10] We would go along and dig a hole, drop the corn, and cover it up with this hoe. We continued to cultivate the corn with the hoe. Later on we made us an old bull tongue and would break the ground with this bull tongue pulled by one pony.

We used to work oxen in two, four, and sixes. The yokes for the oxen were usually made of hickory, of course handmade. Our ox carts were made by taking a log and sawing off at the required thickness of the wheels, making these cuts as near round and of the same size as possible, and then burning a hole through the center of the round block or wheel to fit an axle. The axle would be cut from a log of the right size and at the proper length and back from each end would be cut a shoulder for the spindle and in each end of the axle would be burned a hole through which could be driven a wooden pin so as to hold on the wheel. The rest of the cart was made from small limbs of trees or poles split half in two. We also made our four wheel wagons in the early days in the same manner. (Cherokee 3: 171-76)

Housing

My father started the old Sawney homestead by sharpening a pole axe and cutting down red oak trees and trimming them up and cutting the bark off of them on all four sides to make a square shape and building an old-time double-locked cornered house. Double-locked means that the ends of the logs were so notched that when once put into place they could not be pushed out of place in any direction. No ordinary storm could harm the Indian log houses so built.

This first home was a two-room log house with a hall between and covered with boards made out of timber by my father's hands. He used a tool called a froe.[11] This froe and a wooden hammer he had made out of a hickory bush[12] were all the tools he used in the manufacture of the shingles. My father cleared out about twenty acres of land, and this constituted our farm. The house and other improvements were all built in the same crude way as the small dwelling. Fences were all made of split rails, and gates were handmade by an axe. The wedges used in splitting timber were wooden wedges. Our garden fence was constructed to keep the chickens out and was built of wooden pickets.

Our household furniture was all homemade by father. Our beds, chairs, tables, and shelves were all wooden furniture crudely made by father's hand. In fact, my father became known among the Indians as a real wooden craftsman. He earned some of our living making chairs for other Indians less crafty, and they paid father by laboring on our farm or paying him in meat of some kind or skins of wild fur-bearing animals, such as wolf or fox.

My father would not accept poultry, eggs, and pork in payment for his labor because such things had no market value at all. Conditions in those years were so that such produce was practically worthless. Eggs sold for five cents per dozen, large hogs for two dollars and a half a piece, a cow and calf for eight dollars, and the markets were so far away we could not afford to move this produce for the profit there was in it. (Cherokee, 43: 368-70)

*   *   *

The first house I remember living in was a two-room log cabin. It had a stick and mud chimney where we did most of our cooking. Later we bought a stove, but before 1900 most of the poorer people in the Choctaw Nation did their cooking at a fireplace. Most of them lived in houses made of logs, too.

The average house at that time was of logs and had maybe one or two rooms. Some of the houses had dirt floors; others had floors of split logs. The cracks in the walls, between the logs, were filled with mud, called "chinking." A lot of the houses did not have any windows at all, just one door. In summertime people often knocked out some of the chinking in the walls to let in more air and light. Some houses had openings for windows, without glass. There would be a wooden shutter to close at night and in winter. Some houses had thin skins in their windows to let in a little light but keep out wind and rain.

We burned wood for fuel. Wood was plentiful and easy to get. We got our water supply at the nearby creeks or from springs. Or now and then you'd see a well, the old fashioned kind called a "dug" well. These wells were dug with a pick and shovel and sometimes walled with rock. Usually there was a homemade windlass[13] above this kind of well to hoist the bucket.

Living conditions were not so radically different from what they are now. People just adapted themselves to circumstances, and I imagine that under the same circumstances people nowadays would live about as people did when I was a boy. Of course, we were influenced a lot by the old Indian customs. (Choctaw, 70: 9-13)

Clothing

You have heard them say and recall the age of a boy by referring to him as a shirttail boy. This was because we boys never wore pants until we were about eleven or twelve years old, they were just long shirts. Our clothing was made with a spinning wheel, reel, and loom. We would sit around the fireplace at night at Alex and Becky's house and pick the seed out of the cotton[14] so that it could be carded, reeled, and woven. I never saw any cotton until I got down to Wilson's place.[15] Up in the hills our clothing was made more or less of hides and furs.

The clothing was colored different colors by the use of different barks of the trees. For example, sumac with a little copperas boiled down to a strong liquid made a tan color. Sycamore boiled down would make a red. We could get indigo up at the store at Fort Gibson, and this would make any and all kinds of shades of blue.[16]

The Indians usually wore moccasins up in the hills in the Saline District[17] made from hides and furs. Later they would make shoes. We had no shoe tacks, and we would have to whittle shoe pegs usually out of ash or maple. We would take a cowhide and tan it with bark. If the hair did not come off easily with the bark preparation, we would take ashes and grease and make a kind of soap or lye and throw it on the hide and let it stay there overnight. Then the hair would scrape off easily the next morning. We used hog bristles and squirrel skins cut into threads to sew the shoes. (Cherokee, 3: 174-76)

*   *   *

Our clothing was more or less home spun. Later on we could get clothes at the store at Choteau. The folks had a spinning wheel, reel, and loom. Nights we would sit around the fireplace and pick seed out of the cotton to make our cotton cloth. We had some sheep, and we would shear the sheep, wash it out good in the creek, lay it up to dry, and when it was well dried they would make cloth from this wool. I never did much cloth making but the women would sit for hours carding, reeling, and weaving the different kinds of cloth. They colored this cloth by using different kinds of bark. (Cherokee, 6: 512–13)

*   *   *

The clothing people wore then wasn't so different as you might think. It was chosen for its ability to stand lots of wear, and it was usually rough and comfortable. Most of the Indians and cattlemen then wore a sort of cowboy garb: big hats, cowboy boots, shirts of wool or cotton or calico, trousers tucked into boots. This outfit could be varied as to color and quality to suit the tastes or pocketbook of the wearer. Looking back, I can see that some of the men's styles were sort of funny. Some of the white men, when they wanted to dress up, wore high, stiff collars, string ties, trousers with tight legs. And some wore high-button shoes. (Chickasaw, 70: 12)

Food

After I was big enough to remember things, we had a hard time in getting anything to eat such as flour and other food stuff. My father had to go to Arkansas to get flour, sugar, and coffee and other groceries. We were not the only ones who got groceries from Arkansas. The neighbors around us got their groceries from there. They would all get together and several wagons would go. They would be gone for several days, bringing what we needed for a while, and then they would go again.

We lived on a farm and raised some corn— all the corn we needed for our bread. We did not feed corn to our ponies for there was plenty of grass they could live on during the winter without being fed corn. We needed the corn for our bread and could not afford to feed our corn to the ponies.

Mother used to make meal out of corn. She would put the corn in a mortar that she had, this mortar being made out of a post oak block square on both ends, and which stood on one end. The other end had a bowl in it. This bowl was made by burning it with coals of fire about six or seven inches deep so that it would hold right smart of corn. She would put the corn in the bowl and beat it until she made meal out of this corn.[18] This was about the only bread we had, for we could not get flour when we wanted it so we had to stay with our corn bread. She would make other things out of corn.

She would go out somewhere and dig up some roots, which she called in Choctaw language Lokchok-Ahi, in English it would be called mud potatoes. She cooked it by boiling it, and it was just as good as Irish potatoes are now. At that time we had no Irish potatoes. In fact, we did not know there was such a thing as Irish potatoes out where I lived so these mud potatoes answered the same purpose.[19]

She then would get another root which she called Kantak. I don't know what it would be called in English. The vine of this root looked like a bamboo vine, and it had stickers on it like a bamboo briar. This root had a big head and she would peel the outside of this root and slice the inside, put it on the house top, and let it dry. Then she would beat it like she would corn. It took some time to do this. It would finally turn into what looked like flour. She called it flour. When it was baked, it eat nearly like flour of today. It was good, too.[20]

We had a hard living in those days. We raised some stock but could not sell them, for there was no market for them. Every Indian had stock, and they would not sell them either. It was not worth anything. We could not get enough to buy a good sack of flour out of them if we sold. It was not like today, for the stock brings a good price now but us Indians don't have any to sell. (Choctaw, 1: 225–27)

*   *   *

I was a kid up in what they called the Spavinaw Hills, and later down in the creek bottom along McLain Creek, and we had in this part of the country lots of wild game, wild berries, and wild fruits together with different kinds of nuts. Our game was wild pigeons, quail, deer, turkey, wild cats, panther, bear, mink, muskrats, fox, coyotes, squirrel, and rabbits. Our wild berries were blackberries, dewberries, strawberries, raspberries, grapes, huckleberries, and plums. Our nuts were the hickory nut, walnut, chinquapin, etc. In the little clearings around over the hills in the Saline District we would raise corn, maize, wheat, and some oats.

We did not raise anything for the market, and we simply lived at home with what we had. Our bread was usually corn bread, and to take the place of lard we used Canuchi. The salt for our bread we would get by taking the water from a slough where the water contained salt. This water was then boiled away, leaving just the salt. The corn was ground in a mortar with a pestle. This mortar was made by taking a log about four feet long, standing it on end, and then dishing it out on the upper end, in the fashion of a bowl, and placing the corn in this bowl. The pestle at the lower end was made to fit the bowl or a little smaller than the bowl, and the upper end was larger and much heavier. With the dropping or pounding with this pestle we would crush our corn. After the corn was crushed we would run it through a riddle. The fine part of the corn that passed through the riddle was our meal, the coarse part left in the riddle was our Canhania or, as you call it, hominy grits.[21]

The Canuchi was made from hickory nuts. The hickory nut was placed in the mortar and crushed with the pestle. We would then take and dump the hulls, kernels, and all into a bucket of water and wait for the grease to come to the top and skim it off.[22]

We would bake our bread by smearing it out on a board and hold it up to the fire, to brown on one side and then take another board and turn it over on this board and brown it on the other side. (Cherokee, 3: 171–73)

*   *   *

[To make] sofkey, take flint corn, shell it off of the cob, and when you get ready to use it you put it in cold water. Beat it to take the husks off. That will bring it to grits. When making, put a pot of water on the stove. When it is just about to boil, put the sofkey grits in. When half done, drip some ashes into the sofkey. (We always have a bucket with some holes in the bottom, put ashes in it, and pour some water   over them. The water that drips through the holes is lye.) Keep stirring it until it is done. Put it in a jar and set it aside until next day and drink the liquid. Most people don't like it when it gets sour. I think it's better when it's two or three days old. The men sit around and smoke and drink sofkey. The proportions are three buckets of water in wash pot, one gallon of grits, and one cup of lye.

[To make] sour corn bread, soak sofkey grits overnight in water. Take out and drain the water out. Use a filter or sieve so the water will come out, and leave the corn in. Drain for two or three hours. We beat it then. You could grind it in a food chopper if you wanted to into meal. Take the grits off it and cook like mush; then mix with the meal part. Set overnight after cooking, and it is ready to eat. You put soda in it and salt like other cornbread.

[For] blue dumplings, take one half gallon of strong ashes, sift them, and put in one and a half gallons of water. Put in a gallon of Indian flour corn and keep stirring until the husks come off. Then take out and wash until the water comes clear. Beat or grind to make a meal. Clean some corn shucks or field pea hulls, burn them, and mix with the cornmeal one teaspoon to every half-gallon. That is to make the dark so it shows that it is blue dumplings. Take some water, about half a gallon, and let it come to a boil. Mix the blue dumplings in the boiling water. Then roll it into balls and drop into boiling water and cook till they are done.

Sofkey corn is a flint corn, hard and smooth. Indian flour corn is a large kernel, rough looking, and easy to powder. Both have blue kernels.[23] (Creek, 10: 509–10)

*   *   *

The Indians almost always had small gardens around their places. Two or three acres would be considered a large farm; usually the patches were much smaller. They raised beans, peas, cabbages, and other kinds of vegetables. And they had small patches of corn. Corn formed the basis of many of the Indian dishes. Tom fuller was made of corn crushed, soaked, and fermented. Indians ate lots of cornbread. They made a sort of corn bread in shucks called "shuck bread."[24] Sometimes they mixed nuts, beans, and peas or meat with their "tom fuller." Little by little the Indians grew away from the old ways as the whites settled up the country until finally they got to where they ate about the same sort of foods as the whites did. Very few of them still make the old dishes. If you came to my table you'd see that we eat just about what other poor people do nowadays. (Chickasaw, 70: 9–13)

Fishing

A group of Indians selected a day for fishing and then looked for a stream that could be dammed by poles at two ends.

Six or twelve men of the group were chosen to start early in the morning before breakfast to hunt for a root called devil's shoe-string (Onoleskee is the Creek name), this root being used to obtain the fish. Each man was allowed to dig up only four roots apiece. The roots were beaten to a pulp and placed in a bag. The men would then eat breakfast. The stream was dammed with poles at each end. The roots were soaked in the creek to pollute the water. The root was not poisonous but would make the fish unconscious. The root did not have as much effect on the larger fish so these were shot by men and boys using bows and arrows with light points. The fish would rise and the Indian families would enter the stream and gather as many as they needed. The poles were then removed. This method was later prohibited by the government.[25] (Creek, 2: 56–57)

*   *   *

Beside poisoning streams for fish with roots of devil's shoestring, we had another method of catching them. When creeks are dry and low, a great fish fry day is set. When people gather at a place selected, we would cut and pile branches and limbs of trees across the creek and bind with vine by men pressing down or jumping up and down as to make the limbs press tight.

When all set, enough men are required to lift up while the rest of boys start from other end of stream and scare them toward this brush net until the swimmers reach to net. They would let the net drop which heads off fish from going back to deep water, and of course they would be in a shallow water where bows and arrows come into play. We were ordered to kill only the best and largest fish. This was a great sport.[26]

The Choctaws were very particular in those days as to who (men, women, and children) were eligible to the great fish fry. They believed in signs, and if one was present without having been invited, usually he is promptly excused and would not be allowed around the premises. After gathering at a place located, one man or woman was selected to initiate all those present by using a black or red powder to put a mark on their face. Those not having any black or red paint were not allowed and be ordered away as he was not a member of the fishing society on that day. It was strictly against the fishing rule for an expectant mother or parents to be present.[27] (Choctaw, 1: 209-14)

*   *   *

They would build a fish trap across a stream of water out of large logs and clapboards which made a dam and had a small gate at the bottom for the fish to enter. All the neighbors were welcome to go there and help themselves to the fish, and they would only catch what they could use for each meal. The Indians believe today that the white man came into the country and soon educated the fish. For this reason the fish would go to a shallow body of water to spawn and lay their eggs. At this season of the year, the fish were tame and easily caught, and the Indians would go there and catch what they could use for a meal; but when a white man would find a place like this, he would stay there and catch all the fish, take them home, eat all they could, and let the rest spoil as they had no ice boxes or any way to keep them fresh. In this way, the white man has destroyed the fish and game, and the Indians that live far away from the railroads go hungry today.[28] (Cherokee, 1: 445-46)

Hunting

In my young days, I hunted very often and have killed many deer, but to be a good hunter one would have to get accustomed to their range, where they feed, etc. It may sound foolish and ridiculous for me to expose my way of hunting wild games yet true. It is known to all intelligent people today that every living being, animal, plants, or mineral, was placed here for a cause, and unless we understand its purpose and its use, we cannot prosper much without it. It was placed here for us by nature and is at our command. Therefore, when I wanted to be a hunter I went to a person whom I knew that this party knew where I can get assistance for this purpose.

I was farming that year but did not have much provision to tide me so one day I shouldered my rifle, went hunting, and lost a day from my work, but I did not kill anything that day. On the next day, I knew of a woman who was an herb doctor. My only wish was that she would treat me so I can be a great hunter, and with this in mind I went to her home and explained to her my mission. After a long conversation, I was told that after the treatment all of my hair will turn gray, but I insisted and took the treatment. She went and gathered some kind of weeds and smoked me with this herb once a day for four days. She told the truth as after the treatment my hair turned gray as she said it would, and today my hair is snow hair caused from this treatment.

This was in the year 1907, and after she instructed what to do and how, I have never missed killing a deer.[29] I kill only what I need because I was taught to never kill a deer for sport or waste. After knowing where they range, I can go to the place and wait. After a few moments, I can see one coming up the hill or down depending on where I am hiding, and one would walk as close as ten or fifteen steps from me. Of course, he was killed, and today there is no trouble for me to kill when others fail.

The best time for deer killing is in July or August.[30] He ranged out to graze early in the morning to nine o'clock. After this hour he hides in bushes or in tall weeds and is seldom seen unless one accidently walks up on him. Usually he remains in hiding until about three o'clock in the afternoon when he takes to water and to graze again until about eleven o'clock at night.

Night hunting usually starts about 9 P.M. to 11 P.M., but after this hour, there will be no deer to be seen. He sheds his horn from February first to the fifteenth, and it has been said that after he sheds his horn it is difficult for anyone to find the broken horn.

There is an old saying among the Choctaw tribe of Indians that when one hears a quail on the ground, the deer has grown his horn to about one and one-half inches. If one hears a quail sing or call, resting on a bush about four feet high, the deer horn is nearly grown and is getting fat. When a quail perches high up in the tree, the horn with prongs have grown to full growth and are fat. There is no gall in a deer. Amateur deer hunters do not know this.

A bear is one of few animals that has more intelligence than most animals.[31] He will run from you but when wounded or crippled he is dangerous. The bear usually enters his den in December. Other times he roams around and finds a place under rock or under roots of trees or on a side of a hill or mountain. If he is found in his den, it takes two men to kill him. One of the men must enter the den where the bear is.

If he is to enter the cave, he must be a man with strong nerve because it is not everybody that can enter a den. He must be prepared with a torch or flashlight to locate him to get his position to shoot. After he is located, the hunter aims and fires at the animal. If he is wounded, he is going to rush out of his den. If the man does not have time to get out of his way, he may fall down and lie flat on his stomach and lie still, but if he moves and the bear sees him it is too bad for he will surely kill the man. But if he lies still and not move, the bear will run by him and will not hurt him. As soon as the bear comes out of the den, the man on the outside will shoot him on the hip or the kidney which will cause instant death, but if only crippled or wounded, he is sure to get away.

When he enters his den in December one can hear him as he gnaws his claws he makes a funny noise. The female bear makes her den about January and brings her young cubs in February. The hunters usually listen for the noise and cries of young cubs as they make a noise like a screech owl, and by this means he knows when he hears one. The mother bear will run out when found in den, or if a hunter enters her den to shoot her, she would huddle her young cubs together and hold her head over them. When shot at, she will only clasp her young cubs together and hold her head over them until she is killed. It is pitiful for any one to shoot an innocent mother of young cubs in this position, but she will not make any attempt to run or leave her young ones. This is the way they used to rob her of her young cubs. (Choctaw, 1: 209–13)

*   *   *

A method of hide tanning was to remove the hide from the animal, stretch the hide, and fasten it to poles, stretching and spreading it as tight as possible. The hair was then scraped off with sharp pieces of glass or other sharp objects. It was then rubbed thoroughly with warm hog brains to soften and preserve it. Sometimes wood shavings were mixed with the brains. The hide was then removed from the poles and rubbed between the hands to make it soft. It was rubbed until it became as soft as a rag. The hide was then stretched and hung up again. A fire of green hickory wood was built under the hide, smoking and tanning it. The process of smoking it removed the scent and also tanned it. It was then rubbed again with brains to soften it after the smoking process. It was then ready for use.[32] (Creek, 2: 392)

*   *   *

There were lots of wild horses here, and they belonged to anyone that could catch them. At times the men would get together and go out and round up wild horses. They would cut trees and build a kind of a brush corral with a kind of chute running out from the entrance which was very wide at the entrance but gradually closing in to the entrance of the corral. Then they would locate the horses and start them running, some following and others stationed along to take up the chase as the first horses gave out, and they would run in relays this way until they got them in the corral. There was a man who lived with us named Cook. He always rode a mule, but he was always the man that brought the wild horses into the corral.

Daniel Austin, a cousin of Doc Hastens, half-Chickasaw and half-Creek, went back east to school. Of course, his schoolmates back east were very curious and asked him many questions. He was very witty so one day they were asking him about the wild deer in this country. He said yes, we have lots of deer, but my father never kills a poor deer. They, of course, wanted to know how he could tell whether it was poor or not, he told them his father would just ride along side of them and feel of their ribs, and if they were fat then he would shoot them.

When I was small, the men folks would go on buffalo hunts.[33] My father usually went up in the country around Shawnee. He had a fine horse he called Cheyenne he rode on his buffalo hunts. One time he killed two buffalo and brought the hides home and made rugs of them. We kept those rugs for many years, and I don't know what did finally become of them. (Creek/Chickasaw, 3: 544–45)

*   *   *

In the fall and winter, when the weather was cold, father and I killed and dressed deer and hauled them to Denison, Texas, to sell. We received about ten dollars for each of them. We sold the hides which we had tanned for a small sum. We often went on hunting trips near the present sites of Ada and Roff and would be gone for a week or two. We rode horseback. (Chickasaw/Cherokee, 33: 542–42)

*   *   *

The Indians have always respected the game seasons and did not kill any game during the raising of their young. The Indians probably originated the theory, let every day provide for itself, as each morning the man would get out early in the morning and bring in enough game for that day only. (Cherokee, 1: 445–50)

Notes

1. With the support and cooperation of the Choctaws, Senator Richard M. Johnson established the Choctaw Academy in 1825, under the auspices of the Baptist denomination. In 1841 the Choctaws decided to educate their most promising students in their own nation rather than in northern Kentucky. Carolyn Thomas Foreman, "The Choctaw Academy," *Chronicles of Oklahoma* 6 (1928): 453–80, 10 (1933): 77–114.

2. In *The Rise and Fall of the Choctaw Republic* (Norman, Okla., 1934), Angie Debo describes Robert M. Jones as "probably the wealthiest Choctaw citizen; he is said to have owned more than five hundred slaves, an interest in a trading establishment at Doaksville, a number of steamboats, and five large Red River plantations, of which the largest comprised more than five thousand acres" (p. 60).

3. Southeastern Indians had long lived along rivers. During the Woodland Tradition (1000 B.C. –700 A.D.), in which agriculture started to play an economic role, the southeastern Indians "began to show a decided preference for living near the flood plains of rivers," according to Charles Hudson in *The Southeastern Indians* (Knoxville, Tenn., 1976), p. 62. The village sites of the succeeding Mississippian Tradition (700–1650 A.D.) are also "near the courses or old channels of rivers and streams where the best soil for their kind of agriculture was found" (Ibid., pp. 78–9).

4. Communal labor was traditional among southeastern Indians. James Adair, an eighteenth-century trader, observed that they "obliged every town to work in one body, in sowing and planting their crops, though their fields are divided by proper marks and their harvest is gathered separately." Samuel Cole Williams, ed., *Adair's History of the American Indians* (Johnson City, Tenn., 1930), p. 435. Well into the twentieth century southeastern Indians in rural areas labored communally. This practice became formalized among the Eastern Band of Cherokee Indians, who remained in North Carolina after removal. They organized Free Labor Companies, which moved from one member's farm to another's clearing land, cultivating crops, and making any necessary repairs. These work companies also contributed to the burial costs of members and performed other services not linked to subsistence. John Gulick, *Cherokees at the Crossroads*, rev. ed. (Chapel Hill, N.C., 1973), pp. 88–94.

5. Girdling a tree in this manner prevents the nutrients in the soil from reaching the leaves and branches above the cut. Although it is a very effective way of killing a tree, girdling does not work "instantly." Adair noted that southeastern Indians in the mid-eighteenth century "deadened the trees by cutting through the bark and burned them, when they either fell by decay or became thoroughly dry." Williams, *Adair's History of the American Indians,* p. 435.

6. The narrator presumably refers to the return of Southern refugees from Texas after the Civil War.

7. The fields were fenced to keep out the livestock, which roamed freely foraging in the woods. Traditionally, southern Indians had no livestock and did not fence their fields. Problems developed when white traders brought horses and cattle into their villages because these animals were terribly destructive to the crops.

8. The "cane breaks" of which the narrator speaks were stands of river cane (*Arundinaria*) and not sugar cane.

9. A bull tongue is a heavy plow with a nearly vertical moldboard (the part of the plow that actually turns the soil).

10. A big-eyed hoe has a flat blade with a ring (or eye) at the top into which the handle fits and is, in this way, unlike contemporary gooseneck hoes which have metal sheaths attached to the blades for insertion of the handles.

11. A froe is a heavy knife with the blade at a right angle from the handle. It is used to split shingles from a block of wood.

12. Hickory (*Carya*) is a very hard, durable wood suitable for tools such as hammers.

13. A windlass is a device which consists of a drum, rope, and crank. When the crank is turned, the rope winds around the drum and lifts, in this case, a bucket.

14. Although this family removed the seeds by hand, there were cotton gins in Indian Territory.

15. The narrator went to live with Alex Wilson and his wife after the death of his parents.

16. Both leaves and berries of sumac (*Rhus*) are used for dyes. Colors range from yellowish to dark brown. Copperas, or ferrous sulfate, is added to make the fabric colorfast. The narrator probably refers to the use of hemlock (*Tsuga*) to produce a rosy-tan color rather than sycamore. Madder (*Rubia*), one of the few plants which produces a true red, is not native to Indian Territory and like indigo (*Indigofera*), which grows in more tropical locations, would have been purchased.

17. The Saline District, one of the political divisions of the Cherokee Nation, was located east of Grand River and north of Spring Creek.

18. Traditionally, southeastern Indians soaked dry corn kernels in water and wood-ash lye overnight, drained the kernels, and pounded them in a mortar with a pestle to crack the kernels and loosen the hulls. They then used a basket to separate the grains, which became hominy, from the husks, which were discarded. For meal, they crushed the kernels and sifted the meal. Hudson, *The Southeastern Indians*, pp. 304–5; T. N. Campbell, "Choctaw Subsistence: Ethnographic Notes from the Lincecum Manuscript," *Florida Anthropologist* 12 (1959): 9–12; S. H. Katz, M. L. Hediger, and L. A. Valeroy, "Traditional Maize Processing Techniques in the New World," *Science* 184 (1974): 765–73; Muriel H. Wright, "American Indian Corn Dishes," *Chronicles of Oklahoma* 36 (1958): 155–66; Mary Ulmer and Samuel E. Beck, *Cherokee Cooklore* (Cherokee, N.C., 1951).

19. Mud potatoes (*Sagittaria*) are also called swamp potatoes or duck potatoes.

20. The root of the bamboo briar (*Smilax*), which is also commonly called cut briar, cat briar, green briar, china briar, or tramp's trouble, was widely used as food by southeastern Indians before European contact.

21. Hominy was a staple for southeastern Indians. Traditionally, each household kept a jar of hominy from which people ate whenever they got hungry. The Cherokees called hominy *ganohe · ni* or canhania, the Creeks *sá · fki* or sofkee, and the Choctaws *tanfula* or tom fuller.

22. According to H. B. Battle in "The Domestic Use of Oil Among the Southern Aborigines," *American Anthropologist* 24 (1922): 171–82, one hundred pounds of hickory nuts yielded about one gallon of oil.

23. According to Charles Hudson, four kinds of corn were being grown by southeastern Indians in the early historic period: tropical flint, the cultivation of which began about 200 B.C.; eastern flint, which was introduced about 800–1000 A.D. and which was better suited to cooler climates; dent corn, which was preferred for meal (or Indian flour); and sweet corn. *The Southeastern Indians*, pp. 292–93.

24. Traditionally, the Choctaws cooked their shuck bread, or *paluska holbi*, in hot ashes.

25. Devil's shoestring (*Tephrosia virginiana*) as well as horse chestnuts, or buckeyes (*Aesculus*), attack the nervous system of fish without harming the meat. In *Adair's History of the American Indians* (p. 432), the author related how southeastern Indians used poisons in the eighteenth century: "In a dry summer season, they gather horse chestnuts, and different sorts of roots, which having pounded fine, and steeped a while in a trough, they scatter this mixture over the surface of a middle-sized pond, and stir it about with poles, till the water is sufficiently impregnated with the intoxicating bittern. The fish are soon inebriated, and make to the surface of the water, with their bellies uppermost."

26. Many eighteenth-century observers of southeastern Indians marvelled at the zeal with which the Indians pursued fish downstream toward what Robert Beverley quaintly called a "hedge." *The History and Present State of Virginia*, book 2 (London, 1705), p. 32. Adair claimed that they often drove fish a mile down river "whooping and plunging all the way." Williams, *Adair's History of the American Indian*, p. 432.

27. Many taboos applied to pregnant as well as menstruating women. Frans Olbrechts, "Cherokee Belief and Practice with Regard to Childbirth," *Anthropos* 26 (1931): 17–24.

28. The principle of taking only what was needed was central to southeastern Indian ethics. Many of the myths collected by the late nineteenth-century anthropologist, James Mooney, reflect this principle. Mooney, *Myths of the Cherokee*, Nineteenth Annual Report of the Bureau of American Ethnology (Washington, D.C., 1900); Charles Hudson, "The Cherokee Concept of Natural Balance," *The Indian Historian* 3 (1970): 51–54.

29. In *The Sacred Formulas of the Cherokees*, Seventh Annual Report of the Bureau of American Ethnology (Washington, D.C., 1886), James Mooney recorded some of the rituals connected with hunting. One of these requires the hunter to "go to water," or purify jimself by bathing in the river, and recite the following formula, which Mooney translated from the Cherokee:

> Give me the wind. Give me the breeze. Yû! O Great Terrestial Hunter, I come to the edge of your spittle where you repose. Let your stomach cover itself; let it be covered with leaves. Let it cover itself at a single bend, and may you never be satisfied.
>
> And you, O Ancient Red, may you hover above my breast while I sleep. Now let good (dreams?) develop; let my experiences be propitious. Ha! Now let my little trails be directed, as they lie down in various directions (?). Let the leaves be covered with the clotted blood, and may it never cease to be so. You two (the Water and the Fire) shall bury it in your stomachs. Yû!

The next day, the hunter fasted while traveling to the hunting ground, and, at night, he repeated the bathing and the formula, cooked food, ate, and rubbed his chest with ashes from the fire. On the third day, he looked for game (pp. 369–70).

30. Southeastern Indians traditionally hunted in winter.

31. According to one of Mooney's myths, the bears originally had been human beings but they chose to live in the forest and subsequently acquired the physical appearance of animals. *Myths,* pp. 325–26.

32. Compare with the following description by John Lawson, who observed hide tanning along the Carolina coast in the first decade of the eighteenth century:

Their way of dressing their skins is, by soaking them in water, so they get the hair off with an instrument made of the bone of a deer's foot; yet some use an iron sort of drawing knife, which they purchase of the English, and after the hair is off they dissolve deer's brains, which beforehand are made in a cake and baked in the embers, in a bowl of water, so soak the skins therein till the brains have sucked up the water; then they dry gently, and keep working it with an oyster shell, or some such thing, to scrape withal till it is dry; whereby it becomes soft and pliable.

A New Voyage to Carolina, ed. Hugh T. Lefler (Chapel Hill, N.C., 1967), pp. 216–18.

33. For additional information on hide hunting, see Wayne Gard, The Great Buffalo Hunt (New York, 1959); James H. Cook, Fifty Years on the Old Frontier (New Haven, Conn., 1923); and Carl C. Rister, The Southwestern Frontier (Cleveland, 1928).

Chapter 4 · Entertainment

THE VARIOUS WAYS IN WHICH SOUTHERN INDIANS SPENT THEIR LEISURE
time reflect differences in their degree of acculturation and their socioeconomic class. Highly acculturated southern Indians sought many
of the same kinds of entertainments white Americans enjoyed while
traditionalists continued to play games which were reported by
some of the very earliest European explorers in the Southeast. Occasionally, the interests of the two groups coincided, as perhaps in
horse racing, but generally progressives and conservatives pursued
separate activities and amusements.

The period after the Civil War saw a tremendous growth in
fraternal organizations throughout the United States, and progressives
in Indian Territory participated in this trend. Some groups, such as
the Masons, discredited for a time in the antebellum period as secret
and undemocratic, had a long history. Other societies were of more
recent origins. The American Civil War spawned veterans' organizations, which some southern Indians joined. These fraternal societies
usually had their headquarters in commercial and political centers,
and businessmen and politicians comprised the bulk of their membership.

Much of the entertainment available in the commercial centers of
the five Indian nations had economic overtones. The Indian International Fair, for example, was sponsored by Muskogee businessmen
hoping to attract whites with money to spend and capital to invest

as well as enough Indians, especially Plains Indians, to provide some relatively safe "local color" for visitors.

While the Indian International Fair was primarily a business venture staged by local entrepreneurs, the horse racing that accompanied both the fair and many other events and holidays in Indian Territory had fairly broad popular appeal. Southeastern Indians traditionally enjoyed any sort of contest, particularly if wagers could be made. Apparently, gambling was one Indian vice which whites did not introduce, and attempts by the Indian Police to control it usually proved futile. The Indians bet not only on horse races but also on stalk shootings and ball games. Almost always confined to the hills and coves where conservatives lived, these traditional sports had many aficionados. Stalk shooting provided target practice in a skill which, although no longer needed for survival, provided a link with the remote past. Similarly, the matched ball game gave young men who would have been warriors two centuries earlier an opportunity to prove themselves in a traditionally accepted way. Furthermore, these sports also preserved some aspects of aboriginal social organizations, in which clan and town figured prominently.

Thus, the entertainments southern Indians enjoyed often reflected nearly antithetical attitudes and life-styles. The businessmen of Tahlequah, Muskogee, and other commercial centers had lost touch with traditional kinship ties so they attempted to forge new ones in fraternal societies. Looking to the future instead of the past, they channeled their energies and competitive spirit into economic enterprises designed to bring individual gain. On the other hand, the conservatives engaged in contests that promoted communal bonds and found entertainment in their own rich heritage.

Organizations

Until within recent years, there stood on a rear street at Tahlequah the first and oldest Masonic hall in old Indian Territory and the State of Oklahoma. In the year 1852, the Cherokee National Council granted to the Cherokee lodge of Masons[1] and the Division of the Sons of Temperance[2] now in existence at this place [Tahlequah] two lots on condition that the construction of a hall begin within two years from the date of the act of the council. The hall was completed in 1853, and was then occupied by the Masonic Lodge (which had been chartered in 1847) until the completion of a new and larger hall, which was dedicated in 1890.

Besides the Masonic Lodge, the Knights of Pythias[3] Lodge of Tahlequah held its meetings in the old building for some time, as also did the Odd Fellows Lodge.[4] But in course of time the building often stood vacant, gradually decaying. The desirability of enclosing the old hall within the walls of a fireproof and larger building and preserving it as a historical relic was sometimes mentioned, but no action was taken, and eventually the weather-beaten structure was demolished.

During the period after its abandonment, the upper and lower rooms of the old hall were variously utilized. Public dances were held on the second floor at intervals, while, on the lower floor, services were held by religious denominations.

Then in 1889, a printing office was established in the large lower room. The *Indian Arrow*, which had originally been published at Ft. Gibson in 1888, now became a Tahlequah publication. Upon the walls remained several mottoes placed there by teachers in the Sunday School of the Methodist Episcopal Church South, which had recently completed a brick church. The newspaper was printed in the hall until a short time before the close of 1890, when the presses and material were moved to a new office uptown.

A man was shot while preaching services were being held in a lower room on a night in 1872. The Reverend T. M. Rights, a Moravian minister, was delivering his first sermon in Tahlequah when a shot fired from the outside struck Richard Fields (usually called Dick Halfbreed) in the eye and he tumbled to the floor, apparently fatally injured. However, Fields recovered and lived more than a quarter-century after. (Cherokee, 59: 82–83)

*   *   *

Forty years ago (1896) there was in existence at Tahlequah, Cherokee Nation, the only Indian Grand Army of the Republic Post in the Indian Territory.[5] This post had been organized several years previously. There were then living quite a number of Civil War veterans who had served in the Union Army. The majority of those composing the membership of the post at Tahlequah were Cherokees, once members of the Union Indian Brigade, but there were also some white veterans who lived in and about Tahlequah and who became members of the post.

Officially the post bore this designation: "Captain White Catcher Post No. 2, Department of the Indian Territory, G.A.R." In 1896, the post commander was Savelon S. Bayles, veteran of a Kansas regiment, and the adjutant was Robert Bruce Ross, who had belonged to a company in the Union Indian Brigade in the Civil War.

The meeting place of the G.A.R. Post was at first in the Odd Fellows Hall, which was in the old building originally built as a Masonic hall in 1853. At a later date the members of the post met in a larger hall in the upper story of a brick building on the principal street. Meetings were well attended during several years, but gradually the membership became reduced as one after another of the veterans passed from life, and in course of time meetings were held no more.

The man for whom the post was named was a noted native Cherokee of a bygone time. White Catcher had served as a member of the Cherokee National Council, his home having been in the Tahlequah District. He enlisted in the Union Indian Brigade in 1862, and received appointment as captain of a company. He performed meritorious service, and when the war came to a close was elected as a member of the National Committee, or Senate, from Tahlequah District. Matters of interest and importance affecting the Cherokees demanded attention at the national capital, and, in 1866, Captain White Catcher was selected as one of a delegation of six members to go to Washington. While on that mission, Captain White Catcher served as a pall bearer at the funeral of Principal Chief John Ross, who died August 1, in that year. Some days later, the work of the delegation being completed, the former officer started on his return home, but his death occurred on the way, and he lies buried in the State of Missouri. (Cherokee, 59: 59-61)

The Indian International Fair

The Indian International Fair Association was organized in Muskogee, Indian Territory, in 1875. Mr. John A. Foreman, one of the town's first citizens, was the first president, and Mr. Joshua Ross, a prominent Indian merchant, was the first secretary.[6] These men felt that an enterprise of that type would be of interest and great benefit to the people of the town and also to those of the surrounding country.[7]

The first fair was held that year under a large tent at the corner of what is now Cherokee and Cincinnati streets. The exhibits consisted of all varieties of farm produce and livestock. In the woman's department could be found an exhibit of preserves, jellies, pickles, cakes, and bread. Needlework of all kinds, with a department for children, was included.

At the time the association was organized the intention of the officials was to make it an enterprise for the eastern part of the territory only; but, encouraged by the interest manifested in the new venture, they decided to make it an international affair and include the western tribes, or "Plains Indians." It was then that the location was moved farther east to where the Muskogee General Hospital now stands. A long, barn-like plank building was erected, and the entire grounds including the race track were enclosed with a high board fence.

Horse racing, always a popular amusement among all Indians, was one of the chief attractions. Race horses were brought from adjoining states to compete with the race horses owned by the Indians. The mile race track located where Spaulding Park is now was always in perfect condition for the occasion.

The western or "wild" tribes of Indians came, bringing their herds of ponies with them. The tribes represented were: the Sac and Fox, Comanches, Arapahoes, Cheyennes, Shawnees, Osages, and the Delawares. The first year they camped on the outside of the enclosure, but one night almost all of their ponies were stolen and had to be paid for by the association, and that almost bankrupted the treasury.

The Indians brought their own tents and tepees and set them up inside the enclosure, as they refused to camp on the outside again. They were a picturesque group with their gaily colored blankets they had woven and their imposing headdress. The headdress of the chief was made of eagle feathers, but no one else could wear eagle feathers. Several beeves were always prepared for them, furnished by the association. One beef was slaughtered each morning and divided among them and cooked over their own camp fire. As they all seemed to like their meat rare, they never waited until it was well cooked but would eat it with the blood still running out. The Indians always welcomed visitors to their tepees, and it was my delight as a small child, in company with my little cousins, the Ross children, to wander among their camps.

After a year or so, a larger, more convenient building was erected on the same location. It was a round, two-story structure with four entrances and was called the Dinner Bucket. Large posts supported the upper floor throughout the building. They were always twined with cedar, and the entire interior was decorated with red, white, and blue bunting and evergreens.

The exhibits were tastefully arranged, the woman's department occupying one-quarter of the space. Salesmen from all adjoining states came and displayed their wares. A leading jewelry firm of Fort Smith always had an exhibit with a fine stock to select from.

I think my first great disappointment in life came when, at the age of six, on my first visit to the fair, I proudly went on a purchasing tour with a whole quarter to squander. I selected a lady's gold watch and went to ask my mother's approval. On learning that the price was fifty dollars and it could not be bought for a quarter my disappointment knew no bounds, and my pleasure for the day was ruined.

Along with the race horses came their trainers and riders and also the crowd that followed the racing. The men always slept near their horses to guard them for fear something would be done to injure them. Often a faithful watchdog was tied in the stall with the horse. The riders were a colorful group when they came out on the track with their brilliant satin shirts with their number on the back in a contrasting color. Betting ran high, and thousands of dollars changed hands. A prize was always given to the best woman horseback rider. You could take your choice between the money and a fine sidesaddle. Mr. Ross' two daughters, Rosalie and Susie, each were awarded the prize. Mrs. Will Robinson, now living in Muskogee, and myself were also winners. I rode my own saddle horse that I had been carefully grooming for weeks past. As I was under the required age and do not know how I came to be accepted in the contest, I tried to look as dignified and sedate as possible. The women of the wild tribes were in a class by themselves, as they rode bare-backed and astride. On one occasion when a woman was awarded the prize, she refused to accept a woman's saddle but took a man's saddle.

One of the most attractive things to me was the silver ornaments the men of the wild tribes wore, particularly the chiefs. Crescents, stars, all kinds of emblems cut from pure silver as thin as a knife blade securely attached to a long cord that fastened to their headdress of eagle feathers and hung almost to the ground. I do not know where the silver came from, from which their ornaments were made, but the paints they used on their faces and bodies came from the paint rocks in their own reservations.

They adopted the white man's clothes by degrees. I remember meeting a big six-foot Osage chief after a hard rain one evening. He was clad in a beaded shirt, black broadcloth trousers, a long linen duster, was barefooted, with a gorgeous string of ornaments fastened to his eagle feather headdress that nearly reached the ground, and with his trousers rolled up, he splashed through the mud.

Another thing that thrilled me was the big dinner bell that always rung at Buzz Hawkins' eating tent. Buzz Hawkins and his wife were well-known prosperous Negroes, living four miles west of town. Every year they opened an eating place under large tents. Mrs. Hawkins was a famous cook, and one was sure of a splendid turkey dinner every day for twenty-five cents. I always got a good seat, as I was a fast runner and didn't waste time when the bell began to ring. There were numerous places to eat, but none enjoyed the popularity that the Hawkins' did.

It was in the early eighties that the first merry-go-round made its appearance at the fair. It was a funny thing, operated by little mules that went round in a circle. At first the children were afraid to ride, but after they found out they would not be killed it was hard to get them off.

All kinds of skin games and gambling devices were prohibited, and the Indian Police, who were the only officers on duty, were constantly on the watch, but even then some crept in. No drinking was allowed, and the crowd was always peaceable and happy. The gates were opened at nine o'clock in the morning and closed at 6 P.M. The admission was twenty-five cents for one person and fifty cents for a single rig and one dollar for a double team. I was always glad when my mother was appointed on the committee to judge an exhibit in the woman's department, as we got in free.

The United States flag floated from atop of the main building and could be seen from across the prairie for several miles. A stomp dance was held each night by the Indians, on the second floor of the main building.[8]

The M.K.&T. Railroad, which was the only road through the Territory, gave reduced rates, and visitors from other states were numerous.[9] Distinguished men from Washington, D.C., and officials from the Indian Department always came.

There was plenty of music, as bands from Denison, Texas, Parsons, Kansas, and several Arkansas towns were there and played all day. The bandstand was near the race track, and the horses seemed to be inspired by the music, as well as the people.

The noted Belle Starr and her beautiful young daughter, Pearl Reed, were regular visitors and attracted much attention, partly because of their notoriety and also the way they dressed. Belle always wore a divided skirt, a man's shirt and cartridge belt, and a white felt hat. They were quiet and well-behaved and never seemed to make friends with anyone.[10]

As the distance of what is now called five blocks from town to the fairgrounds was too great to walk, everyone rode. The livery barn operated regular taxi lines to the fairgrounds charging twenty-five cents a trip.

Muskogee had three good hotels. The Mitchell House, located where the Katy Station now is, the Strokey Hotel across the street from it, and the Greenhouse on the corner of Second and Court gave splendid accommodations and were always crowded during fair week. The Greenhouse was a large, two-story frame building in a large yard. It was operated by Mrs. Laslie, a shiny black little Negro woman whose husband claimed to be part Creek Indian. They took only white guests, and no Negroes came in sight except the waiters in the dining room.

Everyone living in town expected their relatives to visit them during the fair and prepared for it, and they were never disappointed.

The fair was held each year the later part of September, lasting one week. It was the outstanding event of the year and was looked forward to in pleasant anticipation for months. It was, in fact, a reunion of friends and relatives that perhaps saw each other at no other time. (Cherokee, 52: 396–404)

Horse Racing

Horse racing was one of the greatest attractions of the fair. Probably the fastest horses in the United States were brought here to the fairs. We had what we called short horses. They only run quarter-mile races. Our race track was half a mile long, but we ran mostly quarter-mile races. Gambling was wide open to the citizens.[11]

They always gave a premium to the best lady riders as a drawing card for the crowds. The fair of 1879 brought a lady here, who was a cousin to Bob Chandler, (I don't remember her name) who was an awful good rider. My wife was also a good rider so they matched a race to run the full half-mile. They rode sidesaddles and wore long riding skirts.

Dr. Fite had a fine horse named Prince. My wife rode him, and the other lady had a horse named Red Buck that she rode. Of course, there was a lot of money bet on the race, and the merchants made up a premium for the winner, which was a fine sidesaddle. Fortunately, my wife won. She kept that saddle for a number of years.

People were much more friendly and sociable then than they are now. On the Fourth of July we had a race here. They made up a premium for the winner and charged an entrance fee for each horse entered. There were seven of probably the fastest horses in the country entered.

Little Danger from Fort Smith, a chestnut sorrel named Gold Dust, and another chestnut sorrel named Gold Digger, and a mare named Brown Lizzy from Rogers, Arkansas, a grey horse named Grey Wolf (which I owned myself), and a sorrel horse owned by Major McCoy all run. When the gun was fired as a signal for them to go, Little Danger got the breaks, and they called them all back and they started again. This time all got an equal start, and it was as close a race as I ever saw. Grey Wolf won by one and a half feet, making the quarter-mile in twenty-two seconds, which was just one second more than the world's record of quarter-mile races. I then shipped Grey Wolf to Kansas City and St. Louis where he broke the track records. The record he made in Kansas City is still unbroken today.

Later, though, there was a man at Webbers Falls owned a black mare named Black Roxey. We matched a race between Grey Wolf and

Black Roxey. This was probably the biggest race ever run here. There was about 6,000 people came here to see the race. It came an awful rain the day the race was to be run, and to my sorrow the race was put off until the next day, and when the race was run, Black Roxey won, but I learned later that they had paid my rider $300 to hold Grey Wolf back. This race attracted more attention than any other race in the Indian Territory. On the following Fourth of July we matched a three-cornered race: Black Roxey and a horse owned by a man from St. Louis, named Big Joe. Big Joe and Grey Wolf were to run, but for some cause Big Joe disqualified. This left Black Roxey and Grey Wolf again, and Black Roxey won. There was a traveling man named Elliotts here from Dennison, Texas, and, as they were planning a picnic at Dennison, he wanted to take the horses there and run them as a drawing card for the picnic. We went down there. I went with Bud Hart, a brother to Ed Hart. Black Roxey and Big Joe were running, and we made it up that one of us would hold stakes, so Bud was holding the stakes and the money began coming in so fast that Bud became confused and made a mistake in change, so they tried to rule him out and let a fellow name Cobb of Vinita to hold stakes. There was already $1500 up, and I said, "No, Bud Hart would hold stakes or there would be no race." So they run, and Big Joe won by thirty feet, and I won $1050. They then matched Black Roxey with Grey Wolf (my horse) and beat me, and then poisoned my horse. (Chickasaw/Creek, 8: 538–40)

Stalk Shooting

This game was known to the Cherokees for many years and was a great gambling game in the early days according to the older Cherokees. The origin and date of the game are not known, but it is still a great sport among the Cherokees. However, the younger generation do not shoot stalks as the Cherokees did forty or fifty years ago. The stalk ground was usually about a hundred and fifty yards long, smooth land and soft dirt.[12] There was not any limit as to the number of members in a team, and I have shot in games where there were fifty men on a side.

The stalks were piled just exactly one hundred yards apart, these piles being three feet long, two feet thick and about three feet high.

The big games were matched weeks in advance so that the event could be noted throughout the country. Many people came from miles around to see the games, and betting took place when the games started.

The members of the teams usually represented two or more communities, as the best shooters were chosen from several teams and made one team. After the teams were chosen, the witcher was chosen by the matcher.

The day before the game the chosen shooters began to come to the appointed place, often coming many miles. The matcher of the game and his backers, or the gamblers, furnished the food, which was usually cooked near the campgrounds.

Every member of the team was not always allowed to shoot, even though he had been chosen, for if the witcher for the team discovered that a member of the team was weak another player was chosen. The witcher was a smart man. He could sure tell if the team was going to win or lose, and he would tell the gamblers in which game they would have a chance to win. I have seen horses and saddles lost in the stalk shootings. They usually made standing bets for, if they did not, the better would back out after the witcher had told which team was going to win.

The bows the players used were made from bois d'arc, and the arrows were made from black locust.[13] The spears were made from wagon seat springs, the length of these spikes being from eight to eighteen inches.

Some of the old timers who shot with me are: Johnson Tyler, George Soap, Sam Foreman, Issac Hummingbird, Bill Downing, Alex Downing, Henry Walkingstick, William Shell, Riley Ragsdale, Ben Squirrel, John Rider, Tom Swimmer, Fixin Blackbird, William England, and Toch Ketcher. The most famous witchers in these shootings were John Hair, Ben Squirrel, Henry Turn, and Thompson Charles. (Cherokee, 90: 136–38)

Ball Games

The old Indian ball game was a favorite game of mine. I still have my ball sticks, which are made of hickory about three feet long bent back into a small loop with skin woven across the loop. The game is very exciting. Two or as many as wish can play. Twenty-two make a good game, eleven on each side. Poles are placed about one hundred yards apart, and the medicine man goes to the center of the ring and starts the game, tossing a small ball in the air. Eleven points wins the game. Each time you hit the end post is a point. The women cheer and pat the men on the back during the game, saying in Choctaw, "Hurry and get it." The ball is never touched by the hand, always hitting or catching with the ball sticks. The players wear only a breech-clout attached to the belt, and at the back a tail attached to the belt which is made from a cow's tail.[14] (Choctaw, 2: 122–23)

*   *   *

When I got to be what the Choctaws call grown, I believe I was about eighteen years of age, I was a large Indian young man of good health and strength. This part of the country was in those days called Gaines County by the Choctaw government. Each of the counties in the Choctaw Nation had what they called Indian ball teams. In other words, the Choctaw of one county would get together and play some primary games of the old-time Indian ball and decide which of the bunch was the strongest and the best players and get them together and make what they called a county team.

The equipment for all Indian teams consisted of two Indian ball clubs. I do not remember the exact length of the handle to this club, but it was, I think, three feet long, made of seasoned hickory. This handle had a thin piece at the end of it, made rather cup-shaped, out of green hickory and dressed down and bent to fit the sides of the handles and was laced to the handle with deer hide or buckskin strings. A good one was made very steady and would stand a lot of abuse.

I was selected for the Gaines County Choctaw team. About twice a year each of these Choctaw counties would have about two games between the county teams. These games were really rough. Any kind of rough treatment, as long as the hands alone were used, was permissible. You were not allowed to use these Indian ball clubs as defensive weapons, but you were permitted to take your opponent with your empty hands and, if you were the stronger of the two, throw him down against the ground just as hard as you were able to. Under no consideration was the Indian ball club to be used, other

than to pick up the small Indian ball and carry or throw it toward
your goal. After many of these county Indian ball games in my
young days , you could see a great many skinned up young bucks,
as they called them in that time.

I was considered the fastest foot racer in what was then called
Gaines County, now Latimer County. I was able to run one hundred
yards in eight and three-quarters seconds. I could take an Indian pony
without bridle or rope or anything but my hands, mount it, and ride
it. (Choctaw, 2: 178–80)

*   *   *

The Cherokee ball games were held during the summer months.
A ball game was very interesting to watch, the ladies being on one
side and the men on the other. A pole about twelve inches in diameter
and about twenty feet long was used, the pole being previously erected
with a medium-sized carved wooden fish about twelve inches long
fastened on top of the pole so that it would turn when hit by a small
yarn ball which was used in the game. The men used raques. The
raques were about fifteen inches in length and about one inch in
diameter, made of hickory or elm, looped on one end. A basket
was formed out of the inner barks just a little larger than the ball.
Each man used one in each hand. His job was to hit the fish on top
of the pole. The ladies were allowed to use their hands, which made
a hard fought game. Each time the fish was hit counted one score,
and seven scores for either side was counted a full game. A game
a day was played for four days. If the men were the losers, they
were required to hunt wild game and fish for a big feast which was
given on the fifth day. On the other hand, the ladies being the losers,
they were to make hominy and sin corn.[15] (Cherokee, 1: 461–62)

*   *   *

The last ball game I know about was in 1921 or 1922, east of Bunk
Pharoah's place, which is Spring Hill. It was really intended to be
a game for fun but ended in a fight between the Arbeccas and Thlop
Thloccos. The king and medicine man makes the match with some
other town's king and medicine man. There is no hard feelings between them at all. They don't know of the grudge between one or
more of their team and one or more of the other team. When they are

playing or before, these players decide to get this grudge fought off and start quarreling or fighting. Sometimes they are told to play ball and fight after it is over, that this is a game for fun and not a fight. Other times the players will take up for their "brothers," and it will be a free-for-all.

When the men play together they have sticks with medicine on them and play entirely different than in a mixed game. In a mixed game they use the pole that is danced around instead of the two goals in the men's game. The men use sticks without medicine while the women catch and throw the ball with their hands. The ball has to hit the cow's head on top of the pole. They have a scorekeeper off to one side who marks on the ground to see who hits the cow's head most, men or women. This game is similar to basketball except there is only one goal. (Creek, 13: 431–33)

*   *   *

There are two different kinds of Indian ball games. The one that they play here at the town is played by both women and men. The other is the matched game, played by picked men.

They have a pole with a horse head or some kind of skull or a fish that has been cut out of a board on the top of the pole. The men use sticks, but there is no medicine on them. The women catch and throw the ball with their hands instead of with the sticks. The ball has to be thrown and has to hit the skull for a score. There is no set score for this game. They just play until they get tired and quit with the ones having the highest score winning. The women try to tear the clothes off the men to hinder them from throwing straight. It is a very rough game but not a dangerous game. If a person gets hurt playing, it is an accident.

Matched game. This game is the next thing to a war. When the town king wants to have a match game with another town, he calls the citizens to come to the town for a dance at a certain time. The king has already decided to have the game and with a certain town. They set a date and yell and dance all night. Some men are appointed to go to the king of the other town with the challenge.

If the king of the other town accepts and agrees on the date to play, all the towns have spokesmen who agree where to camp and where to play ball. They don't play ball at their towns nor camp there just preceding the game. The date is named by the number of suns, not by days.

Then they come back and choose men to play. They always pick the best men, and the number is agreed upon by both towns, and different games might have a different number of players, but both towns of a certain game have the same number.

When one town wants to tell the other something they have runners to take the message, as none of one camp are allowed to go to the other camp except these runners.

The morning of the game they come back to their own camp and make their report. The goal posts are taken to the place where the game is to be and set up by the town it belongs to. Then they dance around it and yell. Next is the ceremony in the middle of the field.

These goal posts are similar to the football goals, but the game is more like basketball except they use sticks instead of their hands and the ball is much smaller.

The teams draw up facing each other in the middle of the field and lay their ball sticks down. A spokesman has been appointed to give them their last instructions as to the rules. He sends them to their positions—guards and forwards for the goal posts and centers—and they are to stay in their places when playing. The same man throws up the ball, and the game is started. The side that throws the ball through the goal posts twenty times makes the score of twenty and wins the game.

Several men have been appointed on both sides to referee the game, and it is their duty to stop any fights that may start if possible. Sometimes they wrestle instead of fighting.

The medicine that they have taken before the game seems to keep them from getting hurt as much as they would have been hurt without it, but even then they are pretty well beaten up and cut up before the game is over. I have never known of anyone being killed, but plenty of arms and ribs have been broken, and there have been scalp wounds four or five inches long. One man was hit between the eyes with the end of the ball sticks. (Creek, 24: 252–55)

Notes

1. The Order of Free and Accepted Masons, probably the largest secret fraternal organization in North America, originated in the eighteenth century.

Although the lodge in Tahlequah was founded and the building constructed before the Civil War, the Masons experienced their greatest growth after the war, when they were joined by several other secret societies mentioned below.

2. Temperance organizations, which proliferated in Indian Territory after the Civil War, are dealt with in Chapter 6.

3. The Knights of Pythias was founded in Washington, D.C., in 1864, as a secret philanthropic organization.

4. The Independent Order of Odd Fellows began in England in the eighteenth century as a secret mutual aid society.

5. The Grand Army of the Republic, an organization of Union veterans of the Civil War, was founded in 1866.

6. Foreman was a white resident of Muskogee who owned a mill and encouraged the building of railroads. Although he was a citizen of the Cherokee Nation, Ross's ancestry was predominently white. He married a Creek woman and operated a business in Muskogee. Angie Debo, *The Road to Disappearance* (Norman, Okla., 1941), p. 232.

7. Angie Debo maintains that the Indian International Fair was mainly a "white man's project" that was intended to promote the growth of Muskogee. The United States agent to the five tribes who was headquartered in Muskogee sanctioned the enterprise because he hoped that it would encourage Indian agriculture, speed acculturation, and enable him to make positive reports. Most conservatives and Plains Indians who attended did so only as spectators. Only in the fall of 1879 did the Indian International Fair provide an opportunity for transacting business of interest to all Indians. At this time, the five tribes and the Plains Indians tried to present a united front against the threat of "Boomers" to occupy the Unassigned Lands adjacent to the Pottawatomie Reservation, which had been ceded by the Creeks and Seminoles in 1866. In response, Secretary Carl Schurz urged them to accept their lands in severalty. Debo, *The Road to Disappearance*, pp. 241–42.

8. Stomp dances are discussed in Chapter 5.

9. The Missouri, Kansas, and Texas railroad (also called the Katy) completed its north-south line, which crossed Cherokee, Creek, Choctaw, and a small section of Chickasaw territory, in January 1873.

10. Belle Starr was a notorious woman outlaw. She had two husbands, Jim Reed and Sam Starr (who was Cherokee), and a number of paramours, including the infamous Cole Younger, who were also outlaws. Although she apparently participated in a number of robberies, Belle Starr received only one six-month sentence. In 1889, she was shot in the back and killed as she rode home alone. Burton Rascoe, *Belle Starr, The Bandit Queen* (New York, 1941).

11. The southeastern Indians enjoyed gambling immensely. In the eighteenth century, Lieutenant Henry Timberlake remarked that the Cherokees "will even lose the shirts off their back rather than give over play, when luck runs against them," and the trader, James Adair, reported, "The Choktah are exceedingly addicted to gambling, and frequently on the slightest and most hazardous occasion, will lay their all, and as much as their credit can procure." Samuel Cole Williams, ed., *Lieut. Henry Timberlake's Memoirs, 1756-1765* (Marietta, Ga., 1948), p. 79; Samuel Cole Williams, ed., *Adair's History of the American Indians,* (Johnson City, Tenn., 1930), p. 429.

12. Stalk shooting gave men an opportunity to develop and perfect a skill which once had been an economic necessity. Although prizes of as much as $200 added an economic incentive, archery largely had been reduced to a sport. In a stalk shoot, the members of each team alternately shot marked arrows into a rack of 200 dry cornstalks. The team whose arrows penetrated at least 150 stalks won. Conjurers, or "witchers," employed a number of means to ensure victory. Wood which had been struck by lightning brought luck when carried in a participant's pocket. Furthermore, short rituals intended to bring success to the conjurer's team and failure to the opponents were conducted. Jack Frederick Kilpatrick and Anna Gritts Kilpatrick, *Run Toward the Nightland: Magic of the Oklahoma Cherokees* (Dallas, 1967), pp. 91-93.

13. Traditionally, southeastern Indians preferred the wood of the locust tree (*Robinia*) for their bows. After removal, they began to use bois d'arc (*Maclura*), which is also called Osage orange and yellow wood.

14. James Adair gave the following description of an eighteenth-century ball game:

> Ball-playing is their chief and most favourite game: and is such severe exercise, as to show it was originally calculated for a hardy and expert race, like themselves, and the ancient Spartans. The ball is made of a piece of scraped deer-skin, moistened, and stuffed hard with deer's hair, and strongly sewed with deer's sinews. The ball-sticks are about two feet long, the lower end somewhat resembling the palm of a hand, and which are worked with deer-skin thongs. Between these, they catch the ball, and throw it a great distance, when not prevented by some of the opposite party, who fly to intercept them. The goal is about five hundred yards in length: at each end of it, they fix two long bending poles into the ground, three yards apart below, but slanting a considerable ways outwards. The party that happens to throw the ball over these, counts one; but if it be thrown underneath, it is cast back, and played for as usual. The gamesters are equal on

each side; and, at the beginning of every course of the ball, they throw it up high in the center of the ground, and in a direct line between the two goals.

Adair reported that he saw some players "break the arms and legs of their opponents." Williams, *Adair's History of the American Indians*, pp. 428-29. For additional information on and analysis of the ball game, see James Mooney, "The Cherokee Ball Play," *American Anthropologist* 3 (1890): 105-32; John R. Swanton, *Social Organization and Social Usages of the Indians of the Creek Confederacy*, Forty-Second Annual Report of the Bureau of American Ethnology (Washington, D.C., 1928), pp. 456-66; Raymond D. Fogelson, "The Cherokee Ballgame Cycle: An Ethnographer's View," *Ethnomusicology* 15 (1971): 327-38; Mark Reed, "Reflections on Cherokee Stickball," *Journal of Cherokee Studies* 2 (1977): 195-200.

15. Adair observed ball games between men and women such as those described by the narrator: "They fix in the ground a large pole with a bush tied at the top, over which they throw a ball. Till the corn is in, they meet there almost every day, and play for venison and cakes, the men against the women; which the old people say they have observed for time out of mind." Williams, *Adair's History of the American Indians*, p. 120. Also see Swanton, *Social Organization*, pp. 467-68.

Chapter 5 · Traditions

THE BALL GAME AND OTHER TRADITIONAL MEANS OF RECREATION were not the only aspects of aboriginal southeastern culture to survive in Indian Territory. Religious ceremonies, medical practices, and town and clan affiliations, which can be traced back to at least the early eighteenth century, continued to be significant in the lives of conservatives. These traditions rarely appeared in their pure aboriginal form because of extensive contact with whites, removal to Indian Territory, involvement in the Civil War, and dramatic social, political, and economic changes on the tribal level. However, the remnants of pre-contact customs served to unify traditional Indian communities and contributed to the estrangement of conservatives from progressives within the five civilized tribes.

Ceremonies focused primarily on personal purification and social rejuvenation, and the most important ritual conducted by southeastern Indians was the Green Corn Ceremony. Originally, the Indians had observed a number of seasonal ceremonies, but by the late eighteenth century they had consolidated these functions into one event. Southeastern Indians held their Green Corn Ceremony in July or August when the new corn was ready to eat. In this sense, the ceremony commemorated the harvest. The participants, however, attached far more significance to the occasion. They extinguished and rekindled their ceremonial fires to symbolize the end of the old year and the beginning of the new. Individuals renewed themselves by purging their bodies of pollution through the use of specially prepared emetics. At this time, members of the community resolved disputes, and their society emerged from the ceremony with order and harmony restored and group identity strengthened. Between annual Green Corn Ceremonies, conservatives met occasionally to reenact particular features of the ceremony, such as dancing and taking medicine. When faced with fundamental changes, such as individual landholding and tribal dissolution, many southeastern Indians sought, at first, to alter the course of events through these ceremonies and, when this measure failed, to find comfort in traditional rituals. Furthermore, some conservatives organized secret societies to perform demanding rituals in order to reaffirm traditional beliefs, values, and relationships.

In addition to maintaining some of their ceremonies, many southeastern Indians continued to rely on herbal medicines and conjurers to prevent and cure illnesses. The premise on which they based such practices was that each illness had a specific cause and a certain cure, both of which were within man's knowledge and power. The spirits of animals brought about some diseases for which plants provided cures. Illness also resulted from conjury, which could be counteracted by more powerful conjury. Whatever the cause, conservative Indians firmly believed that man himself through the use of natural substances and spiritual invocations had the means to combat illness. Removal no doubt altered or perhaps even restricted medical practices since the flora in Indian Territory differs from that in the Southeast, but medicine men apparently managed to provide remedies for most ailments. The expertise of some conjurors extended beyond the realm of medicine and encompassed physical transformation and divinations. Although these witches and prophets aroused fear among most conservatives, their services often proved valuable.

Some aspects of aboriginal social organization also seem to have survived in Indian Territory. Before extensive contact with whites, most southeastern Indian groups had matrilineal kinship systems. In this particular way of reckoning blood relatives, a child belonged only to his mother's family or clan, and his only kinsmen were those who could be traced through her, that is, her mother, her sisters, her sisters' children of both sexes, and her brothers. The child was not related by blood to his father, and his maternal uncle assumed many of the responsibilities that Anglo-Americans associate with the father. By the Civil War, Anglo-American bilateral kinship largely had replaced matrilineal kinship, but many conservatives retained a clan identification and town affiliation, which they inherited from their mothers. Although clans generally had ceased performing traditional legal and judicial functions, kinship often continued to regulate relationships such as marriage. Furthermore, conservatives still placed great value on the family, as their mourning and burial practices demonstrate.

Ceremonies

Every tribal town (tulwa) in the Muskogee-Creek Nation has its chief, heneha, and tustanagee.[1] The chief of a tribal town during a ceremonial dance tells to the heneha what he wishes told to the members of the town (tulwa). It is then the duty of the heneha to talk for the chief at all times. The ones who partake of the tribal medicine are to conduct themselves with the high regard of the medicine used, such as refraining from the use of intoxicating drink. The men are not to touch women or talk to one all during the ceremonial period.

Another tribal town (tulwa) wishing to extend an invitation to other towns gives a short stick to the chief of the town where a dance is being held giving all the information about the invitation thus extended, and then it is the duty of this chief to request his heneha to make the announcement to all that are present giving the date of the ceremonies to be conducted so that anyone wishing may attend.

There is the ceremony often called the Green Corn Dance that is held every summer in the tribal towns of the Muskogee-Creek Nation.[22] This ceremony is held just before any of the members have eaten any roasting ears, but if any of them have eaten some there is a strong medicine to be taken before entering into the festival. The purpose of this ceremony is to take medicine and cleanse the whole body, internally and externally.[3] It is the belief that if corn is eaten before this rite or before any medicine is taken, that many fevers and other sickness will result.

The night before the medicine is to be taken, the men all sleep within the boundary of the ceremonial grounds in their respective places. The next day being medicine day, the men fast and use the medicine, still inside the boundary. Sometimes this fasting and taking of medicine lasts all day long. Some towns fast until noon or until the middle of the afternoon, each town being governed by the chief. The women and children use the medicine also but do not fast, nor do they stay inside of the ceremonial ground boundary.[4] The women on the fast day spend their time in preparing a big feast for the men.

At some time during the day that the herbal medicine is taken, the children also go through a rite which has been a traditional custom. The uncle of the children, as understood in a clan way,[5] uses a needle, pin, or some sort of thorn, usually a berry thorn, to make four long scratches on each of the child's legs and arms. This rite was believed to add strength to a child into old age as well as to tend to make a longer life of a child thus treated. In the early days, these scratches were not treated lightly, but some bare scars where they were done and scratched very deep.[6] This custom is not enforced very much now, and, when it is used, the scratches are not so deep as to make life-lasting scars. When the medicine was being taken and before corn was eaten during the Green Corn Ceremony, the mother of a child took a fresh corn and caused the milk in the corn to run out and rubbed the corn four times on the legs and arms of a child.

When a tribal town (tulwa) decides to move to another location, the chief, heneha, medicine man, and tustanagee sleep one night within the boundary of the ceremonial grounds. These four are responsible for the move of the tribal town. Only ashes under the top layer of the ashes of the old ceremonial fire place to be moved are taken and placed in the place where the new location is to be established. Ceremonial dances are then held. (Creek, 47: 112–25)

*   *   *

Stomp dances. The real Indian name is a stomp dance, but they have added some names to some of the stomp dances.[7] They have a stomp dance the middle of April; the second, the middle of May; the third, the middle of June, and that one lasts all night. Then the king sets the date for them to come back in July (when he thinks the green corn will be ready to eat) and clean the "yard." They all gather at that date with hoes and clean about an acre or more of all grass and weeds and pile them around a pole until there is a big pile four or five feet high.[8] This pile is allowed to rot instead of being burned. Then the king tells them when to come back for the Green Corn Dance. It is usually the next Saturday or Sunday, about the middle of July. If they meet Sunday, they visit that day. Monday, they have two Ribbon Dances by the women. The men do not eat all day and night. That night they take medicine. Wednesday, they sleep all day, and the women and kids stand around. Thursday, they used to go out and hunt; now they go out but have poor luck hunting. Friday, the women have another Ribbon Dance. Saturday, the men do not eat a bite all day, and they dance all night and break up in the morning. After they dance all night, they run to the creek and jump in four times. They must duck their heads under the water with their eyes open.[9]

The men must not talk to a woman. It is a five dollar fine to take a drop of whiskey. "Sick" women just watch the dance from a distance. If any of these rules are broken, the medicine is broken for all who take the medicine, and there will be a lot of sickness and death among them, so they are very careful.[10]

How the fire is made. The ground has been cleaned; nothing unclean has been left on the ground. Some clean dirt, about a wash-pan full, is piled where the fire is to be made and smoothed down on top. Two lines are made, one going exactly north and south, the other going east and west, on the top of the dirt. Some herbs are put in the spaces between the lines. Four two-and-a-half-foot logs are placed with the ends touching in the center of this dirt. Then four roasting ears are placed between them. They use a soft substance that forms in the cracks of trees and is similar to sponge to catch the sparks from the flint that is struck with a kind of file that fits around the hand. More fuel is added to the fire as it is needed, but all these things I have mentioned are completely burned. One fire is made when the first dance is to be held and is kept burning until the next Saturday morning. Then everything is cleared away, and a new fire is built in the same way.[11]

Stomp medicine. There is a big wash pot of hot medicine of mixed herbs and a ten-gallon jar of cold medicine made of red root. The men take partners, and when one takes medicine the other does, too. First, they drink from the hot pot, then from the cold jar and go out to vomit, as it cleans out the system thoroughly.

John Jacobs of Holdenville belongs to Tuckabatchee town. He had a white friend, and they were together almost all the time so this friend wanted to go take medicine, but it was too strong for him. He had to go home after taking some. He was so weak that he had to go to bed for a while, but when he got well he said he never had felt so good and was as strong as an ox. He had accumulated so much poison was why it worked him so hard.

An Indian's heaven. You know the two belong together, the Indian and the stomp dance. The Bible says there are just two places for a person to go after death. There would have to be a stomp ground for me to be happy You couldn't see a stomp dance and not want to dance, too. I love to dance and do every time that anyone else does. I belong to Keligia town but my wife is Arbecca town and church. The husband uses medicine in the wife's town as protection to her. I'm Coon and she is Tiger.[12]

I believe the stomp way is better than the church, for at church a woman is allowed to talk to any man she wants to and to be friends to all. At a stomp dance a woman is not allowed to talk to any man not even to her husband. If something important comes up, he must get permission before he can go talk to her and then only about business. (Creek, 13: 441)

*   *   *

When I was a child I went to the dances, but I was baptized when I was at school so I do not go now. I went to Hanna town or Ponca (Pukon) Tallahassee town, twelve miles southeast of Dustin. That name means "the way peaches are ground."

Early Friday afternoon we would have everything loaded in the wagon and would start to the dance. We would take the cookstove, dishes, groceries, fruit, tent, and everything we would need. We would get there late in the evening and fix camp, build the fire, and cook and eat supper. Then the people would dance from seven till nine and then go to bed.

The next morning we would have the ribbon dance. Only women danced the ribbon dance, and they had all colored ribbons fastened to the tops of their heads and hanging down their backs like streamers. Sunday before breakfast, we took medicine and did not eat roasting ears until after the stomp dance. That afternoon they had the fetta dance. The stomp dance lasted all Sunday night until next morning. After the dance Monday morning, they played ball, but it would

all be over, and everyone would be gone by noon. All the fire would
be out, and none of the wood was left unburned that was in the fire
they danced around as that would be bad luck.

Everyone would be tired, sleepy, and dirty so that when we got
home we just cleaned up and rested. These dances were for health, so
nobody would have fevers and be sick, but if anybody ate roasting
ears without taking medicine he or she would be sick with a high
fever. (Creek, 17: 307-8)

*   *   *

It was against the tribal law for any of the Indians to go to meetings
held by the Reverend Mr. Buckner, a traveling Baptist missionary.[13]
I do not know the years when this took place, but it was before the
Civil War, and I can only remember having known one of the persons
punished. She was Sallie, the mother of Sam Logan. She and Sam are
both dead now.

Several were whipped at the same time that she was whipped,
and for a long time others were whipped. Sallie was kneeling down
praying while she was being whipped with some elm or hickory
sprouts about the size of my finger.

The committee of the Council met after this had been going on for
quite a while and decided that their punishment was doing no good
and that this new religion seemed to be doing no harm. These men
had not been converted themselves, though. They passed a rule to
establish a religious meeting place, and anyone who wanted to could
meet, be converted, and carry on the work. They saw that these
Indians were trying to do right and that it was a good thing. That was
when the Big Arbor was established.[14]

Religion of the stomp Indian. There is an old legend that all the old
Indians believed. There have always been prophets, and there still are
prophets among the Indians. The word stomp ground means "Big
House." God gave them the Big House and the medicine and told them
how to use it.

They obey the Old Testament much more closely than the more
modern ones who have been converted, but lots of persons would
not understand nor sympathize with them. They believed in heaven
and believed that they would go there after death.

The reason that they did not want their women to go to the new church was that they thought it was a church for the white people and not for the Indian. They wished not to lose these things as they considered them good and sacred as they had been handed down through their prophets.

Their dances were to get care for the coming season or undertaking. They believed that if they were not careful to observe the rules there would be an epidemic in the tribe. A person who had helped to dig a grave was not allowed to come near the bed of a sick person for fear that a grave would have to be dug for that person. They were very careful that their women should stay "clean."[15] They were very careful not to eat roasting ears before they had taken medicine, nor to let a person who had eaten of it to touch their dishes, spoons, or dipper as that person was "unclean."

Rating of towns. Tuckabatchee town is spoken of as the Mother of the Muskogee Nation and is first. Arbecca is second, Cussetah is third, and Coweta is fourth. Their number shows their importance in the tribe. Each gathers at his own town, but no two towns meet on the same date so they can all visit the other towns. They do not take medicine when visiting unless they want to, and then it is taken by permission.

Tuckabatchee sacred plates. When the Muskogee Indians came from Alabama they brought everything that was important, and these things were very important as they concerned the medicine and the medicine was the most important of anything to them. These plates are earthen or of baked clay, and they are kept at Tuckabatchee town all the time. There is a little log house about four feet long that was built especially for them.

There are two sizes. The ones that are about eighteen inches in diameter are called Micco Harnega, and red root is the medicine used in them. The Indian that has been careful not to eat the green corn is allowed to eat from these. The others are about six inches in diameter. The barsa is a lily-like plant that grows by the roadside.[16] It is baked or boiled and makes a very bitter medicine. The ones who have dug a grave or eaten green corn wait until the others have taken their medicine and are through. Then they take their medicine and use these plates. A certain man takes care of these plates and also takes care of the fire.[17]

Indian stomp meetings. These Green Corn Dances are held either in July or August. For four days the Indians fast and take medicine. The next four days they eat "white food," which is just flour and water with no salt nor other seasoning. Some of them take a lighter medicine and wash their faces in it, but they do not take as much as before. They have their dances and later have a ball game, then break camp. (Creek, 24: 248–52)

*   *   *

Up to 1914, the rain makers were still active. A large crowd gathered from far and near for the ceremonies, which were held on a creek bank. The Cherokee tribe being divided into seven clans, one of the healthiest men was picked from each clan. One or more wagons were sent out to nearby Indian farm homes to collect food stuffs for the people. A bunch of men were detailed to fish and hunt wild game.

Each of the seven men was given a club about two feet in length which was laid along the side of the creek. The workers then lined up along the creek bank and then jumped in. Swimming out, taking their clubs, swinging them, and following one behind the other in single file, each hit one time seven small trees, which were standing nearby. This was done once a day for from four to seven days.[18] (Cherokee, 1: 464)

Prophets and Witches

In the early days, prophecy was considered a very great attribute among the Creek Indians. In case of a lost or stolen horse, the prophet would call for an article of wear, a blanket, or other garment, the property of the owner of the animal, and after a close inspection of the article would tell the whereabouts of the horse and the best method of its recovery.[19]

The full-bloods believe in the foresight of their prophet. The fee, which varies from twenty-five cents to one dollar, is placed on the gallery of the prophet's house before he furnishes the desired information. Almost every neighborhood or town had its medicine man, who not only introduces his magic and mummery but makes use of wild herbs and vegetable compounds in his practice. But of late years even the full-bloods have begun to lose faith in the medicine man, especially when one uses his magic arts instead of pills and powders.

Many of the Creeks had a superstitious dread of the brass plates belonging to the Tuckbatchees. it was the general belief that contact with these plates meant death, and it was impossible to induce a full-blood to approach their place of concealment or to look at these plates when they were brought forth at the annual festivity. (Creek 70: 193–94)

*   *   *

The Muskogee-Creeks think it an odd thing when twins are born. They believed twins were at times not in their right minds and that they became very dangerous if they were caused to become angry. They were born with a knowledge or insight of things untold, unseen, and unknown. They were naturally gifted with the power to foretell and know these things, and they were taken as odd because they had that power.[20]

In the early days, those prophets and medicine men were never known to mix with anybody or live as the rest of their folks or tribesmen did. Their homes might be good and have beds in them, but the medicine man or prophet selected for himself one of the outside houses, which is sometimes called a smokehouse, or other small house or building which was used as a storeroom for old articles. It was the custom of a prophet to stay to himself, and so he would go out into the old storeroom and sleep there among the trash with old clothes or old quilts thrown together in one corner for a bed.

Wod-ko Ho-mot-tee was one old Indian prophet who lived in this manner near the present Hanna, Oklahoma. He would go around all the year without shoes and hat, and some that have seen his custom tell that, in the house where he slept, he always had a bucket of water nearby, and from the bucket he would take a drink of water whenever he wanted it. In this bucket of water was a snake, and it was actually so, as some have seen it. (Creek 49: 390–91)

*   *   *

The first and present settlement of the Alabama tribe (tulwa) has been around what is now Weleetka, Okfuakee County, vicinity. Alabama Chupco was a well-know medicine man and prophet in his own tribe (tulwa) of Alabama. He was known for his works in the other tribes as well. His real name, Concharty Yahola, was seldom used. Pahos Fixico was another medicine man and prophet also of Alabama tulwa. These two men were old men and had been among those coming from the old home country of Alabama.

These two Indian men as medicine men and prophets were noted as being very, very strict in their beliefs and practices. They were noted for the unbelievable things that they could do, and many of these practices have long been known among the Indians for ages. These two men had the ability to transform into animals or owls, unbelievable today to many.[21] The method or manner of such skill is a secrecy and is unknown to the majority of the present-day Indian. They were noted for their ability to charm snakes by their spell. I have often heard the older people tell about Pahos Fixico and Alabama Chupco. The people told of what they could do and what they themselves told the people. They could pick up poisonous snakes upon first sight, pick rattlesnakes and touch their lips to the mouth of the snake, pick up centipedes with their hands, or they could control and charm the mightiest snakes that could be found in the deeper waters. There are no such snakes in existence now.[22]

The old Indians used the devil's shoestring mixture as a weapon to kill fish (Ha-no-lis-kee in Muskogee-Creek language). The devil's shoestring was a wild plant, but only the long roots were used. The long roots were beaten into shreds, which was placed in water in a large container and set over night. This mixture was very bitter and produced a strong stupefying liquid. The mixture was emptied into a designated spot in the water or river where an ideal fishing spot was known. Any fish coming in the region of the water wherein the devil's shoestring mixture was poured became numb or senseless and floated to the top of the water. Then the Indians used their bows and arrows to successfully gather their kill. The fish thus caught was not poisoned and was harmless to the Indians.

The Alabama Indians fished in the North Canadian River, which is in a south and southeasterly direction from the present town of Weleetka. There was an old crossing called Cha-kee Thakko (Big Shallow) where no fish was ever caught, although it had been tried three or four times. The custom above mentioned for killing fish was used at Cha-kee Thakko.

It was at this time that Alabama Chupco (Concharty Yahola), being the prophet and medicine man, told the Indians of his tribal town that at the spot where the devil's shoestring mixture had been used was a very large hole in the bottom of the river wherein the fish was seeking refuge. He told that no fish would be caught unless the hole had been plugged. Upon investigation, this opening was discovered and closed. Much fish was then caught.

Pahos Fixico, the other prophet, was very curious about the opening in the bottom of the river and attempted to see where it led. He discovered that it was a large tunnel leading downwards so far and then upwards, thence in a level direction. He went as far as he could in the tunnel and came back to tell his people. He told Alabama Chupco what he had seen and why he could not proceed any further than he did.

The water ceased to stand in the tunnel after a certain distance and when Pahos Fixico had gone a little ways in the tunnel he came upon a ball of fire about the size of a human fist located in the center of the tunnel. He was unable to pass this fire. He tried many times to investigate further into the tunnel, but he always said, "I just can't pass that hot ball of fire."

Alabama Chupco decided to see for himself what all the talk about the ball of fire meant, so he entered the tunnel. On his return he told Pahos Fixico that this ball of fire was only the size of a finger-nail when he went there and that it was no longer hot, as he had passed it. He also told that the tunnel came out into the center of the same river but at a different and distant spot. The distance from one entrance of this tunnel was at least seven miles apart. I have been to the spot where the location of one of the entrances to the under-ground tunnel is reported to be. (Creek 52: 411–15)

*   *   *

There was an old woman of the Tahlequah District, who, in bygone years, rode to and fro in the land on the back of a hardy pony. White-headed, with a round, full-moon face and wearing brass-rimmed spectacles, the woman was of rather benevolent aspect, but there were many who looked upon her with fear. It was said by the more superstitious that there was no more powerful conjurer in the Cherokee country. Many anecdotes were related concerning her weird and strange achievements. Some of the tales survive to this day. One of them concerns the alleged ability of the woman to transform herself into the body of an animal, a domestic cat pref-erably, and in that form prowl afar, entering houses and learning secrets otherwise unprocurable. But, in course of time, the witch woman met with a painful experience and abandoned her favorite method of disguising herself.

One day in winter time, when the sky was obscured by dark clouds and snow lay upon the ground with an icy wind from the north, the old woman changed herself into the form of a cat and went to a house several miles distant from her cabin in the hills. When someone opened the door, the strange cat gained entrance and sat quietly with the household cats. With eyes closed and ears open, the old woman listened intently to the conversation, and for awhile all was well. But for some reason the old woman was not in the best of humor. Perhaps she had a headache, caused from having had no strong coffee to drink at breakfast. Anyway, she felt out of sorts but maintained composure until a child trod upon one of her paws, whereupon the strange cat growled and bit and scratched the child so that it screeched in pain. The owner of the house then opened the door and "shooed" the cat, but it refused to go. He then kicked the cat, picked it up and flung it with force far out upon the ground. But instead of leaving, the cat ran back and clawed at the door, emitting fierce yowls. The man inside the house then threw a shovelful of hot ashes and embers out of the door and upon the cat, which was badly singed and ran away, uttering hateful cries.

Several days later some persons passing the old woman's cabin entered to talk with her and found her lying in bed, badly burned about the feet and arms. The old woman said that she had slipped and fallen into the fire, but in course of time the truth came out, and it was found that the witch woman had been burned while in the form of a cat. She finally recovered from her injuries and rode forth again on her favorite pony.

She rode to Tahlequah at intervals from her home down the Illinois River and met acquaintances with whom she talked and laughed after the manner of other old full-blood women of the period, nothing in her appearance indicating that she possessed the strange and peculiar powers attributed to her by the believers in witchcraft and conjuration.[23] (Cherokee 59: 154–56)

Secret Societies

The legend concerning the beginning of the sacred Kee-Too-Wah Society holds the most prominent place of all legendary history of the Cherokees. I shall endeavor to relate it just as it was related to me by full-blood Cherokee chief medicine man of the organization and one whom I number among my closest friends.

Back in the far distant past from some unknown source and cause there arose great strife among the people of the tribe. Chief medicine men of the seven clans were much troubled, and, seeing that all their efforts to overcome the trouble had failed, the chief medicine man decided to go alone up into the mountain and fast for seven days and nights and seek counsel in silence from the Great Spirit as to a remedy to overcome their trouble. He slipped away from the village without anyone knowing of his intentions and went far into the hills alone. The first night of his fast, at a late hour, he heard footsteps approaching in the darkness. He was perplexed, as none of his people had reason to frequent the place at that hour of the night. He called to the object he heard approaching, and to his surprise he was answered in his own language and recognized the voice of the medicine man of the second clan, which is the bear. He came unto the chief medicine man and made it known that he had also came into the hills to seek counsel with the Great Spirit. On the second night of the fast, at the darkest hour, the medicine man of the third clan appeared and joined them, and thereafter each night a medicine man of the consecutive clans appeared until the seventh night, and the council of the seven clans were assembled and each with the same thought as the first, the chief. It was revealed to that council by the Great Spirit for their people to form as one great body bound together for the protection of all and equality of rights, and that body would survive and be known as Kee-Too-Wah.

In this same fast, the message to the council from the Great Spirit said,

The trail of your people will lead toward the setting sun, they will be driven to the edge of the plains, and there the common class of people will discover the remedy, and then with the proper precaution their trail will turn east. At that time the clans will be forgotten, and they will grow weaker and wiser. They will rebel against ancient customs. The eastern trail will lead to peace and liberty for many generations to come. Then it shall come to pass that your people will be oppressed, and the tribe will be wiped from the earth, which will be the end of the trial, the next day thereafter shall come the end of time of all my people.

On the eighth day, or the day following this revelation to them in their council with the Great Spirit, the seven medicine men returned to the village and informed their people of the message they had received. It was then the sacred Kee-Too-Wah was created and has been handed down through the council of the Cherokees through the many centuries unknown to man.

The sacred ritualism of the original Kee-Too-Wah is performed only with the sacred ceremonial fire. When the council of the Kee-Too-Wah is to go in session, the fire keepers start the fire at the council grounds before the sun appears in the east. This fire must not be started with a match but through the old custom.

See-Quah-Nee-Da (Pig Red Bird) was my grandfather. He came from Georgia to Arkansas about 1840, where he resided until about 1852, when he moved to the Illinois District, Cherokee Nation. He was a blacksmith, and from his profession came the family name of "smith," hence the name Red Bird Smith. He was a tribal medicine man and a leader in the Kee-Too-Wah Society the greater part of his life. His death occurred in 1874. During his leadership of the Kee-Too-Wah, the council sessions were always held according to the ancient ritualistic customs and held continuous session for seven days and nights. During my grandfather's leadership of Kee-Too-Wah, the council saw the sign and decreed that the descendants of See-Quah-Nee-Da would inherit the leadership of Kee-Too-Wah. As a boy, my father was taught by the Kee-Too-Wah council as to its sacred ritualistic customs and qualified himself for such leadership, and this council teaching was his only schooling and the medicine men his only teachers. In the removal of the Cherokees from Georgia, the Kee-Too-Wah fire went out. The organization was inactive with the exception of the official council. In the early 1890s my father, with the council, reestablished the fire of the Kee-Too-Wah with the seven clans and returned it to the Cherokees-by-blood. During that period of time, people who were not qualified, to forward selfish motives, built up an organization which was supposed to be the Kee-Too-Wah Society, controlled by some missionaries and designing politicians, which was in violation of the sacred principles of Kee-Too-Wah, as it is a religious organization. To be a member and uphold its principles it is prohibitive as to activity in any other faith and not a political organization.[24]

In 1906, my father in the council of medicine men appointed seven men who were qualified to act on the council and to fast for seven days and nights according to the original ritualistic customs, seeking revelations through council with the Great Spirit as to the reestablishment of the Kee-Too-Wah Society. At the council of the medicine men, the following men were named: Red Bird Smith, John Smith, Joshia Glass, Creek Sam, Charlie Sam, Martin Bowlin, and Will Elk.[25]

When we met and organized as the new official council, my father was appointed as chief or spokesman to preside over the council. During my father's time as chief of the council, Will Elk was the medicine man of the Kee-Too-Wah.

It was the duty of the chief medicine man to examine the members of the new council and ascertain as to which member was to receive the revelation from the Great Spirit in the council of the fast. When his decision was made, I was the one he designated and appointed.

In August 1906, we met in council at the old council ground on the mountain at Buffalotown ten miles east of Gore at the Red Bird Smith schoolhouse. We went into the forest on the mountain and sat down in sacred council, my father opening the ceremonies with prayer, asking counsel of the Great Spirit.

At that time the Cherokees were being oppressed from all sides, their confidence betrayed by the people in which they had placed their greatest trust. My father and other old members of the council were seriously depressed. Their only hopes to survive was through the power that lives behind the sun.

The first night of the council the sky was perfectly clear, no wind, and the forest seemed to be in harmony with the occasion. Only the call of the whippoorwill and the occasional hoot of an owl broke the dead silence of the night. About midnight we observed dim flashes of lightning in the far west, gradually growing more vivid, coming closer. The lightning grew continuous, and we could hear the thunder and a continuous roar, which had all the appearance of a dangerous storm. Under any other circumstances, I would have had fear of it. No member of the council moved or arose from their sitting position on the ground when the storm struck. Its duration was brief, and from the continuous lightning I could see the trees twisting and bending as though they would be torn from the earth, but when the storm had passed none of the trees were damaged, not even a limb was broken, and only a few scattering drops of rain fell.

Not a member of the council had moved, sitting there in silence. I was sitting on the north side of the circle looking northeast. I saw a vision of two little boys naked, one chasing the other in play, and in their scuffle they fell off a ledge of rock about a foot high into some leaves. They got up from their fall, ran down the hill, looking back in my direction laughing, and disappeared in the darkness. The clouds drifted away, and the stars shown out in the heavens clear as crystals. My father said a vision of one naked child appeared before him and said, "I am the thunder," then disappeared.[26]

The council on the seventh night taken place on a high mountain about one-half mile northwest of the council fire. We built another fire, and my father opened the council with a prayer, asking counsel of the Great Spirit. In the early part of the night, my father and Creek Sam were sitting on my left and were discussing the old traditions of their forefathers when it appeared as though a big white sheet fell over me.[27] I arose and walked the trail that wound its way around under the bluff upon which we were holding council. There I observed a small aged man with gray beard who spoke to me in Cherokee as he pointed to a table in the cave and said, "Go eat." The table was served by small spirit women serving our native food, such as wild meat, beans, bean bread, hominy, sweet potatoes with kr-no-hey-ner (which is a soup made from corn) to drink. I seated myself at the table and ate, but during the time I could hear every word that was being said at the council on the bluff above me. When I arose from the table and returned to the council circle, I saw a pair of tigers, a male and a female, standing near looking at us and slowly wiggling their tails. Standing east of us, they separated, the male going north and the female south until they disappeared. I then saw a multitude of people of all nationalities in a great state of excitement caused by these animals. Then the medicine man appeared in a white robe, seeking the trail of the tigers. Many of the people asked the question, "Why is he not excited and has no fear of the tigers?" I then heard a voice say, "He knows something why the tigers cannot harm him." Then there was a message came from the south that the tiger that went south had been captured and safely caged. The messenger then went on north to take the message to the male tiger. When it received it, he went into a rage and began to roar and returned to the south and disappeared.[28] From the top of a hickory tree that stood by the bluff, the limbs of which extended over the ledge where we were holding council, I heard a voice speak, saying, "As you people are here, this is all that is necessary for you all to do, there is nothing but what you all can see."

At this point I came from under the spiritual spell and told the other members of the council of my vision. They said that was what they came there for. Their mission was finished; the council was concluded.

These councils, according to ancient ritualistic customs, are conducted in a fast without food or drink. On the seventh or last night of this council, we violated that tradition by taking to the council ground a gallon bucket of water, as our thirst on the previous night became most intolerable. Just before the council was concluded, one of our party picked up the bucket to take a drink, and to his surprise, the bucket was empty. They had a laugh about the water leaking out of the bucket. I examined the bucket but could find no leak, cast it aside, and thought no more of it. When the council session was concluded, to our amazement, we found the bucket full of water. No one seemed to be thirsty; the water was poured out, and we went our way home.

My father died November 8, 1918. He served as chief of the Kee-Too-Wah until his death, at which time my brother, Sam Smith, succeeded him as chief, with myself as his assistant. In 1902, I was made interpreter for the Kee-Too-Wah and yet hold that position as well as assistant chief, medicine man, and one of the Council of Seven.

This is the original Kee-Too-Wah Society and is not and has never until this time been chartered under the state or national laws. We have in our possession the old peace pipe, the last one made in June 1864, by James McDaniel from stone that was brought from Tennessee, also the original constitution of the Kee-Too-Wah Society that was rewritten by the Kee-Too-Wah Society after the Cherokees came west. Any other organization or body functioning or claiming representation under the name of the Kee-Too-Wah Society are fictitious and impostors. (Cherokee, 9: 492–504)

Medicine

There was not a doctor in the Choctaw-Chickasaw Nation until 1868, when a doctor came, but the medicine men were not such bad doctors.[29] If I had just chills and fever or rheumatism or something of that kind, I would just as soon have an old medicine man now as a doctor of medicine. Of course, it was the herbs and teas of the medicine men that did the good, not their rites. There was a lot of humbug about them. I used to stand around and watch them closely to try to see how they did things, but they were too quick for me to catch on.

The medicine men made cascara from the wahoo bush, which was brushy and grew up seven or eight, maybe ten feet high.[30] The bark was pink and the leaves greenish pink. In May they would cut off the limbs of the wahoo bush and tie them in bundles, then grub out the roots and peel off the bark of the limbs. They made the medicine from the bark and the roots. It didn't taste good.

When we were run down, we would go to the medicine man, and he would give us a half-gallon of this medicine. He wouldn't take money for the Great Spirit wouldn't let him charge for it, but later we could give him a gift.

What the doctors called potaphalene, they made from May apple root.[31] They dug the May apple root, washed it clean, and boiled the root until the strength was boiled out, strained it, and then boiled it down to a thick wax. They made pills out of this.

There was an old woman named Spring who was considered a witch. Some people were afraid of her, but I wasn't. I was just a little fellow and would go to her house and hang around her. She petted me and called me her boy. I think she was a mighty good old woman. She had two or three sons and two daughters. People said that black cats talked to her, but I never did see a black cat at her house.

One time father had neuritis awfully bad. One of Spring's sons told him to go to his mother and she would make him some medicine that would cure it. Father asked, "You think she would make it for me?"

Spring's son said, "Yes, just take her a gallon of lard to put in it, and she'll make it." I went with father and watched. Spring took one root of the bear foot weed and some roots of the bittersweet.[32] She counted these, but I have forgotten the number, and she slipped in some other things, but I didn't find out what they were. After this mixture was cooked, strained, and boiled down, Spring added the gallon of lard. It made a gallon of liniment to be rubbed on. Father used it and got well.

One time one of Spring's daughters was taken sick with an awful pain in her head. Spring did not try to cure her but sent for another witch named Snow. I watched Snow, getting just as close as I could. Snow said that the girl had been shot with a witch ball, and she would have to get it out. I wanted to see it come out. Snow put some kind of roots in water and boiled them, then strained the liquid through a flour sifter. She put this liquid in a pot on the coals and fixed a pillow case over the girl's head so that the steam from the pot would envelope her head. After maybe a half-hour Snow took this off and strained the liquid again. In the sifter there was left a little bunch of human hair tied with a string. Snow told the girl that was the witch ball she had been shot with and now she would get well. I suppose Snow had slipped it in when she was adjusting the pillow slip, but I was watching closely and didn't see her do it.

A man, Ike Sippi, got sick with a killing pain in his left shoulder. I watched a medicine man steam him and rub him. Then the medicine man said that the pain was so bad that he would have to suck it out. He sucked on the spot awhile, then spat out a little stick about an inch long sharpened at both ends and two little pieces of charcoal. This was too much even for me to believe, and I knew the Medicine Man must have had the stick and pieces of charcoal in his mouth. (Chickasaw, 87: 451–54)

*   *   *

As nature would have it, some of the Indian herb doctors of the olden times were just as smart as our best doctors and smarter than most of the quack doctors of our present time. He used herbs that he knew for each case of sickness as there were only a few severe sicknesses known in those days. As time changed, civilization became more intelligent. More and different cases of sickness, epidemics, and contagious disease has been found by scientists. It is now necessary that we have learned doctors who is well posted and scientists to find remedy and control the different cases.

The herb doctors of our days knew how to cure pneumonia by treating with a certain kind of weed which grows only in a certain place. It does not grow or found everywhere. One can take this bush and boil it in water, give the patient about one-third cup full while warm. Then he goes out in the yard to find a suitable place and dig down a hole about twelve inches deep, place in this prepared hole the herb in a kettle or pot, lay across strips of planks or board over the pot, and make a pallet for the patient and have him lie down over the kettle where the pain is and smoke him four times and return him to bed the next morning. Continue the same process for four mornings and give him a warm tea to drink and he will soon recover.

For cough, a bark of sycamore tree is used in one gallon of water. When boiled, sweeten with sugar to taste desired, and give patient one tablespoon full at any time.[33]

We used clean rags to smoke and inhale through nose to break up a cold. After the smoke, the discharge from nose runs freely, which after a while one feel better and soon recover. This was the best method to rid of the cold.

Instead of using sugar-coated pills or some sweetened liquid purgatives to clean out the system, we used the roots of blackroot by boiling and make tea.[34] When lukewarm give patient one cup full every hour until bowels act. After the bowels start acting, give one-third full three times or once a day for three days, which will have him straightened out.

If the patient seems to have or show symptoms of pneumonia and is waiting on a doctor, for temporary relief or first aid treatment I have seen them hold the head of a patient while the other party takes a sharp broken piece of glass and scratches lightly enough to draw blood on the tip end of nose. If as much as two or three drops of blood can be procured in a teaspoon, add two or three drops of turpentine, and give the patient with water. Usually this will bring temporary relief until the doctor arrives.

Rheumatism is caused mostly by bad blood and kidneys not functioning properly. So to give relief I have seen them to break a black or bluish-looking bottle, pick out a sharp piece, fasten to a piece of stick about half-size of a man's small finger about six inches in length, place a tourniquet under arm pit and around arm until vein is plainly seen, cut the blood vein, and let blood run. The first operation, blood will be blackish looking and will continue until reddish color shows, the tourniquet may be loosened, and the flow of blood will be checked instantly. For severe headache, same process is necessary, only the tourniquet can be placed either around the chest or under the armpit or around the neck, and the operation can be on the forehead or on top of head. This will relieve severe headache, but after once operated, same spell will come every year, and of course same process is necessary.

For broken bone, a plaster of clay bandaged or tied around the wound and drop cold water constantly to keep moist as if given a chance to dry will cause severe pain. One can take a certain amount of bark of cottonwood and boil to certain degree and steam the wound will relieve pain.[35] Bandage may be changed but must keep tied until well.

For joint thrown out of socket, I have seen them to take a bunch of roots of cottonwood, boil in water, and steam the injured part four times a day for four days, and on the fourth day the socket will automatically slip back in place. By steaming with this solution, it takes the swelling out and by some method tends to throw joint back in place. (Choctaw, 1: 215–18)

*   *   *

Our tribe was never afraid of any disease. When one felt stiff in his joints, a squaw would take her children to the woods, by a small branch, and gather herbs to brew. She would take the bark from a cottonwood tree and boil it in spring water. Then she would take a hollow reed about thirty inches long and blow in the liquid. This she would do for four mornings. All the time she was blowing in the liquid she faced the east. This is an old custom to always face the east. Our dead are always buried facing the east. While preparing this medicine, the squaw would drink "sofky," a drink made from corn similar to hominy. She felt that would teach her a medicine song for the particular disease she was preparing the medicine for. When the four mornings had passed, she would bring it back to the one who was sick and pour it in a large container, placing a stool in the center of it, then the person wrapped himself in a blanket and sat down while he steamed. The squaw, meanwhile, kept chanting her medicine song. An undernourished child was bathed in this solution and also drank it while the mother chanted her song.

An herb called "heyaneecha" and spring water was our favorite medicine. It was used to clean out our system. By that, I mean in your language, "erp it up." (Creek/Seminole, 32: 182–84)

*   *   *

Sweating remedy. In their treatment of ailments, the native Cherokee resorted to copious sweating. When fevers prevailed or pneumonia as well as other maladies, a piece of the butterfly root was boiled, and the resulting tea given to the sick person in liberal quantities.[36]

It has been said that the butterfly root tea would almost cause a piece of wood to burst into perspiration. It was a hot draught and usually had quick results. The patient perspired most profusely, and often the sick person experienced relief with ultimate recovery.

Portions of the dried butterfly plant root were to be found in many of the log cabin homes of the Cherokees. Those who had not dried and preserved some of the roots were supplied by others who had the foresight to be prepared for emergencies.

The native doctors, some of whom were quite skillful, invariably kept a supply of butterfly root together with other medicinal roots, barks, and herbs. Sometimes the plant was referred to as "chigger weed," the belief prevailing that chiggers or chigoes infested the flowers which appeared upon the plant during the summer.

The plant was never greatly plentiful but was found in sufficient quantity to supply the demand. There were other plants which were productive of perspiration when boiled in water, but the butterfly root was the most powerful and is yet in use among some of the full-blood Indian people of the Cherokee hills.

Slippery elm.[37] An aged man, who recalled the events of the Civil War, related some years ago that after battles the surgeons sometimes had their hands too full to give immediate attention to some of the wounded. In such emergencies the native Cherokee doctors, of whom several were to be found in each of the three regiments composing the Union Indian Brigade, rendered assistance. These native doctors soaked long strips of slippery elm in cold water, and when the strips were well coated with the exudation, they proceeded to treat the wounded persons by passing the strips completely through bullet wounds, chest wounds in particular. Thus the wounds were cleansed of clotted blood and foreign matter, and great relief was experienced by the injured. The slippery elm bark was also used upon other wounds and was valuable in aiding in the reduction of feverish conditions.

Blackberry root.[38] An infusion of blackberry root was and is still in use among the Cherokees for the treatment of intestinal and stomach ailments. The roots were freshly dug, washed, and placed in cold water, and allowed to simmer until a strong tea resulted which, when cooled, was taken in doses of a half-glass, more or less, at frequent intervals, which usually resulted in relief. (Cherokee, 58: 148–86)

*   *   *

Indian medicine was all found in the woods. There were many medicine men at that time. Each medicine man had a different way of treating different diseases. There were no two Indians that doctored alike. The clan that they belonged to had a great deal to do with their doctoring.

When an Indian doctor was called to a certain case, the first thing he wanted to know was the clan that the patient belonged to. They believed that the patient and the doctor belonging to the same clan would not cure. They had to be the opposite clan. There are seven clans among the Cherokee people.

The old timers were very particular as to who handled their medicines, also who prepared the food that the patient ate. People that had helped in any way with a corpse were not allowed in the sick room. (Cherokee, 52: 425–26)

Towns and Clans

In the beginning there were seven sons of the Great Spirit representing the seven heavens. They were blessed and multiplied. Each of the seven sons created a clan, a chief presiding over each clan, subordinate to the medicine man as spiritual advisor.

Thereafter, in marriage, no member of any clan was permitted to marry within his own clan, only to a member of another clan, that the blood may be kept pure within the sight of the Great Spirit.

There was also a great chief of the tribe which presided over the tribe subordinate to the chief medicine man, governing the seven clans, Wolf, Bear, Lion, Terrapin, Bird, Deer, and Savanah.[39] (Cherokee, 9: 492)

*   *   *

My mother belonged to Kealigee town, east of Hannah. My father belonged to Tuckabatche town, north of Yeager. I belong to Kealigee town, as the family always follows the mother both in towns and clan.[40] Mother was (Woka) Coon, so I'm Coon. No person could

marry in his own town but had to marry in a different town. Everyone in that town is related. The husband belongs to the wife's town
in this way:

He goes to the Green Corn Dances, fasts, takes medicine, even if
he happens to be a church Indian. He doesn't have to dance if he is
a church Indian. They fast four days and take medicine, which is a
good physic and is really good for health as it makes men supple and
clears all malaria out. He does this to show that he cares for his wife
and wants to protect her. If the king writes him to be there and for
some good reason he shows he can't be there, he sends some tobacco
or anything they can all enjoy; or else he sends money which is used
for tobacco which they all smoke. That is because he has the right
intentions and is friendly. If he just doesn't want to come, they fine
him a certain amount of money. The king gives him a name; it's no
secret yet like a password in a lodge, and like a lodge they all are
brothers. This name is called a "square name" or "war name" and is
kept on the books instead of his own family name.

Billie West lived north of Bryant, across from where the Victoria
coal mine used to be. His square name was Spokogee Harjo, but he
is not the Spokogee Harjo of the Piankashaw Indians.

If one lives close to one town he doesn't dance with them but goes
back to his own town, no matter how far away that one is. That is
why some go to Shawnee, Wetumka, and other towns during the
time green corn is good to eat. (Creek, 13: 429–31)

*   *   *

When a young man takes his first medicine as a man at a Green
Corn dance, he is given a nickname. There are three arbors for
officers of the town. One of them is the king's arbor. If the Henneha
clan on the south side have a boy that they want named, they pick
the name they want. Sometimes the name is that of a bird or animal,
or sometimes a boy is named by his actions while he is taking the
medicine. Harjo is my father's name and means that he acted drunk,
crazy, or funny while he took the first medicine.[41]

They go to the arbor on the east—Tusknagee—and hold a conference. A certain man calls the boy out by the new name. This man
is the "caller," and the name is long drawn out. The name I remember
is Ho-duuul-ga Ya-hooo-laaaaa (Hodulga Yahola). He goes to that

arbor and to those clansmen. Then he is recognized by that name by the king, who gives him a gift of tobacco, and after that he is always known by that name. (Creek, 24: 255–56)

Marriage

When a young man is out looking for a wife, he used to make a visit to the man who had daughters, and usually takes dinner with the family. The purpose was to investigate to find all he can about the girl that he intends to ask her hand for a wife, by her way of cooking means. If he is satisfied that she is a good cook, he makes about two or three more trips and asks her father about the hand of one of the girls. It was customary that the oldest girl must marry first, then the next oldest, and so on so there was no use in asking for the younger girl when the oldest girl is still unmarried. The father delivers the message to the mother of the girl, and the mother breaks the news to the girl. After the girl decides and gives her consent to the proposal, it must go through the same channel from whence the first news came and finally reaches the ear of the applicant. It took some time before the acceptance or rejection to the hands of matrimony was made known to the hands of the fiancé. When the news breaks out, a big dinner is planned, date set for the marriage, men go out hunting, women began to get ready for the big dinner, and when the day set for the feast time was had, and everybody —friends, acquaintances, relatives, and enemies—were given warm welcome to attend the day of marriage.[42] As a matter of good manners, where there were men gathered carrying on conversation boys under twenty-five years of age were not permitted or allowed to be around under no consideration. They would get together to themselves and practice playing Indian ball game, swimming, hunting, or enjoy some social game together, but it was strictly against the rule to be with the grown persons.

The older folks in their gathering would talk about the present, past, and future times that are to come. They were not educated, could not write their own name, could not talk the languages of other races of people, but by the gift and power they possessed they predicted as to how the country will be after being open up to the white settlers, and from what I have heard and was told it is true by the prophecy of the old timers.

To show they are friends toward each other, one would pull out a tomahawk pipe, fill with tobacco, light it, smoke a few puffs, and hand it to his next man, and so on until the pipe reaches around each man that is present. Or, if the tobacco plays out before making the round, the last man holding the pipe fills it with his tobacco, lights it, and continues as before. That was the way they used to do. While over at some other place some older man would get the young men together, and they would have their entertainment by relating some ghost stories, old fables, or other stories that he may know. (Choctaw, 38: 135–37)

*　　*　　*

Some of the Creek Indians had two wives when I first realized things, that is, I remember seeing and knowing that two women were the wives of certain men when I was a child.[43] (Creek, 65: 270)

*　　*　　*

Clan kin were not supposed to marry. It was against the tribal law, and that law was enforced then, but the younger generation does not pay much attention to the clan kin. In the early days, if two belonging to the same clan lived together and disobeyed this law, they were whipped. They were given fifty licks for the first offense, the second time their noses were cut off.[44] (Creek, 65: 270)

*　　*　　*

Thirty years ago if an Indian couple decided to get married and they belonged to the church, they'd tell all the church members. Then all the church members would decide if they thought it would be a good match, man and wife, and marry them. They had no papers then as they have now, but the preacher would just give them a good talking to. If the church members didn't think it would be a good match, they would marry them, but they would watch them. If the man would mistreat her, her relations would go and get her and take her back home. When they start to go together, they would find out what clan they belong to, and if it was the same, they would say, "We can't go together for we are relation." But if they were not blood relation they could go together. (Creek, 10: 506)

*　　*　　*

At the age of twenty-seven, I was married to Hattie Towie, a full-blood Cherokee, daughter of Ah-Yer-Day-Gee. Her mother died shortly after the birth of Hattie, and she was reared by Jennie Bushyhead, a wealthy Cherokee medicine woman, and grew up under her teaching without any English education. She was a very beautiful and attractive girl about seventeen years of age when I first met her. Our courtship and marriage was according to the old Cherokee customs. When I was courting Hattie Towie, I learned that another Cherokee boy by the name of Joe Waters was also in love with her. I came to believe that she was also in love with Joe so I ceased my attentions toward her.

Jennie Bushyhead, for the interest of her personal motives, encouraged our marriage, and eventually we were married through the influence of witchcraft of evil people that did not have our best interest at heart, though it was against the better judgment of both Hattie and me. We could have made a success of our marriage had we been left alone and not overcome with the power of certain medicine men that were working in behalf of her other suitor.[45] Conditions between us grew more and more intolerable until the final result was separation and divorce, she retaining possession of the one child that was born to us.[46] (Cherokee, 9: 490–91)

Death

When an Indian would die, their people would buy lumber and make the coffin. They would keep the corpse at the house and put it in the coffin. The preaching would be at the house, but they would pray and sing at the graveyard. The old-time Indians would split logs that were about a foot in diameter, notch them, and face them to fit, and build a little house over the grave.[47] Then they wouldn't go to the grave to decorate it like they do now. When several members of the church would have died, they would have a camp meeting and preach another funeral for each of them. One or two on Saturday, one or two Sunday, and one or two Sunday night, till they had preached them all. They would have wine to drink. This meeting could be a year after the death, it didn't matter, but it was at next camp meeting after the death regardless of the time that had passed.

The Scott Cemetery is at Mama's house. It was started in 1889; you can't tell anything about the oldest. The houses have disappeared, and nothing remains but the rocks. You can tell about the ones from 1900 on down. The Indians like to have the dead put close to their homes. This one keeps getting closer to the house for two families bury there. There is a division like a road in the center. The friend's family bury away from the house, and the Scott relation bury each one toward the house. When mother's child died, they buried it in the yard, and this woman was like a sister to her, so when her child died they buried it there with a division between, and the cemetery has grown each year. (Creek, 10: 506-7)

*   *   *

Mrs. Annie Toney, a Cherokee Indian woman, and her newborn infant died. The baby was wrapped in a blanket and put under the bed, and nobody ever knew what became of it. Mr. Auldridge attended the woman's funeral. Her body was placed in a tent where a big fire was built to smoke her, and the Indians marched around the casket all night and made a mournful noise. The casket had holes about the size of a dollar cut in it to let the spirits out, and the corpse was placed in the last wagon in the procession and taken to the cemetery. All the clothing and bedding belonging to her, except one suit for her to wear when she came out, was buried with her.[48] The preacher hid the one suit in the woods after the burial. As soon as the woman died, the other women began preparing a feast and, after the grave was covered, a blanket was spread over it and the food placed on the blanket and the feast began. Eight days after the funeral, the husband killed two hogs and a beef, and another feast was held. The husband took a bath and dressed in a new suit and enjoyed the celebration. (White resident of the Cherokee Nation, 1: 186-87)

*   *   *

Mother told this to me, and I know it is true as she was made a widow by the death of my father about two months before my birth.

After the husband was buried the wife was taken to the home of his people. There was a little house in the back yard that was just large enough to have a bed and chair in it. She was put in there, and guards were kept at the door to keep the widow from coming out. One of the husband's sisters or a woman relative of his looked after her. Her hair was not combed, but every day her head was looked over carefully to see that she did not get lice.

She was not allowed to go to any kind of gathering for four years. After four years had passed she was taken to a social gathering in some home. If there was a brother of the dead man living he married the widow. If not, the next of kin or a man was picked out by the husband's people for her to marry.

When the wife died, the husband was treated in the same way by her people. (Creek, 65: 269)

*   *   *

We did not know what it was to buy a casket for the dead or where lumber could be bought to make coffins for the dead. When one died, men would get together and hew out logs, cut ends to fit, and place it in the ground where the deceased was to be buried. They placed hewn-out logs for bottom or floor, and a quilt or feather bed was placed where the corpse was to lay. They covered over with logs as described and covered with dirt. This was one of the ways that the dead were buried. The memorial, or the Big Indian Cry, was held about six months to one year after the death of member of the family.

When a man lost his wife, he would go bareheaded or wrap his head with a handkerchief and would not wear his hat until after the cry, and afterward he was free to marry again. Likewise of the woman. After her husband was dead, she would remain in the house to herself, all through the day. Meals were brought to her, as she would not eat with the family at the table. She would go the grave once and twice a day to cry, wore black dress and her head uncombed, always mourning. After the cry, she would change dress, friends comb her hair, give her a good word of encouragement, and afterward she is one of the members of the family again and is free to marry if she so desires. Thus ends the rememberances of the deceased love mate of wife, husband, or children.[49] (Choctaw, 38: 134–35)

Notes

1. The Creek *tulwa*, or *talwa*, as John R. Swanton denoted this governmental and ceremonial unit, usually had a chief, or *miko*, a *heniha*, who came from white or peace clans, and a *tastanagi*, who came from red or war clans. The *heniha* often directed public works, supervised certain ceremonies associated with peace, and led dances. The *tastanagi* headed a kind of police

which enforced the laws and punished wrongdoers. Towns also had a number of other officials. Titles and responsibilities varied considerably depending on the size and complexity of the town as well as its own cultural tradition. John R. Swanton, *Social Usages of the Indians of the Creek Confederacy*, Forty-Second Annual Report of the Bureau of American Ethnology (Washington, D.C., 1928), pp. 242–334.

2. James Adair, an eighteenth-century trader among southeastern Indians, gave an excellent account of the Green Corn Ceremony. Samuel Cole Williams, ed., *Adair's History of the American Indians* (Johnson City, Tenn., 1930), pp. 105–17. Other early descriptions include Benjamin Hawkins, *A Sketch of the Creek Country in the Years 1798 and 1799*, Georgia Historical Society Publications, vol. 3 (Americus, Ga., 1938), p. 75; William Bartram, "Observations on the Creek and Cherokee Indians," *Transactions of the American Ethnological Society* 3 (1853): 3–81; and Samuel Cole Williams, ed., *Lieut. Henry Timberlake's Memoirs, 1756-1765* (Marietta, Ga., 1948), p. 64.

3. The "medicine" was made from "red root," which came from a willow (*Salix*) species, and button snake root (*Eryngium yuccaefolium*). Each root was steeped in its own pot. Frank G. Speck, "The Creek Indians of Taskigi Town," *American Anthropological Association Memoirs* 2 (1907): 137–44.

4. In Taskigi town, women and children only washed their hands and heads in the medicine, a powerful emetic which only men consumed. Speck, "The Creek Indians of Taskigi Town," p. 141.

5. Since the Creeks were matrilineal, the uncle who conducted this ceremony would be the brother of the children's mother.

6. Southeastern Indians traditionally employed scratching to strengthen a child. Usually the skin was soaked so that the process would not be as painful as it would be if a thorn or gar tooth were applied to dry skin. "Dry scratching" was used as a punishment. John R. Swanton, *The Indians of the Southeastern United States* (Washington, D.C., 1946), p. 715.

7. Speck describes in considerable detail two Creek dances, the "crazy dance" and the "drunken dance," in "The Creek Indians of Taskigi Town," pp. 138–40. Speck also studied the dances of the Cherokees. See Frank Speck and Leonard Broom, *Cherokee Dance and Drama* (Berkley and Los Angeles, 1951).

8. In Taskigi town, members removed the top level of soil as well and piled it near the southeast corner of the square ground. According to Speck, "This heap of sacred soil symbolized the earth." "The Creek Indians of Taskigi Town," p. 137.

9. Many occasions involved ritual bathing or "going to water." Before extensive contact with whites, southeastern Indians began their daily activities by "going to water." They also bathed before the ball game and ceremonial dances, in treatment of some diseases, and for protection against

bad dreams and evil spells. The details of each of these bathing ceremonies differed, but "going to water" almost always occurred at daybreak after at least one night of fasting. James Mooney, *The Sacred Formulas of the Cherokees*, Seventh Annual Report of the Bureau of American Ethnology (Washington, D.C., 1886), pp. 335–36.

10. Southeastern Indian concepts about purity and pollution governed many of their ceremonies. See Charles Hudson, *The Southeastern Indians* (Knoxville, Tenn., 1976), pp. 317–75.

11. Adair described the laying of the fire in the eighteenth century: "The Archi-magus orders some of his religious attendants to dig up the old hearth, or altar, and to sweep out the remains that by chance might either be left, or drop down. Then he puts a few roots of the button-snake-root, with some green leaves of an uncommon small sort of tobacco, and a little of the new fruits, at the bottom of the fireplace, which he orders to be covered up with white marley clay, and wetted over with clean water." Williams, *Adair's History of the American Indians*, p. 106.

12. This custom may stem from the aboriginal practice in which a man went to live in the household of his wife and her lineage and, if she belonged to another town, within its bounds. Marriage changed neither town nor clan affiliation: man and woman continued to belong to their respective clans and towns. The husband respected his wife's town and clan, however, perhaps because his children belonged to her clan and town through the principle of matrilineal descent.

13. Many Creeks focused their anger at the removal policy on Christian missionaries and Indian converts. In 1836, the council asked that missionaries be expelled by the United States government, which complied, and imposed a penalty of fifty to one hundred lashes on anyone who attended Christian worship services. This official opposition to Christianity ended in 1848, and H. F. Buckner and other missionaries returned. Angie Debo, *The Road to Disappearance* (Norman, Okla., 1941), pp. 117–20.

14. Ironically, the Christian churches adopted the same type of structure —the brush arbor—for their camp meetings that conservative Indians maintained at their square grounds. See Chapter 6.

15. Elaborate rules governed visitors to people who were ill. Pregnant and menstruating women were forbidden from visiting the patient, as were strangers. Mooney, *Sacred Formulas*, pp. 330–31.

16. The narrator is probably referring to bear grass (*Yucca*).

17. The use of sacred plates by the Creeks of Tuckabatchee town in the Green Corn Ceremony was a very old practice unique among southeastern Indians (although the use of medicine bundles by the Seminoles is roughly analogous). Hudson, *The Southeastern Indians*, pp. 369–70.

18. The Kilpatricks recorded a similar rain-making ritual in which the participants recited the following words while they were under water:

Grandfather, I want water!

Grandmother, I want water!

Uncle, I want water!

The Fish wants water!

The Terrapin wants water!

Ne! Now a cloud is coming!

Ne! Now water is coming!

So:!

Jack Frederick Kilpatrick and Anna Gritts Kilpatrick, *Run Toward the Nightland: Magic of the Oklahoma Cherokees* (Dallas, 1967), pp. 31–33.

19. The Kilpatricks reported that among the western Cherokees some medicine men specialized in divining. In their rituals, they employed a variety of objects, including a stone suspended as a plummet, colored beads held in the hand, needles or beads floated on water, and a stick partially immersed in a stream. The most common object used for finding livestock and lost possessions was the plummet, which supposedly moved in the direction of whatever was missing. While observing the plummet, the medicine man spoke prayers such as the following:

Now! Provider!

I have just come to inquire of you.

This, _____, is its name.

You will show me the direction.

Run Toward the Nightland, pp. 113–21. James Mooney discovered similar practices among the eastern Cherokees in the late nineteenth century. *Sacred Formulas*, pp. 386–87.

20. Any child (but particularly twins) could be raised to be a prophet or witch by secluding him for twenty-four days after birth and feeding him the slightly fermented liquid from hominy instead of his mother's milk. Swanton, *Indians of the Southeastern United States*, p. 714.

21. Cherokees believed that if a person consumed only a decoction made from duck root (*Sagittaria*) for four days, he could transform himself into animals, and if he drank the liquid for seven days he could fly and dive underground. James Mooney and Frans M. Olbrechts, *The Swimmer Manuscript: Cherokee Sacred Formulas and Medicinal Prescriptions*, Bureau of American Ethnology Bulletin, no. 99 (Washington, D.C., 1932), p. 30.

22. The narrator probably is referring to the mythical dragon-like snake in which most southeastern Indians believed. See Charles Hudson, "Uktena: A Cherokee Anomalous Monster," *Journal of Cherokee Studies* 3 (1978): 62–75.

23. An excellent study of Cherokee witchcraft can be found in Raymond D. Fogelson, "An Analysis of Cherokee Sorcery and Witchcraft," in *Four Centuries of Southern Indians*, ed. Charles Hudson (Athens, Ga., 1975), pp. 113–31.

24. The narrator is referring to the use of the name "Kee-Too-Wah" by conservative Cherokees who opposed a Confederate alliance in the Civil War. Also called "Pin Indians," these Cherokees were closely associated with the abolitionist Baptist missionaries Evan and John Jones. See Chapter 1. The Downing party also used the name Kee-Too-Wah in the 1870s. See Chapter 8.

25. The narrator's father was Redbird Smith, who reorganized the Kee-Too-Wah Society in the 1890s. Smith led conservative Cherokees in opposition to the allotment of tribal lands to individuals and the dissolution of the tribal government. When political tactics failed, Smith and others attempted to revitalize traditional Cherokee beliefs, practices, and values in order to maintain spiritual and cultural unity. See Robert K. Thomas, "The Redbird Smith Movement," in *Symposium on Cherokee and Iroquois Culture*, ed. William N. Fenton and John Gulick, Bureau of American Ethnology Bulletin, no. 180 (Washhington, D.C., 1961), pp. 159–66.

26. The Cherokees often invoked deities from the Thunder family in their sacred formulas. One of James Mooney's informants explained:

The great Thunder and his sons, the two Thunder boys, live far in the west above the sky vault. The lightning and the rainbow are their beautiful dress. The priests pray to the Thunder and call him the Red Man, because that is the brightest color of his dress. There are other Thunders that live lower down, in the cliffs and mountains, and under waterfalls, and travel on invisible bridges from one high peak to another where they have their town houses. The great Thunders above the sky are kind and helpful when we pray to them, but these others are always plotting mischief.

Myths of the Cherokee, Nineteenth Annual Report of the Bureau of American Ethnology (Washington, D.C., 1900), p. 257.

27. White symbolized peace and happiness. Mooney, *Sacred Formulas*, p. 342.

28. The Cherokees associated the north with defeat and trouble and the south with peace and happiness. Mooney, *Sacred Formulas*, p. 342.

29. The following are among general studies of native American medicine: Eric Stone, *Medicine Among the American Indians*, Clio Medica: A Series of Primers on the History of Medicine, vol. 7 (New York, 1932); William Thomas Corlett, *The Medicine Man of the American Indian and His Cultural Background* (Springfield, 1935); Virgil J. Vogel, *American Indian*

Medicine (Norman, Okla., 1970); C. A. Weslager, *Magic Medicines of the Indians* (Somerset, N.J., 1973). Books and articles dealing specifically with medical practices of southeastern Indians include Robert F. Greenlee, "Medicine and Curing Practices of the Modern Florida Seminole," *American Anthropologist* 46 (1944): 317–28; James Mooney, "Cherokee Theory and Practice of Medicine," *Journal of American Folklore* 3 (1880): 44–50; Mooney, *Sacred Formulas*; Mooney and Olbrechts, *Swimmer Manuscript*; John R. Swanton, *Religious Beliefs and Medical Practices of the Creek Indians*, Forty-Second Annual Report of the Bureau of American Ethnology (Washington, D.C., 1928); Lyda Averill Taylor, *Plants Used as Curatives by Certain Southeastern Tribes* (Cambridge, Mass., 1940). Another useful work is Paul B. Hamel and Mary U. Chiltoskey, *Cherokee Plants: Their Uses —A 400 Year History* (Sylva, N.C., 1975).

30. The narrator is probably using the term "cascara" to refer to a kind of tonic rather than to the buckthorn or bearwood (*Rhamnus*), which is also called "cascara" but grows in the Northwest and yields a laxative. The wahoo bush (*Euonymus*) is also known as strawberry bush, cat's paw, and hearts-a-bustin'-with-love.

31. May apple (*Podophyllum*) is also called mandrake.

32. Bear foot weed (*Polymnia*) is also called leafcup. Another treatment for pain from neuritis or rheumatism involved scratching with a thorny branch of bittersweet (*Celastrus*).

33. The inner bark of the sycamore (*Platanus*), or buttonwood, is used in this remedy for coughs.

34. Blackroot (*Aletris*) is also known as stargrass or star-root.

35. The use of the cottonwood (*Populus*) as medicine perhaps began after removal.

36. Butterfly root (*Asclepias*) had a number of medical uses. It was also called chigger weed, flux weed, pleurisy root, and wirch weed.

37. Slippery elm (*Ulmus*) is also known as red elm.

38. The blackberry (*Rubus*), of course, provided food as well as medicine.

39. Studies of southeastern Indian kinship include William H. Gilbert, Jr., *The Eastern Cherokees*, Bureau of American Ethnology Bulletin, no. 133 (Washington, D.C., 1943); John P. Reid, *A Law of Blood: The Primitive Law of the Cherokee Nation* (New York, 1970); Alexander Spoehr, *Changing Kinship Systems: A Study in the Acculturation of the Creeks, Cherokee, and Choctaw* (Chicago, 1947); Swanton, *Social Organization*.

40. The Creek town, or *talwa*, was not merely a population center. According to Swanton, *talwa* referred to a tribe that had been independent before becoming a constituent part of the Creek Confederacy. See *Social Organization*, pp. 242–334; Speck, "The Creek Indians of Taskigi Town,"

pp. 99–164; Mary R. Haas, "Creek Inter-Town Relations," *American Anthropologist* 42 (1940): 479–89.

41. Adair reported that, in the eighteenth century, Indian names were "expressive of their tempers, outward appearances, and other various circumstances" and were subject to change. Williams, *Adair's History of the American Indians*, pp. 199–202.

42. Traditional southeastern marriages involved an exchange of corn symbolizing the woman's role and deer meat symbolizing the man's. Williams, *Adair's History of the American Indians*, p. 146; Cephas Washburn, *Reminiscences of the Indians* (Richmond, Va., 1869), pp. 206–7.

43. Southeastern Indians often practiced polygamy in the eighteenth century. James Adair wrote, "The Indians are so fond of variety, that they ridicule the white people, as a tribe of narrow-hearted, and dull constituted animals, for having only one wife at a time." Although the national governments of the southeastern tribes outlawed polygamy in the nineteenth century, some Indians continued the practice. Even John Martin, first Chief Justice of the Supreme Court of the Cherokee Nation, had two wives at one time. Williams, *Adair's History of the American Indians*, p. 145; James Franklin Corn, *Red Clay and Rattlesnake Springs: A History of the Indians of Bradley County, Tennessee* (Cleveland, Tenn., 1976), p. 49.

44. Mutilation was a common punishment for sexual offenses such as incest or adultery. Adair reported that, with the first offense, adulterers lost their ears, with the second, their noses and upper lips, and with the third, their lives. Williams, *Adair's History of the American Indians*, p. 152.

45. Conservative Indians often relied on conjury for matters involving love and marriage. Jack Frederick Kilpatrick and Anna Gritts Kilpatrick have collected a large number of formulas and rituals used by the Cherokees and have published them in *Walk in Your Soul: Love Incantations of the Oklahoma Cherokees* (Dallas, 1965).

46. In the period of early European contact, divorce was fairly common among the southeastern Indians, particularly the Cherokees, whose marriages were "ill observed and of short continuance." Williams, *Adair's History of the American Indians*, p. 153.

47. Mortuary customs of the southeastern Indians varied in the period of early European contact. The Natchez conducted elaborate funeral ceremonies for their leaders which included human sacrifices. They buried the bodies long enough for the flesh to decay; then they dug them up, cleaned the bones, and stored the remains in their temple. The Choctaws placed the dead on scaffolds for four months and then placed the bones in a' bone house. The Chickasaws maintained houses for the bones of people who died while traveling and whose bodies could not be returned for interment, and they

buried people who died in their villages in tombs covered with logs and cypress bark. Sometimes warriors would be buried where they were slain, and passersby would add rocks to small mounds over their graves. Hudson, *The Southeastern Indians*, pp. 328–36; Williams, *Adair's History of the American Indians*, pp. 186–94.

48. Adair reported that, unless the traders managed to persuade the family otherwise, "the grave is heir to all." Williams, *Adair's History of the American Indians*, p. 186.

49. Adair gave the following account of eighteenth-century mourning: Their law compels the widow, through the long term of her weeds, to refrain all public company and diversions, at the penalty of an adulteress; and likewise to go with flowing hair, without the privilege of oil to anoint it. The nearest kinsmen of the deceased husband, keep a very watchful eye over her conduct, in this respect. . . . Neither is the husband of the deceased allowed, when the offices of nature do not call him, to go out of the house, much less to join any company; and in that time of mourning he often lies among the ashes.
Williams, *Adair's History of the American Indians*, pp. 195–98.

Chapter 6 · Religion and Education

ALTHOUGH CONSERVATIVE INDIANS DID MAINTAIN TRADITIONS, several factors undermined those remnants of their aboriginal culture. In particular, Christian churches and Anglo-American educational institutions waged war on all vestiges of the Indians' "savage" heritage and attempted to supplant traditional practices and beliefs with "civilization." The impetus for this cultural transformation came from white missionaries with the support and encouragement of the government of the United States and the political leadership of the five tribes. The missionaries, whose ministry began before removal and continued in the West, believed that Christianity and the other trappings of a "civilized" existence were irrevocably joined: a person could not truly live a Christian life unless he wore trousers and a frock coat (or she wore pantaloons, petticoats, and a pinafore), exhibited proper table manners, earned an "honest" living, and if at all possible, spoke English. They thought that schools, preferably boarding schools where children could be supervised constantly, provided the best opportunity to eradicate "savage" attitudes and customs and inculcate "civilized" values. Many Indian leaders, convinced that their people would survive only if they became culturally indistinguishable from whites, supported mission schools and their objectives and often made permission for proselytizing contingent on the establishment of schools. The children of most Indian leaders attended these schools, which in time produced a generation of formally educated leaders who had embraced Christianity. These graduates of mission schools valued Anglo-American education and religion and joined with the missionaries in denigrating the old ways. At the urging of this new leadership, tribal governments instituted networks of public schools, which offered primary through higher education and encouraged the establishment of private subscription schools where public schools could not be built.

Orphans presented an excellent opportunity for missionaries and others intent on "civilizing" the southeastern Indians to implement their plans. Since orphans could not return home to the corrupting influence of parents, teachers were able to prevent any contact with "savage" behavior and to scrutinize every action for the emergence of "savagery." Orphanages resulted from the breakdown of traditional kinship ties and the waning value placed on the family. Kinsmen no longer readily accepted children outside their own nuclear family. In addition to homeless orphans, the dramatic cultural changes the southeastern Indians had experienced produced problems with insanity and alcoholism. Instead of coping with these problems at the family level, many Indians sought external help, which was provided by insane asylums and temperance organizations.

Educational institutions, social reform movements, and philanthropic endeavors generally rested on the Christian religion to which the majority of southeastern Indians subscribed in the postwar period. Ordained Indian ministers conducted services in the native languages, and translators produced Bibles and hymnals for their use. With the language barrier broken, many conservatives came into the Christian fold. However, a significant number of these converts surreptitiously merged their adopted religion and their own cultural traditions. For example, camp meetings, a feature of frontier Christianity, took place when the crops had been harvested, utilized the brush arbor architecture of the stomp ground, and offered the purification and rejuvenation of the traditional Green Corn Ceremony.

While relatively few conservatives totally rejected Christianity, many scorned the white man's education and did not avail themselves of the opportunities afforded them. Economic circumstances also prevented a number of conservatives from enrolling their children in schools. Traditional communities often had fewer people than the requisite for the establishment of a public school, and a subsistence-level existence precluded a subscription school. Even when they had access to public schools, conservatives usually needed their children as laborers. Consequently, education often became the province of the progressives of the five tribes and possibly helped to widen the cultural and economic gap between them and the conservatives.

Churches

The Indians, before they were civilized, believed that there was some kind of a God. But not till they were civilized did they know of the real God and Jesus Christ that they know of today.

After the tribes were moved to Oklahoma (the five civilized tribes) there came into the Territory white missionaries. Among the first to come here in this part of the Territory were some Catholic missionaries. They held their services under arbors made of tree limbs. This was just before the Civil War broke out. The Catholic missionaries did not get many followers.

Then came the Presbyterian missionaries about 1860. Preaching to the Indians among the missionaries were John Lilly and Ross Ramsey, who in 1866 built the first Presbyterian Mission School located about two miles north of Wewoka. There the Indians were taught to read and write English and to worship God.[1]

In 1888 they built of stone their first church house. This church was located on what now is called 506–508 South Mekusukey Avenue. There the Presbyterians held their church services until 1905, at which time they moved to their present location about one-fourth mile southwest of the city limits of Wewoka. With plenty of trees for shade, they built this church of pine lumber with several cook shacks around, which were built by individual families for use in cooking their meals when they come to church, that is, when the meetings lasted any length of time.

In 1923 oil was discovered near this, and later they drilled an oil well on the church property bringing the church plenty of money. So in 1932 they built a nice brick church. The church has the same old bell that was used when it was located on Mekusukey Avenue in 1888, and it is still in good shape.

There were other missionaries, Baptists and Methodists, who came into the Territory after the Civil War.[2] The Baptists have a nice church located about one-fourth mile southeast of the city limits of Wewoka that has also been built since Territory days. There are now many churches conveniently located all over the Seminole Nation.

The Indians generally have from one to two camp meetings a year. They go to the churches, where most families have their own houses to cook in. They always bring plenty of food to eat till the meeting is over. They all like plenty of meat, often killing several cattle and hogs. If you visit their church you are always welcome to eat with them. (Seminole, 68: 450–52)

*   *   *

It does not matter how far out in the woods one may live, he would rather live near to church where he can attend meetings. This has been the practice of the Choctaw Indian that he is not satisfied unless he attends church now and then. While he may not be a minister or church member, he respects the church and is not satisfied unless he gives something.

Since the missionaries came to Indian Territory and preached amongst them, teaching them the right and wrong and to have a place of worship, it has been so strongly impressed on their mind that it seems a disgrace to them when they ignore or refuse to help with the church.

When there is an Indian church, one may notice a brush arbor near the church house, which shows that meetings or Sunday School can be held outdoors when the weather is favorable in the summer time. One of the oldest churches in the county is known as Horn's Corner. This name was given when a man named Horn was killed at this corner, and later a church was organized and was given this name. It is a Baptist church.

In the Territorial days, before the saw mill was known in this country, logs hewn out were constructed into a house where they held their meetings. Hewn-out logs were easily made in those days, as there were plenty of timbers which answered the purpose of lumber, young trees cut into poles for rafters and handmade boards to cover the house, which lasted several years. . . .

At first when the church was built, there were no windows, and a small table was placed in one end of the house for the preacher to preach to his congregation; rough logs placed inside for seats with no lean back; bell would be placed somewhere on the outside, which gave signal to the people when ready for church services.

If in summer time, a brush arbor would be constructed by placing forked poles at an equal distance apart, with poles to weigh down and hold in place, smaller poles then laid across about two feet apart and bush or limbs of trees are cut and thrown on the top which when set up properly would last for two or three summers. (Choctaw, 20: 255–57)

*   *   *

I first attended school near Connerville, in what is now Pontotoc County. I do not remember the name of this school, but it was an Indian neighborhood school. The school was located on the east side of Blue River, and we lived on the west side. I also attended an Indian school east of Lebanon. This school was taught by a white man. It was about this time that I saw my first preacher. I will never forget. My mother told me a preacher was coming to our house, and I began to wonder just what kind of an animal that was. I finally asked her, and she told me it was a man. He was an Indian preacher by the name of Pierceson. He lived near the Washita west of Tishomingo.

The first Sunday the preacher came there was no one there except our own family, but they started to coming in one by one until finally our house would not hold the crowd.

Elie Lone's brother, who had only one name, Lason, was always drunk in those days. He got to riding up to our house on horseback every Sunday while the preacher was preaching. Finally, one Sunday he came into the house and made for the bed. He did not stop when he reached the bed but rolled over to the far side and under it. He came back a while after that and joined the church. Aferwards he spent most of his time reading the Bible.

Finally the preacher, who was a Methodist, suggested that we buy some books. We bought some primers and Bibles, all printed in the Choctaw language since the Chickasaws did not have a written language.[3] Our next preacher, also an Indian, came from Daugherty. He would make the ride every Sunday morning across the Arbuckle, mounted, and on to Lebanon. (Chickasaw, 6: 317–18)

*   *   *

When I was a girl, I attended Elm Hill Baptist Church with my mother, who was a full-blood Cherokee. She was educated and was a leader in the Baptist missionary work for thirty years. She did the interpreting for the ministers who were sent there from the East.

They had the Bible in Cherokee language and would read a verse, then pass it down the line, and every person would read.[4] I was very small, but it impressed me very much. I am still trying to follow out the teachings of my mother and the Bible.

I enjoyed going to church, and most all my people are Baptist. The old church was called the Elm Hill Church, and it is about nine miles east of Stilwell in Adair County. The building has been torn down, but the old family graveyard is still in my memory, and it has grown to be a large graveyard. It was started by our family in 1845. (Cherokee, 30: 160)

*　　*　　*

I used to see the Choctaw ball games and have attended their camp meetings. They still have those camp meetings like they used to do several years ago. They would kill hogs, beef, and get everything ready, and just move over to the church and feed the people. They still follow the old custom. One of the old churches is still there, and they have their meetings at this church yet. It is a Methodist church called the Old Cedar Church. It was a log church house, but they have done away with that one and built a lumber church house, and it is still being used at this time.

I remember some years ago, when the meeting was over and the Choctaws were getting ready to go home, the sheriff of Cedar County was going to arrest one Isaac Reubin. The sheriff's name was Campbell, and he went to this man and told him that he was under arrest, but this man resisted the officer. Then the sheriff pulled his gun and shot at him but missed him. Then Isaac got his gun and killed the sheriff. That was on a Monday morning. He shot the sheriff all to pieces with his own gun, then he got the sheriff's gun and emptied it into him after he had him killed. There has been several Indians killed at this church.

They don't have the Indian cries that they used to have. When they used to have them I went and cooked for them most of the time. They would then have the cries at their home where the grave was. The Choctaws used to bury their dead near the house. They had no cemeteries anywhere then, so they buried at their home and would have the cries at the grave. All the Indians took part in the cries, but they have quit now on account of the white people making fun at them.

I am a full-blood Choctaw Indian and never went to school, not even one day, so I am not able to speak nor read, nor write in English. In fact, I can't read nor write in my own language. I can speak the Choctaw language but that is all. (Choctaw, 70: 46–47)

*   *   *

About four miles east and about two miles north of Stillwell, Oklahoma, near the old home of John Alberty, is a bubbling spring of cold water. It is located in a deep valley nearly surrounded by beautiful hills covered with grass and beautiful trees. To this secluded valley, in the early days of the Cherokee Nation, the old-time Cherokee families from far and near would come in wagons, on horseback, and on foot to be at and take part in the annual camp meeting. Usually the whole family went, taking with them camping equipment and food. They also hunted during the stay at camp. The time of the meeting was usually in August and September because the farming was over, the weather was fine, and grass was plentiful for the stock.

There would be regular worship at 11 o'clock A.M. and at 7 o'clock P.M. These services would sometimes last as long as two hours. It is said that much lasting good was done at these meetings, as shown by the good Christian lives of the people who became Christians at these meetings.

Aside from the religious worship at these meetings was the social side of them. In the long forenoons and afternoons and between the hours of worship, the folks enjoyed themselves, visiting and becoming better acquainted with those living in different neighborhoods.

At this camp there was a long shed with a long table. The cooking was done over an open fire and the meals served under the shed on the long table. (Cherokee, 1: 51–52)

*   *   *

At the present Brushy Mountain Spring, located about eight miles southeast of Muskogee, Oklahoma, my frandfather, John Tate, a minister, started the first camp meeting at this location. It was in 1890. The arbor at first was poles placed in the ground, poles over-head, and then covered with straw. Later they placed logs in the ground and built a roof of split shingles, clapboard shingles, split from logs with a froe. The seats were split logs. This camp meeting operated each year for twenty years. After my grandfather, our preacher was Reverend Coppage. The people in this locality looked forward each year to attending camp meeting, more so than they do now the state fair. I myself attended this meeting for nineteen consecutive years. The meeting lasted usually two weeks. The spring furnished abun-dant, cool, fresh water and does yet. We would take our teams and wagons, load up with flour, meal, lard, meat, chickens, and all kinds of foodstuff, including feed for the teams, and just live at the meeting from the time it started until it finished. It was a great event and took place at the time in summer when our crops were all laid by —July. (Cherokee, 3: 287)

Philanthropy and Social Reform

I was born on Rock Creek, southeast of Sulphur, about 1883. I attended the Indian schools at Sulphur and Davis during the first five years of my schooling. Then mother died, and father sent me to the orphan's home at Lebanon, east of Marietta.[5] This was a home for both boys and girls of the Chickasaws and Choctaws. Our sleeping rooms were upstairs, and the classrooms and dining room were on the first floor.

The girls helped wash dishes and iron, and a woman was hired by the Chickasaw government to do the laundry. A Negro and a white woman did the cooking. There was a Superintendent of Public Instruction, who was appointed by both houses, who devoted his time to visiting the government institutions, and this was one of the institutions he visited. These institutions were supported by the Chickasaw government through the United States Treasury. A sum of $50,000 was paid to the Chickasaws semi-annually for the support of their schools. This money was the interest which ac-cumulated on investments in United states bonds.[6] (Chickasaw, 21: 348–49)

*   *   *

My mother having died in 1902 and my father in 1903, in 1904 my uncle, Morgan Cole, who was my guardian, brought me to this school, and there I first learned my alphabet.[7] Having never left home in my youth in any distance, I had a lonesome time and experienced life that I had never seen before when I came to this school. It happened that I arrived two or three days before the opening of school, and, of course, there were no students. I was doing fine and getting along nicely with the teachers and employees during my two days' stay, and my first acquaintance was William J. Farver, a one-half Choctaw Indian now employed in Federal Building, Muskogee, Oklahoma, who was a postmaster and a store clerk of the school. Not acquainted with him, I took him to be a white man, but to my surprise he could talk the Choctaw language as perfect as I can.

On the day for the students to arrive, they came, and in two days or three the school was filled to capacity. There were about 120 boys, which was all that could be accommodated, and the rest had to return home. School began. The first thing on the docket among the students was the initiation of new or "green" students, as it was called— something similar to the D.D.M. of some colleges, though not severe. It was strictly against the school to fight, and there was an officer of the day always on duty to keep everything in harmony, but at this particular time he was not to be found. I remember a small boy, about one-eighth white, came to me with a faked news that I was wanted by a professor out near somewhere. I went. We went near to the cemetery, which was west of school about one-quarter of a mile, but upon our arrival I did not see the professor. The judge, or the chairman, and members already in session asked me my name, age, my home, and several other questions. I answered all questions in my own native tongue and was instantly told that I was not allowed to talk in my own tongue but must talk in English and that I had committed a break in a rule of school as well as laws of the kangaroo court. I was also charged with "breaking in, in school without permission," "talking Choctaw," et cetera, and the chairman asked, "What is the desire of the members?" Some shouted, "Send him back home." While others cried, "Make him wrestle, fight, or give him a permanent job as water carrier or to empty slop for the teachers and matron."

Here I stood wondering what it was all about or what the final result would be, until one boy about my size walked up and challenged me for a wrestle. We wrestled, and when I got the best of him, up jumped another boy larger than I. And so it continued until you were handled by someone, or if you were somewhat high-tempered and showed fight, of course, you had your hands full. If you out-best your opponent in the fight, same process follows as in wrestling until you are whipped and calmed down. Everything was over and you became a full-fledged member, and you were not to be bothered any more. . . .

Mr. Peru Farver and Charles Kaneubbee were the last two faculty members of Armstrong Academy that served with the World War during the trouble with the "Huns." There were also several of the students of this school enlisted in the army when Uncle Sam called for volunteers. The government was greatly repaid for what it had done for the Indians, as while attending school and under the instruction of military discipline these boys were trained in how to be a soldier and, when volunteered for service, after a short training at the camps, they were ready for the front "Over There" and went to do their bit and "Give Until It Hurt."

I cannot refrain from repeating the same word, when by some reason, this school caught fire from a defective flue while students were eating supper in 1921. I was on the train, and when it arrived at Bokchito, a few of the Armstrong Academy students boarded the train and said the Armstrong Academy went up in flames about 6:30 in the evening. The first school that I attended was at this place. It was home to me, and today I can still see that same old school, the superintendent, teachers, matrons, and students. (Choctaw, 2: 162–69)

*   *   *

My husband was killed in 1894, seven years after our marriage, so I was left with a family to support. In 1894, I secured a job as a matron at the Cherokee Orphans Home near Salina and worked at that job for four years.[8] I had charge of forty-six boys ranging in age from six to ten years. This orphanage burned after I left there and a while before statehood.

Along about 1894 or before, a white man by the name of Whitaker built and operated an orphanage. He secured funds for the operation of this home through subscription of funds, ranging from ten cents up. He spent practically all of his time and effort in this cause. So when the Cherokee orphanage burned, the Indian children were transferred over to the Whitaker home, which had been enlarged from time to time, and were cared for there. Through some action, I don't know the details, this Whitaker Home became what was known as a national home and remained so until statehood. (Cherokee, 2: 460–61)

*   *   *

After we were married we worked at the insane asylum under Bob Woffard. I did the cooking, and my husband was steward and helped care for the inmates. They were all Cherokee Indians. There were eighty inmates at that time. Some of them would not eat and would have to be fed. Some were able to work on the farm. The women would milk the cows. There was one blind woman there, her name was Margaret Galcatcher. She could do lots of work as she was not insane, just blind.[9] (White resident of the Cherokee Nation, 2: 103)

*   *   *

Mrs. Emma Molloy, who visited Tahlequah in 1884, was noted as a temperance lecturer and was a prominent member of the Women's Christian Temperance Union in Ohio.[10] During the period of her stay at Tahlequah, Mrs. Molloy delivered addresses on a number of occasions, and a large number of persons signed the pledge to abstain from the use of intoxicating liquor. Besides addressing audiences in Tahlequah, Mrs. Molloy met numbers of people elsewhere. There were persons who travelled considerable distances to hear her addresses or lectures.

One largely attended lecture was delivered at the Cherokee National Female Seminary, then situated in the Park Hill locality. The students of the institution, neighbors, and people from other places were present. Mrs. Molloy was a speaker of much ability and eloquence and was given close attention.

On another occasion, an address was delivered in the old Park Hill Presbyterian Church, which stood near the site of the early day mission school long maintained by the American Board of Boston, Massachusetts. The church was situated in an open spot surrounded by woodlands. It was filled to overflowing. A larger number of people were present than on any other occasion so far as is known.

From time to time visiting ministers from distant states or cities reached the Park Hill locality and preached in the old church. Women speakers were seldom seen and heard, and for the purpose of listening to a woman a number of persons, who otherwise probably would have remained at home, were present. The Women's Christian Temperance Union of Tahlequah, which came into existence as a result of the visit of Mrs. Emma Molloy, was active during a number of years. (Cherokee, 43: 27–29)

Schools

Levering was a missionary Baptist [school]. The Creeks let the Baptists have forty acres, and they built the boarding school, which was attended without paying tuition. I was too small to go at first as they didn't allow any under eight years to attend. Some were grown boys and girls who could do lots of work. All were large enough to work at something. They cleared land and broke it (plowed it), built barns, raised everything to eat—black-eyed peas, molasses, corn, and all garden truck. There were fifty head of Jerseys to be milked and fed, hogs were raised, so it took lots of corn.

They got up before day and milked, then ate breakfast and went to the bottom to clear land or plow it until nine o'clock. After school they worked until sundown. Fifty big boys did a lot of work. The main man, or superintendent, whose name was Will Wright, was a good manager, the best I ever saw. It didn't cost them much to run that school, and it did lots of good. We worked, but we learned something. (Creek, 14: 405–6)

*   *   *

The New Female Seminary was built in north Tahlequah—begun on November 3rd, 1887, completed on April 18th, 1889—a modern brick building on a lovely site supplied with water from the "Big Spring," with steam heat and inside toilet.[11] It was the pride of the Cherokee Nation, where were gathered 250 Cherokee girls, and they were looking about for the right man, to superintend this beautiful high-class institution of learning. Spencer Stephens was chosen. When given an appropriation to select the proper appointments for the school, Uncle Spencer went to St. Louis, and, among other things, he selected real linen tablecloths and napkins, and silver dishes and knives and forks for the fourteen long tables in the dining room.

Some complained that he was spending the nation's money needlessly, but he told them that young ladies of the best families demanded the best. But politics put him out after that first term as superintendent. There is a tablet in the entrance hall perpetuating his memory and educational efforts.

He was an ideal superintendent. I remember when passing through the halls he found pencil marks on the wall going up the back stairs, and he called Miss Bushyhead's attention to it and told her to find the culprit and make her scrub the marks off. Another time when he went to Aunt Sarah's room on the second floor he found greasy finger marks around the knob. He called Aunt Sarah and told her to scrub around the knob. He was so alert that everything was just right. (Cherokee, 1: 394)

*   *   *

Two miles east of Eufaula, Creek Nation, in sight of the MK&T Railroad, was located Asbury Mission, a manual labor school for Creek Indian boys.[12] The approach to the school grounds led through a beautiful timbered glade. A wide lane separated the large fields of corn, wheat, and oats. Near the house were large, well-cultivated gardens that furnished an abundance of vegetables for the tables. The main building was a brick, three-story structure in a grove of forest trees facing east. Accommodations for eighty boys were provided. Mr. W. N. Martin was superintendent of the school and was assisted by a competent corps of teachers, including Professor R. C. McGee and Miss L. E. Harrell, a sister of one of the Indian Territory's pioneer preachers.

For this special [commencement] occasion, the school rooms had taken on a gala appearance. The pillars in the corridors were twined with evergreens, and spring flowers were in profusion throughout the house. The word "welcome" was formed in evergreen above the door of the auditorium. A charming view toward the east could be had from the upper windows overlooking the entire fields.

The commencement exercises opened at 9 A.M., July 3, 1878, with scripture readings and a song, "Happy Greetings," followed by examination of classes. The result showed exceptionally fine work on the part of both students and teachers. The system of written spelling was believed to be the best that could be adopted. Classes in history, Latin, and mathematics showed marked advancement. The opinion the governing body expressed was that the progress made by the school equalled that of any school of its grade in the states. So pleased were the board of directors with the management and system, that the establishment of still another school would be recommended as soon as the funds of the Nation would warrant, also the establishment of an orphan's asylum modeled after the Cherokee orphanage.

The amount of work done by the boys was worthy of special notice. Under the careful supervision of Mr. Martin, they had planted and cultivated fifty acres of corn, twenty acres of wheat, fifteen acres of oats, and two acres of sugar cane. In the vegetable garden were two acres of sweet potatoes, two of Irish potatoes, and two acres of garden vegetables.

The increased interest in the school, especially by the full-bloods, was manifested by their attendance at the Commencement. . . . Teachers from other schools in the Nation were in attendance and were particularly interested in the primary work. Reverend William McCombs, Superintendent of Instruction in the Creek Nation, addressed the school in the Creek language, followed by Judge Stidham[13] and James Colbert, also speaking in the Creek language. A hearty welcome was extended to all visitors, and an excellent dinner was served, everyone being invited to participate. (Creek 1: 352–55)

*   *   *

In 1877, I came to Okmulgee, Creek Nation, to visit the Parkinson girls who had lived in our town and who were also teaching there at the time. Their father, Jonathan Parkinson, had a dry goods store there. I only expected to make a short visit. Mr. Pleasant Porter, afterward Chief Porter, was living in Okmulgee then. As he was a progressive, intelligent young man, he was very much interested in the Creek schools. When he heard I was a successful teacher in Kansas, he came to see me and asked if I would like to teach in Okmulgee.[14]

As the salary in the Creek schools was $40 a month for a ten-month term, I was not long in making a decision. I resigned my place in Kansas, preparing to teach in Okmulgee the next fall. Reverend William McCombs was superintendent of the Creek schools at that time.

It was necessary that I go to Eufaula to take the examination and get my certificate. Mr. McCombs asked me if I had ever crossed a river when the horse had to swim. I replied that I had not but I thought I could do most anything anyone else could. In company with Mr. McCombs and Captain Belcher, we made the trip and did swim the Canadian River. The trip was made in three days to Eufaula and back.

After I began teaching, Mr. McCombs would come to my school often so that I became worried for fear that something was wrong. Finally I got up my courage enough to ask him if I was not doing the work satisfactorily. He said, "yes," and that he was taking notes on my work so that he could pass it on to other teachers. Miss Edith Hicks, now Mrs. Walker of Muskogee, was also teaching there. I had one little Negro boy in my school. He came, and I allowed him to stay. Every time Mr. McCombs came he would send him home and told me he could not attend school with the Indian children. The little fellow was persistent and would return each time. I told Mr. McCombs that I would be at loss without him as he was my interpreter, understanding the Creek language and I did not. "On these conditions he may stay," Mr. McCombs said.[15]

I had two white pupils, Minnie Fryer, now Mrs. C. H. Finnegan of Muskogee, and her little brother Johnnie. Their father paid tuition, which was required by the law, and they were allowed to attend. (White resident of the Creek Nation, 4: 434–35)

*   *   *

After I was graduated from school, I returned to our home at Goodland, known now as Hugo, and taught the first day school for Indians in that town. I rented a vacant house from Joel Spring and converted it into a schoolhouse. The seats were long, pine benches, and there were no desks. I had a long table made around which the older children sat. The younger children held their books and slates in their laps.

I taught McGuffey's Latest System, cardboard style. A piece of cardboard was hung on the wall with a picture and a description of each lesson. I received $75 a month as my salary from the Choctaw national government.

The next year I married O. S. Lattimer from Lamar County, Texas, and he built our home five miles west of Goodland, now known as Farney, and he also built one large room for a school in our back yard. I named it the Wigwam School and taught school here for three years. This was in 1900. (Choctaw, 33: 85–86)

I got my first schooling there at Springfield, Indian Territory, and there was where I learned to talk the Creek language. The school building was built by the Indians of hewed oak logs and chinked and daubed. It only had one door and that was in the south end. Our teacher was an old sailor by the name of Ross. I don't know how he ever came to this country. He was just wandering through, and they hired him to teach the school. He was the most brilliant and the best-educated man I have ever met. He boarded at our house. We only lived a mile from the school, but having spent his life on the sea and not being used to the land he could not go from our home to the school without getting lost. I always had to go with him and show him the way. He fell in love with and married Susie Walker, a full-blood Creek woman, and they lived there until she died, and a short time later he died. . . .

I attended Asbury Mission one year, and in 1881, when I was sixteen years old, I went to Fayetteville, Arkansas, to the military school there.[16] That was before the Frisco railroad was built. I came up to Muskogee on the Katy and rode an apple wagon on to Fayetteville.

Old Preacher Hill was president of the school while I was there. While I was in school in Fayetteville, the Frisco railroad was built, and one morning in June of 1882, we all marched down to the depot to watch the first passenger train go through. I think it was the hottest day that I ever saw. We had our uniforms on and had to keep our coats buttoned. I boarded with a family named Ellis, but when school was out I went and stayed with Professor Hill. (Creek/Chickasaw, 8: 534–35)

*   *   *

The houses and schools were of log construction with thatched roof. Schools were not much in evidence at the time I was a boy. The only school we had was when someone took the notion that they wanted to build a schoolhouse in some particular locality and went about to employ some Indian that was educated back East to teach the school. The parents of all the children who attended this school paid a dollar a month for each child attending, and this would pay the teacher.

These privately owned school houses and homes were finally improved on, and the log houses or cabins took on puncheon floors instead of dirt floors, possibly one window with glass instead of no windows or possibly a shuttle window, stone fireplace instead of those with straw and clapboards. (Cherokee, 3: 170–71)

*   *   *

My parents were just poor Indians farmers who had been moved from state to state and then to the Indian Territory. Then father had to go to the white man's war at the time I was born, and, when I was large enough to go to school, my chances of getting an education were very poor. I did learn the war father was in with the white men was to free the Negroes from slavery and they were freed. On account of my being unable to get an education, I am here on this reservation, and I am a slave instead of the Negroes.

I was about eight years old when I first attended a little log school on San Bois Creek. I had to go four miles to school. Part of the time I walked, and sometimes I rode horseback on a little pony which father had caught on the Wild Horse Prairie in the Sugar Loaf Mountain and had broken to ride.

I learned to read and write some. We had no grades like Beatrice, my daughter, talks about these days. Some of the children went to school until they could read in a book called a history. When they got so they could read in this book the superintendent of the Choctaw Tribe would send them back east to states to college. Just children of the better-to-do people got to go and get an education. I never went to any other school and not to that one much because father died, and mother and we kids had to work to make a living.

I was never out of the Choctaw Nation, but I have associated with the Cherokees and the Chickasaws who came into our neighborhood, and we lived about as they did in the early days. People with money and an education lived better than we did. They had nice board houses, cook stoves, store-bought clothes that were the best, lots of horses and cattle, but we had a log cabin with a fireplace. We cooked in the fireplace with pots and iron skillets. Sometimes we had pans to eat out of, and sometimes we just ate out of the pots and skillets. (Choctaw, 84: 42–44)

Notes

1. In 1846, John Lilly, his wife and four children arrived in the Creek Nation, where they ministered for two years before moving to the Seminole Nation. In 1859, twenty-two Seminole children were enrolled in the Presbyterian mission school. By 1868, the Presbyterians under the leadership of John R. Ramsey operated four elementary schools among the Seminoles. Edwin C. McReynolds, *The Seminoles* (Norman, Okla., 1957), pp. 282–85, 318–19.

2. Many Seminoles who spent the Civil War in Southern refugee camps became Baptists. McReynolds, *The Seminoles*, p. 319.

3. Soon after they began their ministry among the Choctaws, missionaries translated the New Testament and portions of the Old Testament into the Indians' language which, unlike Cherokee, could be written with Roman letters. According to Angie Debo, in 1837, the American Board of Commissioners published 30,500 tracts, totaling 576,000 pages, in the Choctaw language. *The Rise and Fall of the Choctaw Republic* (Norman, Okla., 1934), p. 62.

4. Cherokee Bibles were printed on the press at Park Hill, which was equipped with type in the Cherokee syllabary developed by Sequoyah.

5. The Chickasaws had enacted legislation in 1876, providing for the operation of twenty-three elementary schools and four secondary schools, including the Lebanon Orphan School. Arrell M. Gibson, *The Chickasaws* (Norman, Okla., 1971), p. 280. Also see Caroline Davis, "Education of the Chicasaws, 1856–1907," *Chronicles of Oklahoma* 15 (1937): 427–28.

6. In 1867, the United States resumed annuity payments of $65,735 to the Chickasaws, who used much of this revenue for schools. Gibson, *The Chickasaws*, p. 280.

7. In 1846, Armstrong Academy, which the narrator attended, opened as a boarding school for Choctaw youths. The school closed in 1861, and the Choctaw capital located in the building. In 1884, the capital moved to Tuskahoma, and the legislature provided that the building be used as an orphanage for boys. Debo, *The Rise and Fall of the Choctaw Republic*, pp. 61, 95, 158–59, 238–39. Also see Angie Debo, "Education in the Choctaw Country after the Civil War," *Chronicles of Oklahoma* 10 (1932): 383–91.

8. The Cherokee Orphan Asylum was established in 1872, and was housed for several years in the building formerly used by the Cherokee Male Seminary. In 1875, the orphans moved into their own structure. M. Thomas Bailey, *Reconstruction in Indian Territory: A Story of Avarice, Discrimination, and Opportunism* (Port Washington, N.Y., 1972), p. 184.

9. See Carol T. Steen, "The Home for the Insane, Deaf, Dumb, and Blind of the Cherokee Nation," *Chronicles of Oklahoma* 21 (1943): 402–19.

10. Organized in 1873, the Women's Christian Temperance Union campaigned for prohibition of alcohol and stricter moral codes. Until a change in leadership in 1896, the W.C.T.U. also supported the Knights of Labor, child labor laws, public kindergartens, women's suffrage, and other progressive causes. Lois W. Banner, *Women in Modern America: A Brief History* (New York, 1974), p. 94.

11. The legislature of the Cherokee Nation appropriated funds to construct seminaries for men and women in 1846. The schools opened in 1851, but lack of sufficient financial support forced them to close in 1856. The Female Seminary reopened in 1871; the Male Seminary did not begin its program again until 1875. The structure of which the narrator speaks replaced the old Female Seminary building, which burned. Gary E. Moulton, *Cherokee Chief* (Athens, Ga., 1978), pp. 159–60; Bailey, *Reconstruction in Indian Territory*, pp. 183–84. Excellent accounts of the Cherokee Female Seminary in the post-Civil War period can be found in Carolyn Thomas Foreman, *Park Hill* (Muskogee, Okla., 1948), and Rudi Halliburton, Jr., "Northeastern's Seminary Hall," *Chronicles of Oklahoma* 51 (1973–74): 391–98.

12. In 1822, the Methodists established Asbury Manual Labor School in the Creek Nation in the East (today Alabama). They closed the mission in 1829. Following a period of hostility to the missionaries in the West, the Methodists reopened the school in the late 1840s. Debo, *The Road to Disappearance*, pp. 85, 97, 120.

13. George W. Stidham was a member of the Creek Supreme Court.

14. Pleasant Porter served as superintendent of Creek schools immediately after the Civil War and as chief from 1899 until his death shortly before Oklahoma statehood.

15. The Creeks provided educational opportunities for blacks, but facilities were segregated.

16. The Creek council often offered subsidies to young men for education in the United States.

Chapter 7 · Economic Development

CULTURAL TRADITIONS, CHRISTIANITY, AND EDUCATION ACTED AS wedges gradually separating the southern Indians into factions. The final blow causing these factions to split was the economic development of Indian Territory after the Civil War. In the course of rapid economic growth, some Indians became very wealthy and completely severed any remaining ties to their aboriginal heritage. These "progressives," as they styled themselves, held in contempt the conservatives who clung to that heritage and the tribal governments which tried, often ineffectually, to restrain their acquisitiveness. Ironically, many of the Indian "robber barons" obtained their wealth largely because of the traditional landholding practices embodied in tribal law. Since citizens of the Indian Nations held land in common, any citizen could use as much land as he wished, but he could not sell the land to a noncitizen. The common ownership and inalienability of realty allowed capitalistic Indians to embark on various enterprises without investing capital in land and guaranteed at least a few Indians a share of the profits from outside corporate investments.

Many avaricious Indians acquired extensive landholdings. Since real estate could be leased to noncitizens, these progressives often brought in tenants to improve the property, and then, when the leases expired, they resumed control. Consequently, a few individuals established title to vast tracts of land. Often the acreage was used by citizens and noncitizens to whom it was leased as pasturage for cattle, and ranching became a major economic enterprise in the years

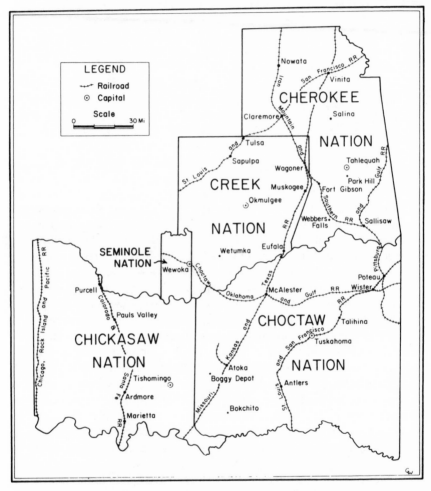

MAP 6. Railroads in Indian Territory. (Adapted from John W. Morris, Charles R. Goins, and Edwin C. McReynolds, *Historical Atlas of Oklahoma*, 2d ed., Norman: University of Oklahoma Press, 1976. Used by permission of the University of Oklahoma Press.)

immediately following the Civil War. Indian ranchers frequently leased ranges they did not need to Texans, who had to drive their herds through Indian Territory to rail terminals in Kansas before the completion of the north-south railroad in 1873. Even after 1873, many ranchers from Texas leased land in Indian Territory or on the Cherokee Outlet.

The construction of railroads through Indian Territory altered far more than ranching; indeed, the economic development of Indian Territory hinged largely on improvements in transportation. Before the Civil War, the southern Indians had rebuffed overtures from railroad companies to lay tracks across their lands. Wagons, stagecoaches, steamboats, and ferries filled the Indians' transport needs, and the governments of the Nations feared the disruptive influence of the railroads. In the nineteenth century, however, the United States was entering a new economic age characterized by a national economy, large corporations, a nationwide network of railroads, and a merging of political and economic interests. Consequently, the treaties negotiated with the five Nations after the Civil War reflected this new economic age. In particular, the treaties provided for rights-of-way for two rail routes—one north to south, the other east to west—through Indian Territory. Not content with mere rights-of-way, the railroads began lobbying for land grants, ostensibly to offset building expenses but actually to increase profits through speculation. The United States Congress, which equated railroad profits and national good, dutifully complied. Since all land other than the rights-of-way belonged to the Indians rather than to the United States, Congress qualified the grants with a provision that the railroads would receive title when the Indian title had been extinguished. Thus, the powerful railroads and their friends in Congress became the enemies of Indian sovereignty and the proponents of individual ownership of land. Until the Indian titles could be extinguished, the railroads had to rely on Indians or intermarried noncitizens to establish claims to townsites and other valuable property, and they had to be content to speculate in leases. This practice placed a number of Indians on the railroad payrolls and in the camp of those who favored allotment of land and dissolution of tribal governments.

The men who owned the railroads were interested in aspects of economic development other than transportation. These tycoons quickly realized that Indian Territory had the potential to produce great wealth through its natural resources. Although exploitation of the region's greatest resource, oil, had only just begun at the time of statehood, the earth held other treasures with which major American corporations became intimately acquainted. Coal beneath the surface and timber above augmented profits from the railroads. Once again, the corporations depended on Indians to stake out claims, although national governments generally tried to exact royalties on minerals and timber.

Ranching, railroads, mining, and logging brought prosperity to a few Indians; many, however, were passed by. Often traditional communities became even more isolated as economic and political activity shifted to locales on rail routes. Conservatives looked on in dismay as railroad tracks snaked across the land, the earth opened to yield coal, and fallen timber bared rocky hillsides. Tribal governments' inability to deal effectively with the economic forces assailing them or the collusion of tribal authorities, United States agents, and corporate interests further disheartened conservatives. Most alarming, perhaps, was the growing number of non-Indians who came to Indian Territory as tenants, cowboys, railroad workers, loggers, or miners and remained with their families. The day would come when these noncitizens would demand land and a role in government, and that demand would seal the fate of the Indian Nations.

Ranching

I have from the time I was a little boy been interested in the cattle business, and I have studied it from every angle and from its beginning to its present day. I never did much farming in my life, that is, extensively, as I have always worked on the range and ranches and am still today engaged in the raising of the cattle on my miniature ranch of 1,100 acres, compared with the ranches in my early manhood.

After the war, cattle were very expensive on the northern markets and were scarce in those parts, while in Texas cattle covered the plain and prairie by myriads.[1] There were no facilities to market these cattle other than to drive them through, and this they tried by grazing them through the Territory to points in Kansas. They suffered great losses with their herd and more so when the Texas cattle came into Kansas and spread what they called the Texas fever among the native cattle of that state. The farmers along the trail objected seriously to this method and went about in a way unlawful to stop it. They would sometimes take the cow punchers and hang them and would cause the cattle to stampede in order to break up this practice. The cattle were kept moving at first with little halt through the Territory, and those that did get through were very thin, foot sore, and weary and were anything but ready for the market.[2]

Having failed in this system, they took to the idea of grazing them slowly through, taking possibly eight or nine months. There was plenty of blue stem grass, sage grass, and buffalo grass, and by slowly grazing them they would be rolling fat when they arrived in Kansas and they would be fit for the market. This proved much more practicable. The cattle would gradually become more acclimated and be in the pink of condition. I have seen thousands and thousands of these cattle on the plains and prairies being grazed and driven through the land to market to Wichita, Kansas, and Abilene, Kansas, where the railroads would handle them. It was during these days that a trail was blazed by a half-breed Cherokee who had refugeed in Kansas and started selling goods and supplies that he hauled in wagons to the wild Indians on the plains between Wichita, Kansas, and the Washita River. His name was Jess Chisholm, and they called the route he traveled the Chisholm Trail, and this became notorious to all the cattle men because they followed practically this trail from Texas to Kansas. I used to travel this trail some and would come into it at what is now known as Cleveland, Oklahoma.[3] This method of marketing cattle ceased in about 1875, and ranches were set up on the plains on unassigned land, I mean by unassigned lands, lands which had not been assigned and was known and called government land.

With the subduing of the wild Indians, buffalo herds disappearing, and the railroad operating, cattle were shipped from Texas to the Indian Territory, and by 1880 ranches of all sizes and description were in progress. These Texas cattle were of all sizes and colors, long horns, Mexican types, et cetera. Some were wild and half-wild, and many of them were branded before arrival in the Territory, which necessitated each ranch maintaining a brand record. Each ranch had its particular range, and some of these ranges overlapped, like the Lazy S would overlap the F.S., and so on. I will tell you of these and other ranches later on.

On each new ranch were a number of buildings which consisted of the superintendent or foreman's house, cook shacks, bunk houses, sheds, and corrals. Most of these buildings were built of log and the corral of split rail. I know of one ranch where lumber was hauled from Kansas to build the house for the owner so that he could have for himself a plank house. The lumber was hauled by ox teams to the ranch.

Employees on the ranch consisted of superintendent or foreman, cow punchers, horse wranglers, cooks, and salt boys who kept up the salt licks. The number of employees varied in accordance with the size of the ranch.

We would have our spring and fall roundup and the cattle driven to their home range that did not belong to us. We could tell by the way branded to whom they belonged. On these roundups we would always take the chuck wagon along and would be gone from home some two or three weeks at a time. We cooked and ate at no particular spot, being just the time where we were caught, and at night we would roll up in our blankets and sleep on the ground. Got up at break of day, get out chuck, in the saddle, and start riding again. All calves would be branded, and we knew ours from the rest because they would be following their mothers that were in our brand. Those that were not following the mothers of our brand but of other brands would be driven along with their mothers to their home range.

The range hands, all of them, were jolly good fellows. They dressed picturesquely with large brim hats with high crowns, a large handkerchief around their necks, high-heel boots, shirts usually of some bright color, and chaps over their trousers. This was the comfortable dress for the cow punchers, and each had its particular part in a cowboy's life. The hats were used to protect them from the rays of the sun, and they were beneficial in heading off a cow or starting a bucking bronco. The handkerchief which they wore about their necks were often used in caring for their wounds and those of the doggies, the high-heel boots kept their feet from slipping through the stirrup on their saddle, the chaps protected their trousers and legs from the whipping of the high grass, which at times was half high to the sides of a horse, and the heavy shirts not only protected them from the sun but from insect bites of all kinds. There was little education and refinement was among them. They loved to play pranks on each other and, not because I was a cow puncher myself, I am compelled to say that they were brave men, hated a thief and a coward, and despised lawlessness in any form. [4]

The cattlemen formed an organization at Caldwell, Kansas, along in 1881, and I favored it very much because I knew that soon the Cherokee Strip and the Oklahoma Country would be opened to white settlers due to much talk. We cattlemen bitterly opposed it because we knew it would tear up our ranches and bring the cattle industry to another degree of dissatisfaction making it unprofitable. [5]

I remember when only a mere boy of my first job on the ranch, and for this job I was paid six dollars a month. Later on, I received ten dollars a month and so on until I began to know my cattle and became a buyer and bought thousands of head for the ranch where I was employed. By this means and my allotment, I myself engaged in the cattle business. (Creek, 9: 360–65)

*   *   *

Everything was a free cattle range with no fences. Our range extended from Glenoak, located east of Bartlesville in Washington County, to Skiatook in Tulsa County. Cattle raising has existed in the United States since the early colonial days. It was first started along the eastern coast but was replaced by agriculture and forced to move westward. After the buffaloes were slaughtered, leaving the vast pasture lands without animals to consume the excellent grass, this was an ideal place for the cattlemen. The Plains Indians were placed on reservations in the Indian Territory. They had depended upon the buffalo for their livelihood, for food, clothing, and shelter, and, after the disappearance of the herd, the Plains Indians were comparatively easy to keep upon the reservation, where they were fed by the government of the United States. This made it possible for the ranchmen to occupy the region with some degree of safety.

The Indian Territory was a splendid area for the ranching industry, considering the climate, soil, and land system. The winters were mild, enabling the cattle to feed on open range throughout the year. The soil produced a good quality of grass, and the free range for the cattle made this the popular cattle country. This new country was thinly settled and was not used for agriculture, which was another advantage for grazing the herds. The water supply was fairly abundant.

We had our disadvantages to face also. The hungry Indians sometimes made a raid on the ranchmen, and the cattle rustlers were to be dealt with. There was no protection of the law. The cattlemen were forced to live by their own law, and their only protection was their faithful Winchester and six-shooters.

My father owned a small ranch with about five hundred head of cattle. His brand was RM. Lon Everetts and John Legal were two of his cowboys. Captain DeNoya, a Texas cowman, also stayed at our place. My father had worked on the Robert L. Owens ranch south of Caney, Kansas, before his marriage. Their brand was OH.

The cowboy's work took him out in all kinds of weather, and he was at home in the saddle, as he spent long hours on horseback, riding the range and looking after the cattle. The stock were much different from the peaceful, quiet cattle of this age. They were small, wild creatures that were liable to become unruly at times. The cowboy's duty was to "ride fence" and keep it in repair. Often the ride would last for two or three days. The cowboy would then cook his grub over a campfire and roll up in his blanket and sleep under the stars.

The roundup was held in the spring and fall of the year. At this time each ranch sent their outfit to the roundup. The cattle were driven together in one big herd, then divided into smaller herds where the calves were branded. Each ranch had their individual brand, and the calf was determined by the brand of its mother. The calf was thrown, tied down, and the red hot branding iron applied to its side. Unidentified calves were known as "mavericks" and were divided among the different cattlemen. A remuda of at least two horses for each cowboy was taken to the roundup. When one horse was tired out, the rider roped another and continued his work. The chuck wagon was another important feature of the roundup. The cook served hot coffee and meals at all hours.

When the outfit left for the roundup, we never knew when they would return nor how many of them would return. The cowboy felt the responsibility of his herd and fought for them as if they belonged to him. Any differences to be settled between their employer and another outfit was an individual battle for each loyal cowboy.

Our ranch house, like all others in this section of the Indian Territory, was a two-room house built of logs with a porch on two sides. The bunk house for the cow hands was also built of logs. My father usually kept four cowboys. The cattlemen were generous and hospitable, and a stranger was always welcome.[6] (Cherokee, 23: 387–93)

Transportation

After the war, the mail was carried from Fort Gibson to Fort Smith on horseback. The route didn't follow the Military Road.[7] The old route ran between where the M.O.P. Depot and the stores in Vian now stand.[8] In a few years the horseback route was abandoned, and a stage line was established. The stage coaches were drawn by four horses. There were certain regular stops along the stage routes where passengers could board or leave the stage coach. Every few miles there was a stage stand where they changed the horses and also changed drivers. There was a stage stand just at the south edge of what is now Sallisaw, and another was Coody's Station near where Greenwood Junction is now located. Joe Coody had a big corral there and kept and fed the stage teams and also boarded the drivers. The Indian Territory stage coaches only went to the Arkansas River, and the passengers and mail were transferred across the river by steamboat where an Arkansas stage coach met them. (Cherokee, 10: 490–91)

*   *   *

One of my pleasant pastimes was watching for the old stage coach. The driver sat on top and drove four horses. They changed horses every ten miles, and Camp Creek was where they changed first after leaving Fort Smith. The horses were driven in a gallop all the time. The harness consisted of collars, hames, tugs, and the lines.[9] The driver carried an ox whip that he could hit the lead horses with. The old stage was swung on springs and rocked from side to side as it whirled past. It had a luggage carrier on the back and a door on each side. The seats faced each other in the stage, and the passengers sat face to face. (Choctaw, 65: 409–10)

*   *   *

A ferry crossed the Arkansas River at Tamaha. It was first a cable ferry and later a steam ferry. The railroad used to carry the mail to Vian and then a man drove a stage, carrying passengers and mail from Vian to Tamaha and had to cross on this ferry.

In the Blaine bottom, downstream from Tamaha, there was a ferry that crossed the Arkansas River which was run by a man named Foreman. If I remember, he was part Cherokee Indian. The first steel bridge I ever saw I helped to build. It was across the San Bois Creek on the old road from Skulleyville to McAlester.

Through this part of the country, when I was a boy, there was only two main roads of importance. All other roads were just trails from neighbor to neighbor. These two main roads were the Texas Road to Texas and the road going to McAlester.[10]

Towns in those days were miles and miles apart. I know of the road south to Texas, but I lived near the road to McAlester. This road branched off the Texas Road out of Skulleyville about five miles and ran west across San Bois Creek. A good old friend of mine of the name of Charlie Newberry, a full-blood Choctaw, ran a store on San Bois Creek. The bridge I helped to build was near his store. This road went on to Fort Sill, but I never went farther than McAlester. Mr. McAlester ran the store at McAlester.

I have seen lots of steamboats on the Arkansas River and remember, when we would hear them whistle, how we would all go to the river to see them go past. After I grew up, I used to go down to Tamaha and watch the steamboats unload. I remember the names of some of them, the Jennie Mae, Lucy Walker, and the Border City. There were others, but I have forgotten their names. (Choctaw, 84: 45-46)

*   *   *

When the boats whistled for the landing, the whole village would turn out to meet and to greet it. They carried both passengers and freight. The merchants would cart their merchandise away from the landing about as fast as it was unloaded by the roustabouts.

Some of these boats came from as far as New Orleans, Memphis, and Little Rock when the river was up, this being usually in the month of June. Most of the boats, however, from Little Rock and Fort Smith tried to run on a schedule of once a month. Sometimes some of these boats would steam on up the river as far as the Nevins Landing with merchandise for Fort Gibson and Muskogee, Indian Territory. If the river was so that the boats could not get up the river due to low water, the freight was unloaded at Webbers Falls and then hauled by freight wagons to Fort Gibson and Muskogee. (White resident of Indian Territory, 8: 3)

*   *   *

In 1870 the Congress of the United States passed this act authorizing the government to give a patent deed to any railroad building their road through this Indian Territory to every other section of land on each side of such railroad track.[11]

The Frisco and Katy railroads began a race, each wanting to finish their road bed across the Territory first.[12] The Frisco stopped their mad rush coming south when the Katy road beat them to the Indian line. The Katy built their road right through the middle of my father's farm. Each road employed at least 400 to 500 track layers. They laid the tracks and ties very often right on top of the ground without any grading whatsoever. These madmen worked just exactly like fighting fire. Night and day, rain and storms did not stop these mad fire-eating workers. Right there on that job, I saw more men with shirts looking black on account of being thoroughly dripping with perspiration than I have ever seen before or since.

The Cherokees protested this act of Congress giving so much acreage to the railroad, and after many heated court battles carried finally into the Supreme Court of the United States, the Cherokee Nation won on the ground that Congress had no authority to sell or give away lands patented or deeded to this Nation.[13] (Cherokee, 23: 49–50)

*   *   *

After the Cherokees became interested in politics, all of the powers of granting or allowing any public utilities were given to the councilmen and Senate of the Cherokee Nation. Any public utility could have the man elected, who would favor his or their interests by buying votes. This happened when the railroad law went into effect. The Kansas City Railroad was held at Siloam for years.[14] At that time the legislature was composed mostly of full-blood Cherokees. But after the next election, most of the men who were sent to the Council and Senate were mixed-blood Cherokees. They were the ones who voted that the lines of said railroad be extended through the Cherokee Nation. The full-bloods were never in favor of the railroads. (Cherokee, 43: 299–300)

*   *   *

The town of Downingsville was born just a mile west of where we built our first log cabin, about a mile south of Cabin Creek and about two miles south of the present town of Vinita. The first Frisco survey showed their crossing of the M.K.&T. near the new town of Downingsville, south of Cabin Creek, but Cornelius Boudinot,[15] then the leading Cherokee attorney, Johnson Thompson, Colonel J. M. Bell, and others got busy with the railroad officials and had the survey changed about three miles north, to where the present town of Vinita is now located. They then fenced off two miles square at the crossing and prepared for a townsite to be built wherever the road might cross. They were successful in getting the crossing moved, and the town soon moved northward to the railroad crossing.

There was so much friction came up over the way Boudinot and his bunch had handled the location of the town that the Cherokee Nation stepped in and declared it unlawful, tore their fences down, and proceeded to lay off a townsite at the place the railroads had crossed.

The town of Downingsville was plotted by the Cherokee Nation in 1871, and the first town lot was sold in February 1872, to Martin Thompson. This was at the new location. The town went under the name of Downingsville for some time, and through the efforts of Cornelius Boudinot, who had gone as a delegate to Washington, he had it changed to the name of Vinita. He had known the noted sculptress, Vinnie Ream, in Washington and had the town named after her.[16] (Cherokee, 2: 270)

*   *   *

The first hotel in Muskogee was owned by Mr. Metchard; it was located just southwest of where the M.K.&T. depot now stands. It was built of log, with the logs standing straight up and down. The roof was made by stretching a tarpaulin over the top. The next business house was built by Atkinson and Robert. It was the first general mercantile store in Muskogee. The first drugstore was owned by Mr. Cummings and Dr. Williams. The Patterson mercantile store was located on Agency Hill and later moved to Muskogee. George Elliott was first postmaster in Muskogee. The post office was located in the Atkinson-Robert store.[17]

I saw the first M.K.&T. passenger train that run to Gibson Station. Everyone for miles around were there to see it. The railroad at that time went no further north than Gibson Station. Lots of the people that came to see it were afraid and would not come very close. Several teams hitched to wagons ran away, but no one was injured by them. An old Indian known as Coolboy was drunk, and the engine pooped off steam scalding Coolboy. He started running, and as he passed a saddled horse he lost his balance and fell against the horse. The horse kicked Coolboy and broke his leg. (Cherokee, 1: 138–39)

*   *   *

Jeff Archer, brother of John, had the first store in Tulsey town. Had set it up in 1883 in a tent on what is now Main Street, between the Frisco tracks and First Street, while the railroad was building in. He sold chiefly staples, such as cheese, crackers, sardines, and canned goods. The next, another tent store, was set up at what is now the southeast corner of First and Boulder by John Thomas who sold only hard cider. It was only after the railroad was already in that H.C. Hall set up his store, although he is usually credited with having the first store in Tulsa.[18]

Almost all mercantile business was done on credit, bills being paid once annually. An Indian, no matter what other faults he may have had, was always a man of his word. If he promised to pay on a certain date, he would be on hand ready to pay on that date. If he had no cash he would bring cattle or horses and always more than enough to settle the account, giving the merchant the better of the bargain always. (Cherokee, 1: 146–47)

*   *   *

I went to school in 1882 and 1883 at the Colbert Neighborhood School east of Berwyn. During the time I was here, Colonel George Harkins came to our school and made a talk. He said, "It won't be long until big iron horses will be running through here." I arose and asked what he meant by an "iron horse." He explained that he meant a train. I had no idea then what he meant, for I had never seen or heard of a train. He went on to say that people would come in here from everywhere, and if we were not prepared to care for ourselves they would knock the dirt from under our feet. That very thing has happened to me. I have lost all the land I alloted to the white men. I now live in an old log house which my father built in 1887, but it belongs to some Negroes at present. (Chickasaw/Creek, 33: 543–44)

Natural Resources

We moved back to Wilburton and worked in the timber on Jones Creek. We were shipping the logs to Fort Smith. Some were used for ties, bridge timber, and things like that. The biggest logs were on Poteau River. One big bur oak tree of eight or ten feet was all that a team could haul. We got post oak, hickory, sometimes walnut, and the big bur oaks. A royalty was paid to the Indian government for the timber, just as a royalty was paid to them for the coal.[19] D. C. Cole of Hartshorne was the head man on the timber for the sixty-five miles from McAlester to Wister. He had subcontractors under him. In 1895 the Choctaw, Oklahoma and Gulf Railroad started west for Shawnee. We made ties on Salt Creek and Little River for four months.

My parents were missionary Baptists, and whenever a man wanted something to eat, he got it. These strangers were nice men apparently and always paid their way, but we did not quiz them, as it was considered improper and sometimes unhealthy. Father always said if a man wanted to tell you his business you would not have to ask him, and if he did not want to tell it, he would not.

I never worked for the cattlemen until after I was twenty-one, for mother considered them rough, undesirable company for a young boy. After I was of age I worked for cowboys some.

Old Number One was the work train which hauled bridge timber when they were making the Choctaw, Oklahoma and Gulf Railroad. Number Two was the first engine which hauled passengers. Frank Holly was the engineer of the train, and Landers Smith was the conductor. (White resident of the Choctaw Nation, 22: 55–57)

*   *   *

It must have been about a fourteen-mile haul to the railroad where we took the lumber. It was at a little place called Moyers on the Frisco Railroad where we hauled the lumber and unloaded. They then loaded it on the cars and shipped it somewhere else. We made good money on the haul.

This sawmill I am speaking of was located on the mountains west of Jumbo. The timber was fine, large, yellow pine timber, and there were a good many white oaks there. I do not know whether the sawmillers paid for the timber or not, but they sure did cut some fine pine timber, and I guess they made lots of money out of it,.

We lived in tents for a long while, then we built us box houses. They were called sawmill shacks.

We had no furniture, just only what we brought in our wagons and did not need much, for we were camping out most of the time anyway. The sawmillers do not have nothing but camping outfits anyway, for they are moving from one sawmill to another every few days, so we did not need but very little furniture.

I was not old as I am now so I worked around the mill while the boys hauled lumber. The lumber was cheap at that time. We could buy all the lumber we wanted at $5 per thousand. Second-grade lumber was not known, as they burned up the second-grade lumber; then they took only first-grade lumber. Of course, they wasted lots of lumber, but I do not guess it cost them anything to make the lumber out of the fine timber they were cutting. At this sawmill, they had no school nor even church, and the children grew up wild around the mill; they were raised up without an education at that time. . . .

When I went to Jumbo, there were lots of wild game on the mountains, deer, turkey, and lots of fish in the creeks. It was no trouble to kill a deer or a turkey at any time a man wanted to eat one of them, and there was plenty of fish in the creeks. The boys at the sawmills lived on them, and some of the boys killed a few bears back in the hills. There were no white people much out there when I first came there—none out on the farms, a few sawmill hands around the mill was about all the white people.[20] (White resident of the Choctaw Nation, 22: 122–24)

*   *   *

Along about the year 1885, a party of men from Minneapolis, Minnesota, came to this country on a wild turkey hunt. I got acquainted with one of the men by the name of Edward D. Chadick who was looking for all the outcroppings of coal around in this country.

This party of men had come to McAlester on the new railroad which had just passed through that part of the country called the M.K.&T. Railroad Company, and they had gotten acquainted with a settler by the name of J. J. McAlester. Sometime later the town of McAlester was called by his name. This J. J. McAlester also was an intermarried citizen of the Choctaw tribe.[21] After the M.K.&T. Railroad had come along there, McCurtain[22] staked off some land for his home, built his house, and started to dig him a well. After they had dug this well part of the way, they came upon a large vein of coal, and of course this man Mr. Chadick was notified about this. Mr. Chadick located a lot of coal outcroppings around where Wilburton now is, and the idea came to him that if it were possible to get a railroad built through this country it would be a great thing in the movement of the coal.

So after the turkey hunt was over, Mr. Chadick went to Philadelphia. In those days that was the great headquarters for railroads. He explained his findings in this Indian country to men of that city. The Lehigh Railroad Company of Philadelphia financed Mr. Chadick. A company was organized in the year of 1888, and Mr. Chadick brought back to this country a party who made a survey of the prospective railroad right-of-way. The prospect of this railroad and the finding of coal was the reason for the location of what is now Wilburton.

The original name of this railroad was the Choctaw, Oklahoma & Gulf Railroad, which later was changed to the Rock Island. As best I remember, this road went through this county in the year of 1890, and it was operated then from what is now called Wister to what is now called South McAlester. There seemed to be a great argument with the department about these men being granted with the privilege for this right-of-way, so these men just ran their road two miles or possibly not quite that far from what was then McAlester and made their stop. This of course made another settlement spring up around this new station. Therefore we now have what you would call two towns. The first one, or the old town, was called North McAlester, and the new town was named South McAlester. These names exist today. (White resident of the Choctaw Nation, 15: 306–8)

*   *   *

I came originally from Pennsylvania. My father before me was a Pennsylvania man born there in the early part of the nineteenth century. We lived at Mount Pleasant. Mother was a native of the state, too. Her maiden name was Barbara Snyder. She and father both died before I came to the Indian Territory, and they are both buried there at Mount Pleasant. Father's name was Jonathan Nichols.

I came to the Choctaw Nation in 1898. I was a meat cutter by trade, and when I heard through a friend of mine named James Cooper that a man named Foster who owned meat markets at McAlester and Hartshorne in the Indian Territory needed a meat cutter, I decided to come and see if I could get a job. Cooper wrote me that Foster wanted a man who wouldn't drink, and I knew I could fill the bill to that extent, and I knew I was a good meat cutter.

I went to McAlester over the M.K.&T. Railway. Then I got on a C.O.&G. train[23] and came to Hartshorne. Hartshorne was a booming little mining town then. It was about eight or nine years old. It had some big mines and strip pits working around it, and business was good.

I got the meat-cutting job all right. The shop was right in the middle of the town, where Venter's Bakery is now. I worked there two years. It was the most interesting job I ever had up until that time. It was as exciting as an indoor job could be. I had all sorts of people for customers: the miners, Polanders, Lithuanians, Russians, Italians, Negroes, Dutch, Germans, Irish, Scotch, Bulgarians, and almost any other sort of people you could name and Indians, too. I knew lots of Indians: Dave Thomas, Bill Ervin, Bud White, Perrys, Moores, Folsoms, a man named Hocklatubby. One Choctaw named John Pulcher was, I think, sheriff of Gaines County.

And there was an Indian woman who was a teacher out at Jones Academy. I think her name was McCurtain; she may have been some relation to the Green McCurtain who was a Choctaw high chief for so long. She certainly was a clever, friendly woman. She bought meat from me time and again.

At that time Hartshorne was a real frontier town. It was incorporated and had its own city government, but it was cut off from the United States Government, and a white man had no actual legal security. We didn't really consider our homes and property secure until after Statehood.

The town itself was a sort of freak of circumstances, as you might say. If it hadn't been for the discovery of coal around here the town would probably never have been built. The Choctaw, Oklahoma and Gulf Railway Company was the firm which opened and developed the mines here. The railroad was built through this valley in the last part of the eighties. Someone prospecting for the company discovered coal. I never did get it straight just who found the vein of coal at Hartshorne. A man named Captain Jack Mitchell was said to have found a lot of coal in this part of the country, though I do not believe he found the vein at Hartshorne where the old mine number one was sunk. Maybe it was John Grady.

As I understand it, the C.O.&G. put in a mine at Alderson first in 1889. Coal was reached in Hartshorne at number one in April of 1890. By 1896, just before I reached the town, the mine at Alderson was said to be producing about a thousand tons a day, and the one at Hartshorne as much or more, and remember that this was produced under crude, primitive methods of mining. I never mined any myself, but a man can't live for years around a mining town and not absorb some knowledge of mining customs and practices. The work was slow; most of it was done with a pick and shovel. There were no machines to undercut the coal then, no electric motors to rush the coal-laden cars to the mouth of the shaft. The cutting was done by hand with a pick. The cars were pulled by mules. The miners wore smoky, oil-burning lamps. Coal mining was then old-fashioned in its methods and dangerous, but there was something about it that grips my imagination as I look back into the past. The world will never see the likes of those days again.

When I came to Hartshorne, there were about five hundred men working at shaft number one here, so I was told. Wages weren't high, but a company man got a little over $50 a month, and a digger might make much more, sometimes as much as $100 or more.

The population of Hartshorne was said to be nearly four thousand people. There was a wooden school standing where the brick high school is now. This wooden building had three or four rooms. The Choctaw, Oklahoma and Gulf Company built the schoolhouse. Up until the time I came to Hartshorne, or maybe a year or so before, it had been a subscription school. But the people got together and decided to handle the thing in a more businesslike way. The miners were to pay so much a month into a school fund; married men paid $1, and single men 50 cents. People not working at the mines paid $1.50 for each pupil whom they sent to school.

So you can see that this was still a frontier town when I first came. It had its own peculiar customs and ways. It was a product of circumstances. The discovery of coal made it. Miners, ranchers, Indians, merchants, and farmers made up its population. The town had a personality of its own, different from the places I had known back East. (White resident of the Choctaw Nation, 70: 60–64)

*   *   *

I grew up to do nothing but work, hard work, and when the coal mines began to open up throughout the country, I thought I would like to work in them. My first job was water boy on a strip pit at a place which is now Krebs. Strip pits gave way to underground work, and I got a job pushing little cars back under the ground, to be loaded with coal by the miners, then taken to the "lift," or elevator. Then as mines began to develop more and more I became a full-fledged miner and worked at McAlester, Krebs, Alderson, Haileyville, Hartshorne, and Wilburton.

The mines, in the last few years, do not operate enough for one to make a living at the business. Besides, my age is against me, and I can't do the work as I used to. I got so I could not provide food, clothing, and shelter for myself and family and applied to the Indian Agency for help, and they moved me here on the reservation three years ago. We have plenty to eat, a good house to live in, but the bedding and clothing given us has been worn out by the United States Army and the C.C.C. boys. (Choctaw, 84: 47)

*   *   *

In 1893, the coal miners started organizing and called their organization the Knights of Labor. In 1894, they called out a strike for recognition of their labor union.[24] Three-fourths of them did not pay for a permit to stay in the Choctaw Nation. The coal operators knew this so they went to the Indian Government and had them put the coal miners out as intruders.

Women were loaded into flat cars like cattle regardless of their condition, and they were all sent over the state line. Some of the men came back on the same trains with the ones who put them out, but the more loyal ones stayed out. The strike was lost inside of ninety days, as the Knights of Labor was such a new organization that they did not have enough funds to hold out. (White resident of the Choctaw Nation, 22: 57)

*   *   *

Speaking of coal mines, the discovery of coal, in my opinion, brought about the settlement of the Choctaw Nation by whites years earlier than it would otherwise have occurred. The Indians all around me didn't seem to pay much attention to the white people coming into the country in such large numbers. Later, they saw that it meant the Choctaw government would have to give way in time to the white man's government, and this knowledge split them into two factions, or parties. One side was in favor of progress, of accepting the white man's ways and opening up the country. "What if Statehood came," they argued, "wouldn't it be a good thing?" The other side wanted this country for the Indians; they wanted Indian government, Indian ways, the land held in common by the tribe as a whole.

None of my kin folks had land where there was coal, but if I understand it right the royalty from the coal was paid, right at first, to the Indian on whose claim the mine happened to be located. That gave some of the Indians more money than they had ever known before, and naturally these Indians thought the white men were all to the good. Progress was a great thing.

Then later, as I understand it, arrangements were made for the coal royalty money to be turned over to the tribal government and be held in common. Some of the Indians never did quit objecting; they wanted the old ways, and I guess if they had been given their wishes they would have run the whites out of the country altogether.[25] (Chickasaw, 70: 13–14)

Indian Entrepreneurs

I leased my new place west of Oolagah to a white man, I do not recall his name, for ten years. He was to break the land, build a good three-room house, barn, dig a well, and plant an orchard.

He began to break sod and build a fence. While digging a post hole, he struck coal. This was a great surprise to the people, for we did not know there was any coal in this country. I took a crew of men and put in a few prospect holes and discovered coal.

I then went to Tahlequah by train, and, as I knew the law, I took a mining lease from the treasurer of the Cherokee Nation giving me a permit to lease the outside capital by paying into the treasurer, at the rate of 25 cents per ton, royalty. It was soon rumored that I had struck coal on my place, and in four days men called me from Independence, Kansas, to lease it. We talked the matter over, and I gave them a ten-day option on it, which they accepted. They mined it for about ten years. This was the first and biggest industry that had struck this country.

We had a town site law at this time.[26] The Iron Mountain railroad ran through Oolagah, and the Frisco railroad was built as far as Tulsa. We had not struck oil as yet, but oil men were becoming interested.

I went to Braggs, Indian Territory, and bought fifty head of yearling steers and shipped them to Oolagah. At that time there were no stockyards there, so I jumped them out of the car. My business was growing, so I hired Jake Lipe to keep my books and work in the store as a clerk.

My children had been attending the neighborhood school, and I decided to send them away for higher education. I could see the advantage of a good education and wanted my children to have the best. I sent my oldest son, William, to a business college and hired Mr. Lipe and his sons to help me in the store and with my business until William finished school. I sent Eddie, the youngest boy, to business college at Webb City, Missouri, and Ellen, my only child by my second marriage, went to a ladies' college at Lexington, Missouri. My second wife was Maggie Sanders, who I married in 1888.

When my children returned home, they were well equipped to face the future. William took my place behind the desk, and we started business together. Eddie was unsettled, and we tried to get him to settle down in some kind of busines. He was well qualified to hold a choice position, and we needed him.

I thought I could use him in the store, but he was not interested. I had several business enterprises at that time, was handling cattle on a large scale, operated a large merchandise business, and had opened up a coal mine. He could have worked in any of these enterprises, and we needed his assistance badly.

I decided to send him to medical college, for I realized this was a good profession and it looked like easy money. He was dissatisfied with this arrangement and decided he preferred to be a farmer and stockman. I bought more cattle, for we had acres and acres of range. This was just prior to Statehood, and we had plenty of money. I bought Eddie two good cow horses and a $50 saddle.

John Derickson had a big ranch south of Oolagah, so I took three Cherokee boys, Bruce Mitchell, Roy Walker, Kute Tucker, and my son, Ed, Jr., we went to the ranch where I bought 200 coming two-year-old steers for $22 per head. Derickson had the finest ranch in the country.

I traded my livery barn to Ed Halsell for fifty brood mares. Ed was a big rancher and a good business man; he could see the cattle business was at an end and began to sell his cattle. This was after the government cancelled our lease on the Cherokee Strip, agreeing to pay the Cherokee people for it. Ed saw a chance to turn his horses into some Cherokee Strip money and sold the barn to John Taylor for $1,000 cash when John drew his Strip money.[27]

When the Missouri Pacific Railroad came through the country, the law provided a location for a town every six miles. The towns between Fort Smith, Arkansas, and Coffeyville, Kansas are: Hanson, Vian, Braggs, Fort Gibson, Wagoner, Ross, Inola, Tiwah, Claremore, Sageeyah, Oolagah, Talala, Watova, Nowata, Delaware, and Lenapah. These towns were all laid off, and the size of each town was 640 acres. The lots were to be sold only to citizens of the Cherokee Nation. We then elected officers, and I was elected the first mayor of Oolagah, Bill Taylor was my clerk, John Taylor was the first marshal, and Charlie Roberson was his deputy. Under the tribal laws of the Cherokee Nation, it was lawful for the mayor to perform marriage ceremonies, and I had the pleasure of remarrying three couples who had formerly been married in Texas. Under our tribal laws, a white man must be married in the Cherokee Nation to become a citizen. These couples were Bob Harris and his Cherokee wife, Walter Willis and his Cherokee wife, and John Amis and his Cherokee wife.[28]

Our town site laws were in full operation, and some improvements were started on the 640-acre townsite under my supervision. With the help of the marshal force, I cut the fences and removed all the unlawful constructions and opened up the streets. At that time Oolagah was the best-looking little place in the state. We had constructed the little stone jail to hold the bad men. As the town was opening up people were buying the town lots. With the aid of outside capital, the coal business was booming, farming was a leading industry, and farm teams were flowing in from every state in the Union, and the improvements of the town lots made Oolagah appear to be a thriving little town.

My sons and I were doing a land office business. I saw teams in Oolagah so thick you could hardly cross the street. This was during harvest time, and the teams were hauling wheat and coal to the railroad in Kansas and western Oklahoma. Two or three years later Collinsville was started. They were soon operating coal mines and advertised for teams. People came from different parts of the state and camping places were scarce between Oolagah and Collinsville. I then took full charge of my coal mines and farm, which I operated until about 1933, just before the Depression, when we sold our business. At the time Oolagah was booming I owned about one-half of the town. (Cherokee, 46: 79–85)

*   *   *

Under the old Choctaw law governing mineral deposits, my father traced out the veins of coal deposits between the Poteau River and Arkansas line. He sank some small shafts or dug slopes and built log pens as "improvements" one mile apart to establish his claims and control before allotment to the coal deposits in an area lying between Fort Smith, the Poteau River, and west of the Frisco railroad in Leflore County.

I organized the First National Bank of Poteau, Oklahoma, in 1904, the first national bank on the extreme east side of the state. I secured leases and drilled in the first gas wells in the field known as the Leflore County Gas Field in 1910, piped the gas into Poteau, and induced the first gas plants to come in there on extreme east side of the state.

I organized and helped furnish the capital to build the first electric light plant on extreme east side of old Indian Territory in 1905. Hugo, Wilburton, and Fort Gibson were the only towns east of the M.K.& T., which had electric lights at that time.

Immediately after the Civil War, my mother's brother Jesse Riddle, an enrolled Choctaw citizen, obtained a permit to operate a toll gate on Backbone Mountain on what was then known as the Texas Road leading south out of Fort Smith, Arkansas, to Paris, Texas, the only improved mountain road in Choctaw Nation. (Choctaw, 73: 288–89)

*   *   *

Father took his bride to Doaksville, their first home. He began the practice of medicine, and in that capacity he operated the first drug store, which was just a long shelf in one corner of his office. They lived here about four years then moved to Perryville, the stage route crossroads from Fort Smith to Fort Washita and from the Kansas line to Denison, Texas. We were living at Perryville when the Missouri, Kansas and Texas Railroad was built through here. Father continued his practice of medicine and run a store, too, during these times.

Father said that in the early days the Choctaw Indians used to pick up coal from the top of the ground and take it to the blacksmith shops and sell it. They even loaded up wagons and took it as far as Fort Sill and Arbuckle and sold it. They knew nothing of mining and simply picked up the coal without any effort on their part.

In those days there was a tribal law forbidding white men prospecting for coal in the Territory. Father told an interesting story of how the governor of the Choctaw Nation once ordered out the lighthorsemen against J. J. McAlester, Tandy Walker, and other who were trying to build a coal line to Krebs. This was a violation of tribal laws, and the governor determined he would take extreme measures to stop the would-be railway builders. Just as the troops were getting close,

Dad warned his friends, and they got away to a place of safety, leaving Indian Territory until the trouble quieted down. Then the federal government intervened, and the trouble was ended and the road built through.[29]

Dad's first venture in the coal operating business was in 1874. He bought his first interests at Krebs from two Indians and paid them $50 for it. Later on, he and J. J. McAlester became operators of large interests.

In 1882 we moved to Savanna and was living there when the big mine explosion occurred in 1888 that nearly destroyed the town of Savanna and injured and killed hundreds of miners and residents.

We then moved to South McAlester, and father entered into a new profession in 1875 along with the old. He and Captain Granville McPherson established the first newspaper in the Choctaw Nation, the *Star Vindicator*, a small paper, which was printed with an old Washington hand press. The newspaper business broke up when Captain McPherson took his press to Texas in 1880.[30]

Father quit practicing medicine in 1881, and opened up the mines in Savanna, leasing the same to the Gould interests.[31] He operated a general merchandise store in 1896. We returned to McAlester and lived there until father's death. (Choctaw, 68: 435-37)

Notes

1. Joseph G. McCoy estimated that a steer which brought $80 to $90 in Eastern markets would have sold for $5 in Texas. *Cattle Trade of the West and Southwest*, ed. Ralph P. Bieber (Glendale, Calif., 1940), p. 94.

2. A number of cattle trails linking Texas ranges with Kansas stockyards crossed what is today Oklahoma. The two earliest and most treacherous trails crossed the nations of the southeastern Indians. The east Shawnee trail followed the Texas Road, while the west Shawnee trail left the Texas Road at Boggy Depot and entered Kansas on the west bank of the Arkansas River. Both trails traversed hilly, forested terrain and crossed deep rivers with steep banks. These natural impediments to moving large herds coupled with Indian opposition to the drives forced cattlemen to seek a better route farther west. Edwin C. McReynolds, *Oklahoma: A History of the Sooner State* (Norman, Okla., 1954), p. 152-61. Also see Edward Everett Dale, *Frontier Trails* (Boston, 1930).

3. The Chisholm Trail crossed the western Chickasaw Nation from north to south along a line parallel to the tracks later laid by the Rock Island

Railroad. See Sam P. Ridings, *The Chisholm Trail* (Guthrie, Okla., 1936), and Wayne Gard, *The Chisholm Trail* (Norman, Okla., 1954). To the west of the Chisholm Trail was the Great Western through the lands of the Kiowa, Comanche, Cheyenne, and Arapaho.

4. The life of the cowboy is described in Reginald Aldridge, *Life on a Ranch: Ranch Notes in Kansas, Colorado, the Indian Territory, and Northern Texas* (New York, 1884); Theodore Roosevelt and Frederick Remington, *Ranch Life in the Far West*, reprint ed. (1888; Flagstaff, 1973); Evan G. Barnard, *A Rider in the Cherokee Strip*, ed. Edward Everett Dale (Boston, 1936); and Arrell M. Gibson, "The Cowboy in Indian Territory," in *The Cowboy: Six-Shooters, Songs, and Sex*, ed. Charles W. Harris and Buck Rainey (Norman, Okla., 1976).

5. The Cherokee Strip Live Stock Association obtained a charter from the State of Kansas in 1882, and a five-year lease from the Cherokee Nation. The Cherokees generally favored the arrangement, which provided income for the government, and resisted initial attempts by the United States to purchase the land and open it to white homesteaders. The Cherokee Strip Live Stock Association supported the Cherokees and even offered to buy the land, but the United States ultimately won. In 1893 the United States paid the Cherokees $8,595,736.12, or $1.40 per acre, for the Outlet. In the land run which followed, 100,000 people participated. McReynolds, *Oklahoma*, pp. 266, 299. See Edward Everett Dale, "Cherokee Strip Live Stock Association," *Chronicles of Oklahoma* 5 (1927): 58–73; and William W. Savage, Jr., *The Cherokee Strip Live Stock Association* (Columbia, Mo., 1973).

6. Studies of the cattle industry include Edward Everett Dale, *Cow Country* (Norman, Okla., 1942), and *The Range Cattle Industry* (Norman, Okla., 1930); Neil Johnson, *The Chickasaw Rancher*, ed. Arrell M. Gibson (Stillwater, Okla., 1961); Edith Wharton Taylor, *Money on the Hoof— Sometimes* (Fort Collins, Colo., 1974); Norman Graebner, "Cattle Ranching in Eastern Oklahoma," *Chronicles of Oklahoma* 21 (1943): 300–11.

7. The first surveyed road in what is today Oklahoma was the military road marked off in 1825 between Fort Smith, Arkansas, and Fort Gibson on the Grand River.

8. The Missouri Pacific Railroad runs through the town of Vian, which is west of Sallisaw.

9. The collar cushioned the horses' necks; the hame holds the tugs, which connect the collar to the coach; the lines are the reins, which control the horses.

10. The Texas Road developed while Texas was a Mexican province and became increasingly important as a north-south route after the province became a state. It ran from Colbert's Ferry on the Red River to Boggy Depot, then to Fort Gibson, and north to Kansas and Missouri.

11. The treaties of 1866 provided for right-of-way for one north-south railroad and one east-west railroad. Even before the treaties were signed, Congress began granting to the railroad companies sections of land with clear titles contingent on the extinguishing of Indian titles. The building of railroads through Indian Territory is dealt with in the following works: James L. Alhands, "Construction of the Frisco Railroad Line in Oklahoma," *Chronicles of Oklahoma* 3 (1925): 229–39; Donovan L. Hofsommer, ed., *Railroads in Oklahoma* (Oklahoma City, 1977); J. F. Holden, "The Story of an Adventure in Railroad Building," *Chronicles of Oklahoma* 11 (1933): 637–66; V. V. Masterson, *The Katy Railroad and the Last Frontier* (Norman, Okla., 1953); H. Craig Miner, *The Corporation and the Indian: Tribal Sovereignty and Industrial Civilization in Indian Territory, 1865–1907* (Columbia, Mo., 1976), and "The Struggle for an East-West Railway into the Indian Territory," *Chronicles of Oklahoma* 47 (1969): 560–81.

12. The 1866 treaties provided that the first railroads to reach the boundary of Indian Territory from the north and east would receive the rights-of-way. The Katy (Missouri, Kansas and Texas) reached the northern boundary and the Frisco (St. Louis and San Francisco) reached the eastern boundary first. The chief controversy between these two lines was over where their tracks would cross.

13. In 1871, Congress enacted legislation stipulating that charters for railroads would be granted even in the absence of treaty provisions. In 1882, Congress began granting rights-of-way and sections of land to additional railroads. The Cherokees sued, and, while they were awarded damage payments, the Supreme Court failed to grant injunctions against further construction. Miner, *The Corporation and the Indian*, pp. 112–15; Angie Debo, *The Rise and Fall of the Choctaw Republic* (Norman, Okla., 1934), pp. 110–31.

14. The narrator refers to the Southern Kansas Railway Company, which had competed with the Katy for a north-south route through Indian Territory. Congress granted a right-of-way to this company in 1884. Miner, *The Corporation and the Indian*, pp. 29–30, 110.

15. Elias Cornelius Boudinot was a major promoter of railroads, often at the expense of the Cherokee Nation, of which he was a citizen.

16. See O. B. Campbell, *Vinita, I.T., The Story of a Frontier Town of the Cherokee Nation, 1871–1907* (Oklahoma City, 1969).

17. See John D. Benedict, *History of Muskogee and Northeast Oklahoma*, 3 vols. (Chicago, 1922); and Grant Foreman, *Muskogee: The Biography of an Oklahoma Town* (Norman, Okla., 1943).

18. See Angie Debo, *Tulsa: From Creek Town to Oil Capital* (Norman, Okla., 1943); and C. B. Douglas, *The History of Tulsa*, 3 vols. (Tulsa, Okla., 1921).

19. In 1869, the Cherokees passed a law requiring that logging and mining companies pay royalties to the tribe. The Creeks and Choctaws soon followed suit. The Choctaws encountered difficulties, however, when their supreme court repeatedly threw out royalty legislation, thereby permitting the corporations to pay token royalties to individuals who claimed land containing resources. Miner, *The Corporation and the Indian*, pp. 58-76. With respect to coal, a compromise was effected by which the Nation and the mine owner shared royalties equally. Debo, *The Rise and Fall of the Choctaw Republic*, p. 128.

20. For a discussion of the problems created by the lumber and railroad tie companies, see Daniel F. Littlefield, Jr. and Lonnie E. Underhill, "Timber Depredations and Cherokee Legislation, 1869-1881," *Journal of Forest History* 18 (1974): 4-13.

21. See Paul Nesbitt, "J. J. McAlester," *Chronicles of Oklahoma* 11 (1933): 758-64. For a less flattering characterization, see Miner, *The Corporation and the Indian*, p. 61.

22. Apparently, the narrator is still talking about McAlester and not Green McCurtain, a Choctaw chief who favored nationalizing mining interests.

23. The Choctaw, Oklahoma and Gulf Railroad.

24. The miners struck over a 25 percent reduction in wages. Debo, *The Rise and Fall of the Choctaw Republic*, p. 130; McReynolds, *Oklahoma*, pp. 268-69.

25. The best study of coal mining in Indian territory is Gene Aldrich, "A History of the Coal Industry in Oklahoma to 1907" (Ph.D. diss., University of Oklahoma, 1952). Published sources containing relevant information include Frederick L. Ryan, *The Rehabilitation of Oklahoma Coal Mining Communities* (Norman, Okla., 1935); and Arrell M. Gibson, *Wilderness Bonanza: The Tri-State District of Missouri, Kansas, and Oklahoma* (Norman, Okla., 1972).

26. The Cherokees refused to sell blocks of land to railroads for townsites. Instead, they restricted the privilege (and profit) to Cherokee citizens. As a result, some Cherokees claimed large tracts of land and then leased them to railroad companies, white businessmen, and other non-Indians.

27. Cherokees received a per capita payment from the sale of the Cherokee Outlet to the United states in 1892.

28. Although these particular marriages may have been for more romantic reasons, white men often took Indian wives because of the privileges afforded intermarried citizens of the Indian nations.

29. Although the Choctaw Supreme Court ruled unconstitutional the law under which McAlester and his associates had been convicted, Chief Coleman

Cole ordered it executed because of his intense opposition to mining. Debo, *The Rise and Fall of the Choctaw Republic*, p. 128.

30. The *Star Vindicator* favored territorial government, allotment of land, and white settlement of Indian Territory.

31. In addition to vast mineral leases, Jay Gould controlled the Katy and Frisco railroads. Miner, *The Corporation and the Indian*, p. 100.

1. Voting in Wewoka. Courtesy of Photograph Archives, Division of Library Resources, Oklahoma Historical Society.

2. Choctaw Camp Meeting. Courtesy of Photograph Archives, Division of Library Resources, Oklahoma Historical Society.

Chapter 8 · Allotment and Statehood

THE INFLUX OF NON-INDIANS INTO THE NATIONS CREATED A NUMBER of problems. The benefits of citizenship including schools did not extend to these people, and they could neither vote nor appear as litigants in Indian courts. Gradually, noncitizens began demanding a government in which they could participate and that would not restrict the ownership and free use of land. Joining this agitation were the "boomers," white farmers who wanted Indian lands divided into parcels and allotted to individuals with the excess being opened to white settlement. In 1889, the "boomers" scored an initial success when the United States staged a "run" for homesteaders into the unassigned lands. This run only seemed to whet the "boomers'" desire for more land, and they increased pressure on Congress to extinguish Indian titles. Also in 1889, Congress passed a law providing for the allotment of land belonging to all Indians in present-day Oklahoma except the five civilized tribes and a few small Indian groups soon to be included in supplemental legislation.

The political climate in Washington, D.C., proved favorable for the "boomers" as well as for white and Indian entrepreneurs who wanted to be free of the restrictions governing land in the Indian Nations. In 1893, Congress established a commission headed by Senator Henry L. Dawes to negotiate the allotment of lands belonging to the five southern Indian Nations and the dissolution of their tribal governments. At first the leaders of the five Nations refused to negotiate with the commissioners, but most weakened when they saw that Congress intended to move ahead with the division of land.

3. Muskogee about 1900. Courtesy of Photograph Archives, Division of Library Resources, Oklahoma Historical Society.

Their fears were confirmed in 1898 with the passage of the Curtis Act terminating Indian governments without the consent of their citizens.

In general, highly acculturated, well-to-do progressives came to favor allotment and statehood, while traditionalists staunchly opposed the plan. Bitter factionalism developed which, in some cases, led to armed resistance. When force failed to alter the course adopted by both the United States and the Indian governments, conservatives responded in a traditional Indian way: they withdrew and refused to participate in their governments or receive allotments. Through illegitimate councils, secret societies, and ancient ceremonies, they sought to isolate themselves from those who had ceased to share their values.

Statehood followed the allotment of lands and the dissolution of tribal governments. Some Indians worked for the admission of a separate Indian state named "Sequoyah," but Congress tabled the measure. In 1907, Oklahoma Territory and Indian Territory were admitted to the union as one state, the State of Oklahoma.

Factionalism

Since the Civil War, the Cherokees had been divided into two parties. The Downing party, founded and headed by Lewis Downing following the war, stood for the new order of things, for the settlement of the affairs of the Indians, and for an equal distribution of all lands and property. The National party was headed by the full-blood Indians and a few others who wanted a return of the old system of Cherokee government, was opposed to the allotment of lands, and in no way wanted to be infringed on by the white man.[1]

Thomas M. Buffington made his first race for chief of the Cherokee Nation on the Downing ticket and was opposed by Wolf Coon, a full-blood Cherokee, on the National ticket.[2] The question at issue in this election was allotment of land and was a hard fought one. At first, it was wagered that Buffington would win with a landslide, but the question of allotment was a much bigger one to the average Indian than had been figured, and when the vote was counted, Wolf Coon was only 302 votes behind.

He immediately contested the election through his attorneys Frank Boudinot and Daniel Gritts, and the election was referred to a committee composed of Senator C. V. Rogers of Cooweescoowee,

4. *W. C. Rogers Delivering Inaugural Address at the Cherokee Capitol, 1903.* Courtesy of Photograph Archives, Division of Library Resources, Oklahoma Historical Society.

Hitcher of Goingsnake, and Councilors James Bonaparte Wodall of Delaware, Ben Hilderbrand of Cooweescoowee, and Waters of Flint District. This committee did not take action until sometime later.

Chief Samuel H. Mayes and his executive officers then turned the reins of government over to Chief Buffington, who announced his executive secretaries to be Willis O. Bruton of Muldrow, Jeff T. Parks, and Andrew B. Cunningham of Tahlequah. The meeting then adjourned to the public square in Tahlequah where members of the tribe had gathered to listen to their new chief's first message.

Looking calmly over the crowd, many of whom were his bitter political enemies, the chief addressed them in words carefully chosen, urging them to lay aside personal petty grievances and to work together that the best thoughts and most patriotic endeavors might be welded for the benefit of the Nation as a whole. He spoke of the treaty which the Cherokees had by a majority vote ratified early in the year. The treaty had been drawn by the Indian leaders together with members of the Dawes Commission, but Congress had failed to approve it. He urged more time to be given in which Congress might consider it. He asked the council to appropriate money for the payment of delegates' expenses to Washington that they might confer with the president and members of the Congress relative to Indian laws and measures being considered at the capital, asking that not more than two delegates be sent.

In his message, he declared the tribe had three high schools, 124 primary schools, and one orphan asylum. He urged that more money be provided for the school system, as in many instances teachers had had to discount warrants received for their services.

When the report of the action taken under the new chief's direction was taken to Washington, all the recommendations were allowed by President McKinley except that appropriating $3,000 for delegate expenses at Washington. This had to be paid from the delegates' own pockets.

The committee appointed to investigate Wolf Coon's charges against Chief Buffington went into session shortly after the close of the National Council and met with J. George Wright, head of the Dawes Commission, who, after carefully considering all angles of the petition, listening to arguments presented by lawyers of the plaintiff and defendant, decided the charges were without foundation and threw them out. . . .[3]

The white man was rapidly taking possession of the country given by treaty to the Indian as his as long as grass grows and water flows. No longer was he merely a visitor in a foreign country. He was a resident by choice. He came and brought his family with him, he built himself a home, he cultivated the soil, he monopolized business. A survey of the Indian Territory in 1900 disclosed that there was 101,000 Indians of all tribes, as compared to over 396,000 whites. The Indians' count naturally took in all men enrolled in the tribes, many of whom were entirely white but who had intermarried. The term of "squaw man," referring to such, had been dropped. There were too many of them. Many white men, not members of Indian families, had been adopted by various tribes and thus given rights of citizenship.

Although Chief Buffington was only one-eighth Indian, he had spent his life among them, was their leader, and naturally strove to prevent this rapid absorption of his tribe by another race.

Cattle were being shipped in and grazed on the Indian's land without the consent of the tribe. True, taxes were collected on many of them, but many came in tax free, a white man giving an Indian a small fee to report the cattle as his own.

Congress was demanding the enrollment of the Indians, and commissions were appointed whose duty it was to enroll them. The question of whether the government was going to pay the Cherokees for various things the Cherokees believed the United States owed them was a moot one and one which continually demanded the chief's attention. Various contracts with lawyers were placed before the Indians providing a percentage of the immense sum was to be paid to the lawyers.[4] Railroads building into the Indian Territory were claiming every other alternate section of land for their own under terms with the government drawn up in 1886, which provided that when the Indian land ceased to be the property of the Indian it should be given to the railroad.

W. C. Rogers, himself a Cherokee, who succeeded Thomas M. Buffington as chief of the Cherokees and who owned three stores, one at Vera, another at Talala, and another at Skiatook, Indian Territory, invoiced at $30,000, refused to pay his merchandise tax, and his stores were closed by officers representing the tax collectors for the Cherokee government. The merchandise tax, which Rogers was refusing to pay, had been bringing much money into the Cherokee treasury and aiding materially in financing the government of the Indians. Rogers obtained a court order permitting him to open his store at Talala so that he might dispose of perishable groceries. In this stand he was supported by many other Cherokees. He retained as his lawyer Mellette and Smith, W. H. Kornegay of Vinita, and Luman F. Parker, James S. Davenport, and W. T. Hutchins. They carried it through the courts and obtained a decision favorable to their client. Thus came to an end the merchandise tax in the Indian Territory, destroying much income tax for that tribe, as most of the store owners were white men from the East.[5]

The question of statehood at this time was rife. Most of the white people in the eastern half and practically all in the western half of what is now Oklahoma were demanding statehood. Bills were introduced in Congress which, had they been approved, would have permitted the western half to enter as a state with the power to annex any and all of the eastern half. To offset support of these bills, Chief Buffington spent most of his time in Washington. "Our people are willing for the western half to become a state," he declared, "but we are not ready for statehood on our side. We want more time to prepare for the changes which statehood will bring about."

Mineral and oil rights of Indians to land in the Territory was a much argued question. The chief contended that when the government gave the Indians the Territory, all rights had gone with it, both above and below the surface. Another Cherokee treaty was introduced into Congress giving each Cherokee surface rights to eighty acres of land. This Chief Buffington bitterly opposed, declaring, "Our enrollment is not yet complete, but it has reached the stage where we, our people, number only about 30,000 Cherokees and freedmen, and we own nearly 5 million acres of land. To offer of us only eighty acres is an outrage."

A committee appointed by Chief Buffington to work with members of the Dawes Commission in drawing up a treaty that would meet approval immediately began work. President McKinley had again vetoed the bill passed by the National Council appointing L. W. Buffington and James Keys, pro-treaty men, and Red Bird Smith and Wolf Coon, anti-treaty representatives, as a committee to meet with the congressional representatives in Washington to harmonize treaty problems.

Under the chief's guidance, a treaty was drawn up with the Dawes Commission approving it, and on November 6, 1901, the council again met in regular session. This treaty under the Cherokee laws became known as the "Allotment Bill" as it provided solutions on problems of allotment which had been vexing previous to this time.

A bitter fight was waged in the council to prevent the passage of the bill, but under the skillful direction of the chief, aided by J. C. Starr, Gideon Morgan, and George W. Mayes, it was finally passed on March 4, 1902. Congress was in its closing days when the bill reached it, and Speaker Henderson refused to allow it to come up in the House. He would not recognize any speaker who favored bringing it on the floor, and Chief Buffington once more sensed defeat.

Calling together Senator Quay, Secretary Hitchcock, Tams Bixby, and Judge Springer, Chief Buffington asked an audience with President Theodore Roosevelt. This was granted, and the committee spent several hours closeted with the president. At last, he consented to bring administrative pressure upon Congress to consider the bill and pass it at once. Speaker Henderson was called in and after much manipulation agreed to bring the bill before the House on Monday, June 30th. Everything else was laid aside as the House took up the question, and it was passed quickly and intact.

Satisfied, the chief returned to his people, where he set the election day for their ratification as August 7, 1902. At last the chief was satisfied that he had obtained a treaty which would meet the approval of his people; however, many of them headed by the full-bloods bitterly fought its adoption. Chief Buffington, Hooley Bell, Too-quah-stee, and others led the fight for its adoption, making speeches throughout the Territory, supplying papers of the Territory with articles favoring it, and answering arguments presented against it.

The Cherokees swarmed to the voting precincts on election day, and 6,716 of them cast their votes. The council was called into immediate session, and on August 14th revealed the official count as being for the treaty 4,340, against the treaty 2,376. Chief Buffington had at last won his fight. His home precinct had supported him with an almost eight-to-one vote in favor of the treaty, 1,826 for and 214 against.

Delighted that through years of effort both as a member of the Senate and as chief of his Nation he had succeeded in bringing about a necessary end, he returned to his home resolved to enjoy himself a few weeks before setting to work to wind up the affairs of the Nation in the shortest possible time. (Cherokee, 79: 121–31)

*   *   *

The Choctaws, in common with the other tribes, had their dissensions and their differences. This unhappy state of affairs originated before they emigrated from Mississippi to the Indian Territory and continued on through the years to the dissolution of tribal existence. The National party, the faction opposing the ratification of the removal treaty, and the Progressive party, those favoring the removal treaty, each continued the opposition to the philosophy of the other; however, the Progressive party was the victor in all the leading issues of that period.[6] The more wily of the politicians would align themselves with the Progressive party and thereby assure themselves of the support of the powerful heads of that party, while those politicians who professed to be the representatives of those who placed the continuation of tribal existence above all other issues would in each instance meet with organized opposition from the more powerful Progressives. The last clash between the National and Progressive parties occurred in 1892, when the issue of whether or not the land which had been held in common by the Choctaw tribe should be partitioned.[7] The Progressive party favored the partition, while the Nationalists sought to prevent it and thereby prevent the dissolution of tribal existence. Wilson Jones and Jacob Jackson were contenders for the office of principal chief, Jones for the Progressives and Jackson for the Nationals. Green McCurtain, a former principal chief and a pronounced Progressive, took the field in support of Jones. The campaign became so heated that a display of armed support appeared in the interest of both contenders. The husband of the subject of this sketch, Martin Whistler, was a participant in these armed forces in support· of Jacob Jackson who was his stepfather and who lived in the same general locality west of Shady Point. However, it is said no group killings resulted from the campaign, and after the election Jones was declared elected as principal chief.[8] Both candidates were Choctaws; Jones, it is said, was of a submissive character, while Jackson was well educated and very aggressive. It is said that he had served as clerk or secretary of state for several terms. . . . [9]

Despite all the wealth which had been placed in the laps of the Choctaws through the inheritance of the Choctaw Nation with its wealth of natural resources, this poor old full-blood Choctaw woman finds herself in her advanced age with nothing but one hundred and sixty acres of land, which she can neither sell nor eat, nor can she find a properly equipped farmer to whom she can rent it with the view of making it productive of a living for her. She is highly intelligent and wonders if, after all, it would not have been better had the Nationals had their way.[10] (Choctaw, 67: 179–82)

*   *   *

Under the Choctaw law, an Indian could settle on a piece of land, no matter how large, and improve it, and if he did not get within a quarter of a mile of someone else's improvements, the land was his to use as long as he wished. But no individual really owned land; it belonged to the tribe as a whole.[11]

But even before 1900 we voted on whether to allot land to individuals.[12] This question was also a source of trouble between the two factions of Choctaws. There was bitter feeling on both sides, and even some killing. I was a member of the council at Tuskahoma the year Green McCurtain and Tom Hunter had such a close race for the position of high chief—1902, I think it was. Lots of the followers of Hunter thought that he really won the election; they hinted at trickery. That's how bitter things were.

The allotment of land started about 1904, whether some of the Indians wanted it or not.[13] The number of acres an Indian got depended on the estimated worth of the land in question. I got 320 acres. Then after the allotment was over the Indians held a vote on whether we should have statehood or not, but I, for one, saw that our election meant little. Statehood had been inevitable ever since the discovery of coal in the Choctaw Nation.

And I just want to say this before I am through: I felt safer against robbery and violence when I was under the Choctaw law than

I do now. A man never had to worry about thieves because an Indian wouldn't steal. There are more killings in one year now than there were during all the years of the Choctaw rule. (Choctaw, 78: 489-90)

*   *   *

In 1902 he [Josiah Billy] served as interpreter in the Choctaw National Senate and was a witness of the very tense situation which was created through the bitterly fought contest between Tom Hunter and Green McCurtain for the governorship. In that instance, the outgoing governor, G. W. Dukes, who favored the election of Hunter, allied himself with the Hunter forces and vacated his office and turned it over to Tom Hunter during the week that the votes were to be cast. Hunter took over the office and organized the Council without counting the votes. This caused great confusion and violent disputes in the building and on the grounds. The United States marshal, who was in full sympathy with the Hunter faction, took over the capital and caused a troop of Negro soldiers to be brought in to assist him in maintaining peace.

Indian Agent Shoenfelt, however, gave his support to the McCurtain faction and sent to Washington asking that a company of soldiers be sent to the Choctaw capital at Tuskahoma to take charge of affairs. The authorities at Washington immediately responded to the request of Agent Shoenfelt, and troops were rushed to the scene of the conflict to preserve peace. Upon the arrival of these troops, a conference between representatives of the contending forces was held at the Gilbert Thompson Hotel. That conference resulted in an agreement that the Council House be turned over to the councilors, it having been closed to all save the supporters of Hunter in the interim. Upon the announcement of the agreement made at the conference, a mad rush was made for the Council House by both factions; however, physical combat was averted, and the election for the office of governor was entered upon in an orderly manner, the result being that McCurtain was found to be elected governor.

Josiah Billy recalls the great oratorical ability to Jacob Jackson, a well-educated Choctaw Indian, who served as the Choctaw national secretary for a period of three two-year terms and was often heard in the Choctaw legislative halls with profound attention and respect.

In 1892 he had been an opponent of Wilson Jones in a race for the governorship and, doubtless, would have won that race had Wilson not had the irresistible force and assistance of Green McCurtain.[14] Jackson was a member of the Nationalist party, a party which fought at every step to maintain tribal existence. (Choctaw, 54: 390–92)

Resistance

Mr. Crawford Anderson remembers with remarkable clarity the occasion when Governor Wilson Jones authorized the formation of companies of militia to effect the arrest of the non-Progressives, or Snake Indians, who had banded together for the purpose of killing the leading men in the Progressive party.[15] The situation in the vicinity of Talihina and on down to Antlers was very tense. A large number of the non-Progressives had congregated at the home of Dick Locke at Antlers, all armed to the teeth, and were openly defying the tribal authorities.[16] Mr. Anderson was a member of one of the companies of militia serving under Captain Gilbert W. Thompson. The militia had camped at a small village called Davenport, a point about three miles distant from the home of Dick Locke, and had proceeded on to Antlers on the following morning. Upon approaching the home of Dick Locke, the militiamen were fired upon from all parts of the interior of the house, from the windows, doors, and from every other opening through which a gun could be projected. The militia then opened fire. This exchange of bullets was continued for some time, and then a truce was called, and a conference between Captain Thompson and Dick Locke was held. It was agreed in this conference that the conspirators would submit to arrest without further resistance. The entire band was then placed under arrest and sent to Paris, Texas, under escort to be placed in the federal jail at that place. In spite of all the shooting which had taken place before the truce was called, no one had been seriously injured, but the house which sheltered the conspirators was practically demolished.

Upon the submission of the offending parties to arrest, Captain Thompson directed most of the militiamen to return to their homes. Some of these men who were not fortunate enough to have funds with which to pay train fare were required to walk, some of them as far as fifty or sixty miles. Mr. Anderson, however, together with some four other comrades was provided with the necessary funds and arrived at their homes in Talihina late on the same evening. Here they found a large assemblage of people awaiting the arrival of the train, all eager to learn of the result of the battle of which they had heard vague rumors during the day. Many of this group were sympathetic with those who had been taken to jail. This caused a well-founded fear that reprisals against the militiamen who had just returned would follow. Mr. Anderson and his companion militiamen quickly made their way through the crowd and then separated to go to their respective homes, which were at varying distances and directions from the railroad station.

Such was the fear of Mr. Anderson of being ambushed on his way home in the darkness, which had by that time appeared, that he avoided walking the well-beaten road and kept at a distance of from one to two hundred yards from it.

Upon his arrival at his home, he informed his much alarmed wife of his fears for his personal safety, which he felt were justified, and after eating his evening meal he made his way to a secluded spot to spend the remainder of the night. In this manner, he very probably cheated his would-be assassins out of an opportunity to carry out their murderous designs.

This already tense situation was made the more so when it was learned that the conspirators, who had submitted to arrest and had been taken to the federal jail at Paris, Texas, had been liberated on the day following their arrest and were again free to renew their offenses against the peaceable processes of the tribal authorities. They immediately resumed holding secret meetings in which they laid their plans to assassinate the leading man in the Progressive party.

A young white boy, whom the Indians thought did not understand the Choctaw language and therefore it was of no consequence if he did hear them, overheard and understood the conversation had by a band of the conspirators in which it was planned to kill several of the leading Progressives, Mr. Anderson and Gilbert W. Dukes being among the number to be killed.[17] Upon fully satisfying himself of the correctness of what he had understood the conspirators intended to do, this boy very indifferently mounted his pony and rode off in the direction of his home, which incidentally was in the opposite direction to that of the homes of Anderson and Dukes. This act on the part of the boy was designed to dispel any suspicion which the conspirators might have felt that he had understood their conversation and would notify the proposed victims. After reaching a point where he was out of sight of the Snakeheads, as they were sometimes called, this boy put spurs to his pony and by a circuitous route quickly arrived at the home of Governor Dukes and made known to him the plans which he had overheard.

Upon being apprised of those plans of the Snakes through the bravery and sagacity of that young boy, Governor Dukes immediately notified the remaining named proposed victims, and they all met at the home of Governor Dukes and maintained a guard throughout the night, expecting each minute to hear the approach of their would-be assassins. The night passed without incident, but a survey of the ground not far distant from the home on the following morning revealed tracks freshly made which told in unmistakable language that the boy's warning had been timely, well founded, and the means of foiling the purposes of the conspirators and perhaps of saving the lives of the proposed victims. Presumably the stealthy Snakes, aided by the darkness of the night, had made a reconnoiter of the premises and thereby found their would-be victims greater in number and much better entrenched than they had expected to find them. An attack in accordance with their prearranged plans was seemingly not warranted.

It is a well-known fact that a Territory-wide slaughter of the leading Progressives in all parts of the Choctaw Nation was to take place on that same night. Fortunately, however, with the expectation of the killing of five leaders in what was then Gaines County, the plans of the conspirators were frustrated.

On another occasion, a group of the Snake Indians had congregated in an isolated place, and after they had held their powwow, all spread their blankets upon the ground and prepared to spend the night in sleep. One man had been designated to stand guard near the sleeping conspirators. The now watchful Progressives in some way learned of this bivouac, advanced upon it, found the irresponsible guard soundly slumbering, quietly seized him, and then noiselessly advanced upon the main body of the group whom they found lying close to each other all wrapped in their blankets. The Progressives, being equal if not superior in numbers, surrounded them before they awoke, and then each Progressive, with gun cocked and ready for instant firing, commanded the renegade Indian lying closest to him to arise and surrender.

In this manner, the arrest of a considerable number of those who had proven themselves to be menaces to the lives of those with whom they did not agree upon tribal matters was affected without the loss of life. Such wholesale arrests occurring at about the same time aided materially in quelling the uprisings and finally brought peace and tranquility back into the lives of those who for months had lived in constant fear for the safety of themselves and for the safety of their families due to the sneaking way in which the renegades carried their vindictiveness into effect.

In that group arrest, it is interesting to note the personal experience of Mr. Anderson. The particular Indian lying closest to him at the time the signal for the awakening of the sleeping Indians was given was commanded by Mr. Anderson to arise and throw up his hands. He arose from a prone to a sitting posture and then put down his right hand as though in an attempt to seize a gun. At that instant Mr. Anderson commanded him to drop that gun or he would fire. This latter command had the effect of causing the Indian to again reach for the sky with his hands and elicited the information that, as he was a cripple on crutches, he was merely reaching for his crutch and not for a gun as Mr. Anderson had thought. The instantaneous response to the second command of Mr. Anderson is all that stood between the still sleepy Indian and instant death, for Mr. Anderson was not at that time in a mood to unnecessarily put himself up as a target for the gun of a renegade Snake Indian.

Following this group arrest, the non-Progressives were not so bold, and their meetings were scantily attended. The appearance of several Progressives in the vicinity of the meeting place would cause a gradual departure of the Snakes from the meeting place for their several homes.

There was an element of justice in the cause of the non-Progressives. The only fault to be found is in the method adopted in the promotion of that cause. They had been warned by the opponents of conformity with the terms of the Dancing Rabbit Creek Treaty in their far off Mississippi that it was useless to give up their lands upon which rested the remains of their ancestors; that if they moved to the new Indian Territory they would again soon be asked to give it over to the white man.[18] So it is not in the least surprising that they felt a spirit of rebellion arising within their bosoms when they realized that the warnings given to their fathers in Mississippi by the nonconformists were well founded and that the promises which were made as inducements to remove to the new Indian Territory were in process of being abrogated. (Choctaw, 12: 334–44)

*   *   *

I was born in 1893 on the Louis Smith allotment near Mallette in the Creek Indian Nation. However, my first childhood recollections center about Raiford where we lived. I remember sitting at the side of the road in order to watch the United States laws pass by with their Snake Indian prisoners, who were being taken to Eufaula. Ours was a farming family.

"Snake Indians" is the name applied to those who practiced the philosophy of Chitto "Crazy Snake" Harjo, Creek Indian, warrior, and statesman. He fought against the law of the white man and was the leader of several rebellions, the last in 1907. It was in some of the earlier uprisings that these Crazy Snake Indians, who often had more Negro blood than Indian, were captured.[19]

Speaking of Crazy Snake Indians, my uncle Bill, Father's brother, married into the Creek Indian tribe. Of this union Ivory Guin was born in 1898, and was put on the roll for allotment the same year. His mother died shortly after his birth.

One day in the late summer of 1903, Dad and Uncle Bill decided to cut the tall grass to be found on Uncle Bill's son's allotment. Uncle Bill's son was named Ivory. This grass was to be used as hay. It so happened that Ivory's allotment was near Hickory Ground.[20] This ground was situated near the small town of Salem and was at that time headquarters for the Crazy Snake outfit, and it was later made the Creek capital by "Crazy Snake" Chitto Harjo. Uncle and Dad, after making the trip, had but little time that first day to mow hay. They made camp in a small woodland and used their wagon to sleep under.

The first night they were startled to hear the zing of buckshot uncomfortably near, in fact a bullet went into their campfire. They jumped to their feet, ran a short distance, and hid behind trees.

Soon about ten Negro Snake Indians on horses entered the circle of their campfire. One of these Negroes sang out, "Hello, white man!

We burn you before day." The savages started dancing about the fire, yelling and gobbling as they did so. This commotion summoned other Crazy Snake Indians from Hickory Ground. My dad and uncle heard them swiftly approach on horses. They didn't have anything but an old muzzle loaded gun to stand off their foes so they decided the best thing to do was to retreat. This they did. They went to the home of a friendly Indian of the name of Billy Cheeks. He lived on the North Canadian about four miles from the place of the attack. The next morning Dad and Uncle Bill returned to their camp, got their wagon and team, and came back home. (Creek, 80: 218–20)

*   *   *

Wylie Jim Boy of Okemah, Sam Haynes of Okmulgee, and Eunice Harrison of Wewoka were the only Indian police I remember. It was about the time of the Dawes Commission that they were started, and one of their duties was going with the Dawes commissioners, who were afraid of the Indians and outlaws. The police wore Winchesters and six-shooters and a star pinned on them. They went to different families and stayed a while. They stayed with my father quite a while, then went to another place, and tried to get everyone enrolled, but a few were left out.

The Snake Indians never did come up and enroll, but the Dawes Commission had names from the town chiefs and sat in their offices and enrolled them. Every town had a town chief to represent it at Okmulgee, and he had every name and number of members of his town. The Dawes commissioners called on him to get the names to enroll.

The Snakes were against the new treaty and wanted to stay with the old treaty. That was the cause of the Snake uprising. Porter made a complaint, and the government sent soldiers in here. The soldiers didn't know whom to get nor where to find them, so they had some Indians to go and help them. I rode with them about a month, and we gathered a whole lot from Wetumka, Henryetta, Sasakwa, Okemah, and the last at Eufaula. When they were all rounded up they were loaded in a box car and sent to Muskogee to the jail.[21] The soldiers were of the cavalry.

We camped around and guarded them before they were sent to Muskogee. Soldiers, big tent, horses, and we Indians made quite a camp. The Snakes didn't like me to this day for my part in it. (Creek, 14: 398–99)

Withdrawal

After the enrollment of the five civilized tribes of Indians, particularly Choctaws in this case, to be allotted lands to them by the United States government, there were a few Choctaws who opposed this movement, as well as those who were against Indian Territory to become as a state. Being opposed to the movement of what the government is to do, there was an organization or party formed by these people who declared themselves as against the allotment of lands to the Indians and declared themselves "a band of Snake Indians," or "Ishki Oshta Clan," and would not yield to the allotment of lands. They were in favor of the land to be held in common, not to be owned by any one individual, firm, or corporation, that one may move on any certain piece of land to make improvements and live on as his home. If he desired to move to some new location, he had the privilege of selling the improvement, but that he was not required to dispose of the land.

This was some of the ideas that these parties or clans had written in their constitution they had adopted; hence, they did not care to be interfered with by the government. It was at this time when the government allotted Willis Toby, a full-blood Choctaw Indian, 150 acres of homestead land, where he finally lived and made this his home until he died.

Mr. Toby was a Methodist minister and a leader of the band of Snake Indian Clan, who finally settled down on this track of land that the department had set aside for him. After settling down, he held several Snake Clan meetings where Creeks, Seminoles, and Cherokees participated in holding of these meetings, and a big feast was given to the public and a grand time was had, although no one was allowed to look on while the meeting was in session, only the members.[22] Most of the people in the community with the influence of Willis Toby belonged to this organization. Later the organization was disbanded.[23] (Choctaw, 91: 317–19)

*   *   *

My Great Aunt Molly More made a tour and visited her whole family of relations and told them not to allot, that they were able to make their own living without the help of the government.

Grandfather's mother was a Garland. Sage Garland made two trips to see if we wanted to allot, as he could take it over Molly More's head if we wanted to. I was eight years old at that time. My step-father, E. M. Longstreath, said he thought we should take the allotment, but we never did.

We moved to the Cherokee Nation to keep from allotting, and Grandfather quit writing to all the relations who allotted. He and his people had pulled away from the Choctaw Tribe on account of the treatment and abuse of the government, as they had signed three treaties but had been driven back and back until they did not want anything to do with the government nor with anyone who had anything to do with the government. (Choctaw, 83: 45)

*   *   *

This allotment treaty was another law that was passed by the legislature of the Nation which was not approved by the Cherokees. Like the railroad law it was allowed by the Council. The Cherokees among the full-bloods protested the law. This protest caused another election by popular vote to decide. In the following election, several thousands of Cherokees did not vote. They did not vote because they did not have any confidence in what the representatives of the United States government had agreed to do in the former dealings. The government of the United States had broken so many treaties with the Cherokees that they at that time did not have anything to do with this law. They were called the Nighthawks.[24] These people not voting caused this law to be passed over the ones who were not in favor of it.[25] (Cherokee, 65: 17–18)

Statehood

It was in 1893, Congress provided for a commission to treat with the five tribes to give up tribal government and not hold their lands as common property but to accept allotments of land and become citizens of the United States instead of citizens of each tribe. This commission was known as the Dawes Commission, and Henry Dawes was the first commissioner or rather the first chairman of the commission.[26] It took some time for this commission to begin to function. Surveyors came to the territory and begin to lay townships, towns, and villages, et cetera. Quite a little while, I would say five years, after the Dawes Commission went into effect before allotments were made. I enrolled I believe in 1898 and filed for my hundred and sixty acres in 1899. Each one of my children did likewise.

I nor any of them experienced any difficulty in proving up, as we were all born here and everybody knew we were citizens. I enrolled at Okmulgee, Indian Territory. . . .

The people just could not get satisfied with the Territory laws. They chose to elect their own officers to rule them instead of the Territory laws. People out of the Territory were sent in by the government to rule and did not know or have any idea of the conditions that existed in the Territory.[27] As far back as 1891, people began to want the Oklahoma Territory and the Indian Territory taken in as one great state.[28] They quarreled and fussed and fumed around for a length of time and some wanted just Oklahoma Territory as a state and leave the Indian Territory as it was.[29] The people continued to argue not only here in the Territory but also at Washington. In 1905, the tribes called a convention at the Muskogee, Indian Territory (and, while I think of it, we used to call Muskogee Arkansas Town) on August 21, to form a constitution for a state composed of Indian Territory separate to that of the Oklahoma Territory. Our Creek chief, Pleasant Porter, a neighbor of mine for years and with whom I had been deer hunting many times, was selected and elected president of that convention, and we had a Creek poet by the name of Alex Posey who was elected secretary.[30] Out of the five tribes I believe all sent delegates to the convention, except possibly one, and I believe that the one absent was the Chickasaw tribe. Of course, Sequoyah was a Cherokee, and it was he who composed the Cherokee alphabet and, in order to pay tribute to him, they voted to call the Indian Territory the State of Sequoyah, and it was to have forty-eight counties. The result of this convention was brought by representatives of the five tribes before Congress, but for some reason they never acted.[31]

Now you see Oklahoma Territory wanted a separate state, the Indian Territory wanted a separate state, and neither one got what they tried to get. In 1907, a bill was passed in Washington to include both territories into one state and that it should be called Oklahoma. Delegates from the Indian Territory and the Oklahoma Territory met at Guthrie, Oklahoma Territory, and both territories did become one state. I have heard people say that Oklahoma became a state in 1907, but I claim it was 1908 because the officials did not take office until January 1, 1908.[32] (Creek, 9: 368–72)

Notes

1. This statement is an oversimplification of the Cherokee party system. In order to attract support from conservatives, the old Downing party assumed the name Keetoowah in 1879, and opposed the Independent National party, which had grown out of the old Ross party. The Independent Nationals were victorious in that election. By 1883, the parties were the National, which won, and the Union. The Downing party reappeared in 1885 and elected the principal chief. The Downing candidate, Joel B. Mayes, was reelected in 1891 over candidates of the National and Liberal parties. Samuel H. Mayes of the Downing party won in 1895, the election immediately preceding the one of which the narrator speaks. Morris L. Wardell, *A Political History of the Cherokee Nation, 1838–1907* (Norman, Okla., 1938), pp. 335–49.

2. Wolf Coon had refused to sign an 1899 agreement with the Dawes Commission concerning allotment of land and dissolution of tribal government.

3. Senator Henry L. Dawes died in 1903, and Tams Bixby followed him as chairman of the commission. In 1905, the commission was abolished except for the position of chairman. Bixby continued as sole commissioner until 1907, when J. George Wright, who had been Indian inspector representing the Department of Interior, assumed the position. The office was abolished in 1914.

4. A major issue in a number of elections was the retainer and fees paid attorneys.

5. In 1905 Rogers refused to call an election because the demise of the government was imminent. The Cherokees went to the polls anyway and elected Frank J. Boudinot principal chief, but the Department of Interior refused to recognize Boudinot.

6. The Progressive party of the 1892 election was a relatively new party organized in 1872. The members of this party, however, usually descended from proponents of the removal treaty, occupied the same socioeconomic class, and shared the same values. Angie Debo, *The Rise and Fall of the Choctaw Republic* (Norman, Okla., 1934), p. 164.

7. The immediate issue prompting the hostility and violence of the election of 1892 was disbursement of funds resulting from the sale of the Leased District to the United States. In general, however, the National party opposed white immigration and allotment and favored tribal sovereignty and national control of natural resources. At its inception and through the election of 1894, the Progressive party also opposed territorial government. Debo, *The Rise and Fall of the Choctaw Republic*, pp. 164–74.

8. On September 11, 1892, a group of Nationals assassinated four Progressives in Gaines County. The United States agent, Dr. Leo E. Bennett, arranged a temporary truce. Periodic violence continued into 1893.

9. Although Wilson N. Jones had little formal education and spoke no English, he had served as a district school trustee and national treasurer. He also was reputed to be the wealthiest man in the Choctaw Nation. Jacob B. Jackson had attended college in the United States before entering public service. He had served in the Senate and currently was national secretary. For biographical sketches of these men, see H. F. O'Beirne, *Leaders and Leading Men of the Indian Territory* (Chicago, 1891).

10. Compared to many Indians, who completely lost their allotments through fraud, this woman was perhaps fortunate. See Angie Debo, *And Still the Waters Run: The Betrayal of the Five Civilized Tribes* (Princeton, 1940).

11. See Norman A. Graebner, "The Public Land Policy of the Five Civilized Tribes," *Chronicles of Oklahoma* 23 (1945): 107–18.

12. On August 24, 1898, by a vote of 2,164 to 1,366, the Choctaws ratified the Atoka Agreement, which provided for allotment of land and termination of tribal government. Debo, *The Rise and Fall of the Choctaw Republic* p. 262.

13. Choctaw allotments began in spring 1903.

14. Green McCurtain was a member of a prominent Choctaw family which had produced two other chiefs, Edmund and Jackson. Generally regarded as a man of integrity even by those who disagreed with him, McCurtain continued to guide the Choctaws after statehood.

15. The following episode occurred after the contested election of 1892, while the term "Snake Indians" generally refers to conservatives who organized in 1896 to resist allotment. Since many of the same people were involved in both episodes, quite conceivably the term came into existence earlier.

16. V. M. Locke was an intermarried citizen who later became superintendent of schools.

17. Gilbert W. Dukes was principal chief from 1900 until 1902.

18. The Treaty of Dancing Rabbit Creek provided for the removal of the Choctaws west of the Mississippi River.

19. Chitto Harjo's followers primarily were Creek conservatives. Freedmen usually favored allotment and statehood. Angie Debo, *The Road to Disappearance* (Norman, Okla., 1941), p. 376.

20. Hickory Ground was Chitto Harjo's town.

21. In 1901, the followers of Chitto Harjo attempted to reestablish effective tribal government. Their council passed laws against taking allotments and hiring or leasing to whites and ordered all who had received certificates of allotment to surrender them. The lighthorsemen appointed by this government arrested and whipped several violators. The Snakes became so dis-

ruptive to the work of the Dawes Commission that sixty-seven were jailed and tried. They received suspended sentences. Debo, *And Still the Waters Run*, pp. 54–58. Also see Mel Hallin Bolster, *Crazy Snake and the Smoked Meat Rebellion* (Boston, 1976).

22. The Four Mothers Society to which the narrator apparently refers was organized about 1895. At one time, the society reportedly had 24,000 members from the Cherokee, Chickasaw, Choctaw, and Creek Nations. Debo, *And Still the Waters Run*, p. 54.

23. Willis Toby, along with the Cherokee Redbird Smith, the Creek Chitto Harjo, and other representatives of the Four Mothers Society, testified before a United States Senate committee on conditions in the Indian Nations. They pleaded in vain for restoration of the government and their undivided land. Debo, *And Still the Waters Run*, pp. 151–56.

24. The Nighthawks were also called Keetoowahs.

25. See Daniel F. Littlefield, Jr., "Utopian Dreams of the Cherokee Fullbloods: 1890–1930," *Journal of the West* 10 (1971): 404–27; and Thomas, "The Redbird Smith Movement."

26. See Loren N. Brown, "The Dawes Commission," *Chronicles of Oklahoma* 9 (1931): 71–105, and "The Establishment of the Dawes Commission for Indian Territory," *Chronicles of Oklahoma* 18 (1940): 171–81.

27. In 1898, Congress abolished tribal courts and placed Indians under United States jurisdiction.

28. Congress passed the Organic Act creating Oklahoma Territory in 1890. At that time, the Territory included the Unassigned Lands, which had been opened to homesteaders in 1889, and the panhandle. "Boomers" continued to pressure Congress to open additional land to white settlement. By 1907, Oklahoma Territory included all the land now in the State of Oklahoma except that belonging to the five civilized tribes and the small tribes northeast of the Cherokee Nation. Edwin C. McReynolds, *Oklahoma: A History of the Sooner State* (Norman, Okla., 1954), pp. 292–97. For information on the "boomers," see Dan W. Peery, "Captain David L. Payne," *Chronicles of Oklahoma* 13 (1935): 438–56, and "Colonel Crocker and the Boomer Movement," *Chronicles of Oklahoma* 13 (1935): 276–96; and Carl C. Rister, *Land Hunger: David L. Payne and the Boomers* (Norman, Okla., 1942).

29. See Thomas H. Doyle, "Single Versus Double Statehood," *Chronicles of Oklahoma* 5 (1927): 18–41, 117–48.

30. See Leona G. Barnett, "Este Cate Emunkv: Red Man Always," *Chronicles of Oklahoma* 46 (1968): 20–40, for an account of the career of this legislator, educator, interpreter, poet, journalist, and employee of the Dawes Commission (who sometimes used his Creek name).

31. Congress tabled the proposed constitution. See C. M. Allen, *The Sequoyah Movement* (Oklahoma City, 1925); and Amos D. Maxwell. *The*

Sequoyah Constitutional Convention (Boston, 1953), and "The Sequoyah Convention," *Chronicles of Oklahoma* 28 (1950): 161–92, 299–340. An earlier attempt to organize a united Indian government also failed. See Allen G. Applen, "An Attempted Indian State Government: The Okmulgee Constitution in Indian Territory," *Kansas Quarterly* 3 (1971): 89–99.   ]

32. President Theodore Roosevelt proclaimed Oklahoma the forty-sixth state, and Charles N. Haskell took office as governor on November 16, 1907. See Charles Wayne Ellinger, "The Drive for Statehood in Oklahoma, 1889–1906," *Chronicles of Oklahoma* 41 (1963): 15–37; and Roy Gittinger, *The Formation of the State of Oklahoma, 1803–1906* (Norman, Okla., 1939).

Epilogue

The aftermath of allotment and statehood confirmed the worst fears of conservatives. Feeble attempts by the federal government to protect Indian land titles by prohibiting sale of allotments (or portions of allotments) for a specified period of time failed miserably. Unscrupulous whites demonstrated remarkable ingenuity in circumventing the letter and spirit of protective legislation. Since guardianships of Indian children and incompetents entailed the administration of their estates, the most helpless in the Indian nations became the most exploited. Horror stories of the abuse of guardianships abound, none more poignant perhaps than that of three children who lived in a hollow tree and foraged for food while their guardian enjoyed the returns from their property. The discovery of oil on land previously deemed undesirable and therefore allotted to the poorest Indians brought more fraud and scandal, and few conservatives ever realized any profit from the Oklahoma oil fields. Most conservatives continued to eke out a living as best they could in the remote parts of the state and avoided whites and progressive Indians.

Progressives, on the other hand, often benefited from the allotment of land and from the oil boom in the early days of statehood. Unencumbered by restrictions on the alienation of allotments, many speculated freely in real estate, mineral rights, and oil leases. Rather than losing what they had accumulated under the tribal governments, these progressives continued or expanded their economic activities. Some became wealthy; a few even reached the upper echelons of national corporations. Since they shared the values of white Oklahomans, progressives quickly became assimilated into the dominant white society, and only a romantic pride in their Indian ancestry separated them from the boomers' descendants.

The "marriage" of a white cowboy and an Indian princess during festivities marking Oklahoma's admission to the Union symbolized the joining of two cultures, two traditions, and two peoples. But in the state of Oklahoma, Indians were a relatively small minority. Among the Indian population most were progressives who soon became culturally (and often physically) indistinguishable from whites. Thus, in reality, Oklahoma statehood meant the triumph of Anglo-Americans, not the blending of two cultures.

Because of the preponderance of whites, Indian peoples seemed to disappear along with their nations. While tribal governments may not have contributed significantly to the conservatives' ethnic identity, Indian nations did give their ethnicity formal expression. With the demise of Indian national governments, the citizens of the five civilized tribes lost their collective voice, and white Americans found it easier to ignore them, the problems they faced, and the traditional practices and beliefs they maintained. Finally in the late 1930s, state and federal officials began to implement programs to improve the economic plight of traditionalists, and the 1960s and 1970s gave rise to community organization and assertion of Indian rights among traditionalists. Current emphasis on tribalism and cultural pluralism has aided the resurgence of traditionalists and, in addition, has encouraged whites and progressives to explore the heritage of the five civilized tribes. These reminiscences are a testimony to that heritage and a tribute to the Indian people themselves —the richness of their lives, the acuity of their intellect, and the depth of their feelings—who make the Indian nations well worth remembering.

Bibliography

Abel, Annie Heloise. *The American Indian as a Participant in the Civil War*. Cleveland, 1919.

_____. *The American Indian as Slave Holder and Secessionist*. Cleveland, 1915.

_____. *The American Indian Under Reconstruction*. Cleveland, 1925.

Aldrich, Gene. "A History of the Coal Industry in Oklahoma to 1907." Ph.D. dissertation, University of Oklahoma, 1952.

Aldridge, Reginald. *Life on a Ranch: Ranch Notes in Kansas, Colorado, the Indian Territory, and Northern Texas*. New York, 1884.

Allen, C. M. *The Sequoyah Movement*. Oklahoma City, 1925.

Allhands, James L. "Construction of the Frisco Railroad Line in Oklahoma." *Chronicles of Oklahoma* 3 (1925): 229–39.

Anderson, Mabel Washbourne. *Life of General Stand Watie*. Pryor, Okla., 1915.

Andrews, Thomas F. "Freedmen in Indian Territory: A Post-Civil War Dilemma." *Journal of the West* 4 (1965): 367–76.

Andrist, Ralph K. *The Long Death: The Last Days of the Plains Indian*. New York, 1964.

Applen, Allen G. "An Attempted Indian States Government: The Okmulgee Constitution in Indian Territory." *Kansas Quarterly* 3 (1971): 89–99.

Bailey, M. Thomas. *Reconstruction in Indian Territory: A Story of Avarice, Discrimination, and Opportunism*. Port Washington, N.Y., 1972.

Banks, Dean. "Civil War Refugees from Indian Territory in the North, 1861–1864." *Chronicles of Oklahoma* 41 (1963–64): 286–98.

Banner, Lois W. *Women in Modern America: A Brief History*. New York, 1974.

Barnard, Evan G. *A Rider in the Cherokee Strip*. Edited by Edward Everett Dale. Boston, 1936.

Barnett, Leona G. "Este Cate Emunkv: Red Man Always." *Chronicles of Oklahoma* 46 (1968): 20–40.

Bartram, William. "Observations on the Creek and Cherokee Indians." *Transactions of the American Ethnological Society* 3 (1853): 3–81.

Bass, Althea. *Cherokee Messenger: The Life of Samuel Austin Worcester*. Norman, Okla., 1936.

Battle, H. B. "The Domestic Use of Oil Among the Southern Aborigines." *American Anthropologist* 24 (1922): 171–82.

Bearss, Edwin C. "The Civil War Comes to Indian Territory, 1861: The Flight of Opothleyoholo." *Journal of the West* 11 (1972): 9–42.

Benedict, John D. *History of Muskogee and Northeast Oklahoma*. Chicago, 1922.

Berthrong, Donald J. *The Southern Cheyennes*. Norman, Okla., 1963.

Beverley, Robert. *The History and Present State of Virginia*. London, 1705.

Bolster, Mel Hallin. *Crazy Snake and the Smoked Meat Rebellion*. Boston, 1976.

Botkin, Benjamin A., ed. *Lay My Burden Down: A Folk History of Slavery*. Chicago, 1968.

Britton, Wiley. *The Union Indian 'Brigade in the Civil War*. Kansas City, Mo., 1922.

Brown, Loren N. "The Dawes Commission." *Chronicles of Oklahoma* 9 (1931): 71–105.

————. "The Establishment of the Dawes Commission for Indian Territory." *Chronicles of Oklahoma* 18 (1940): 171–81.

Campbell, O. B. *Vinita, I.T.: The Story of a Frontier Town of the Cherokee Nation, 1871–1907*. Oklahoma City, 1969.

Campbell, T. N. "Choctaw Subsistence: Ethnographic Notes from the Lincecum Manuscript." *Florida Anthropologist* 12 (1959): 9–12.

Collier, Peter. *When Shall They Rest? The Cherokees' Long Struggle with America*. New York, 1973.

Constitutions and Laws of the American Indian Tribes. Wilmington, Del., 1973, 1975.

Cook, James H. *Fifty Years on the Old Frontier*. New Haven, Conn., 1923.

Corlett, William Thomas. *The Medicine Man of the American Indian and His Cultural Background*. Springfield, Mass., 1935.

Corn, James Franklin. *Red Clay and Rattlesnake Springs: A History of the Indians of Bradley County, Tennessee*. Cleveland, Tenn., 1976.

Croy, Homer. *He Hanged Them High*. New York, 1952.

Cunningham, Frank. *General Stand Watie's Confederate Indians.* San Antonio, 1959.

Dale, Edward Everett. "Cherokee Strip Live Stock Association." *Chronicles of Oklahoma* 5 (1927): 58-73.

_____. *Cow Country.* Norman, Okla., 1942.

_____. *Frontier Trails.* Boston, 1930.

_____. *The Range Cattle Industry.* Norman, Okla., 1930.

_____, and Litton Gaston, eds. *Cherokee Cavaliers: Forty Years of Cherokee History as Told in the Correspondence of the Ridge-Watie-Boudinot Family.* Norman, Okla., 1939.

Davis, Caroline. "Education of the Chickasaws, 1856-1907." *Chronicles of Oklahoma* 15 (1937): 427-28.

Debo, Angie. *And Still the Waters Run: The Betrayal of the Five Civilized Tribes.* Princeton, N.J., 1940.

_____. "Education in the Choctaw Country after the Civil War." *Chronicles of Oklahoma* 10 (1932): 383-91.

_____. *The Rise and Fall of the Choctaw Republic.* Norman, Okla., 1934.

_____. *The Road to Disappearance.* Norman, Okla., 1941.

_____. "Southern Refugees of the Cherokee Nation." *Southwestern Historical Quarterly* 35 (1932): 255-66.

_____. *Tulsa: From Creek Town to Oil Capital.* Norman, Okla., 1943.

De Rosier, Arthur H., Jr. *The Removal of the Choctaw Indians.* Knoxville, Tenn., 1970.

Doran, Michael F. "Negro Slaves of the Five Civilized Tribes." *Annals of the Association of American Geographers* 68 (1978): 335-50.

Douglas, C. B. *The History of Tulsa.* 3 vols. Tulsa, Okla., 1921.

Doyle, Thomas H. "Single Versus Double Statehood." *Chronicles of Oklahoma* 5 (1927): 18-41, 117-48.

Duncan, Robert Lipscomb. *Reluctant General: The Life and Times of Albert Pike.* New York, 1961.

Ellinger, Charles Wayne. "The Drive for Statehood in Oklahoma, 1889-1906." *Chronicles of Oklahoma* 41 (1963): 15-37.

Fischer, LeRoy. *The Civil War in Indian Territory.* Los Angeles, 1974.

_____, and Kenny Franks. "Confederate Victory at Chusto-Talasah." *Chronicles of Oklahoma* 49 (1971-72): 452-76.

Fogelson, Raymond D. "An Analysis of Cherokee Sorcery and Witchcraft." In *Four Centuries of Southern Indians.* Edited by Charles Hudson. Athens, Ga., 1975.

_____. "The Cherokee Ballgame Cycle: An Ethnographer's View." *Ethnomusicology* 15 (1971): 327-28.

Foreman, Carolyn Thomas. "The Choctaw Academy." *Chronicles of Oklahoma* 6 (1928): 453–80, 10 (1933): 77–114.
_____. "The Light-Horse in Indian Territory." *Chronicles of Oklahoma* 34 (1956): 17–43.
_____. *Park Hill*. Muskogee, Okla., 1948.
Foreman, Grant. *Indian Removal: The Emigration of the Five Civilized tribes of Indians*. Norman, Okla., 1932.
_____. *Muskogee: The Biography of an Oklahoma Town*. Norman, Okla., 1943.
_____. *Sequoyah*. Norman, Okla., 1938.
Franks, Kenny. *Stand Watie and the Agony of the Cherokee Nation*. Memphis, Tenn., 1979.
Gard, Wayne. *The Chisholm Trail*. Norman, Okla., 1954.
_____. *The Great Buffalo Hunt*. New York, 1959.
Gibson, Arrell M. *The Chickasaws*. Norman, Okla., 1971.
_____. "The Cowboy in Indian Territory." In *The Cowboy: Six-Shooters, Songs, and Sex*. Edited by Charles W. Harris and Buck Rainey. Norman, Okla., 1976.
_____. *Wilderness Bonanza: The Tri-State District of Missouri, Kansas, and Oklahoma*. Norman, Okla., 1972.
_____, ed. *America's Exiles: Indian Colonization in Oklahoma*. Oklahoma City, 1976.
Gilbert, William H., Jr. *The Eastern Cherokees*. Bureau of American Ethnology Bulletin, no. 133. Washington , D.C., 1943.
Gittinger, Roy. *The Formation of the State of Oklahoma, 1803–1906*. Norman, Okla., 1939.
Graebner, Norman A. "Cattle Ranching in Eastern Oklahoma." *Chronicles of Oklahoma* 21 (1943): 300–11.
_____. "The Public Land Policy of the Five Civilized Tribes." *Chronicles of Oklahoma* 23 (1945): 107–18.
Graves, Richard A. *Oklahoma Outlaws*. Oklahoma City, 1915.
Greenlee, Robert F. "Medicine and Curing Practices of the Modern Florida Seminole." *American Anthropologist* 46 (1944): 317–28.
Gulick, John. *Cherokees at the Crossroads*. Rev. ed. Chapel Hill, N.C., 1973.
Haas, Mary R. "Creek Inter-Town Relations." *American Anthropologist* 42 (1940): 479–89.
Halliburton, Rudi, Jr. "Northeastern's Seminary Hall." *Chronicles of Oklahoma* 51 (1973–74): 391–98.
_____. *Red Over Black: Black Slavery Among the Cherokee Indians*. Westport, Conn., 1977.

Hamel, Paul B., and Chiltoskey, Mary U. *Cherokee Plants: Their Uses—A 400 Year History*. Sylva, N.C., 1975.

Hawkins, Benjamin. *A Sketch of the Creek Country in the Years 1798 and 1799*. Georgia Historical Association Publications, vol. 3. Americus, Ga., 1938.

Hicks, Hannah. "The Diary of Hannah Hicks." *The American Scene* 13 (1972): 2-24.

Hofsommer, Donovan L., ed. *Railroads in Oklahoma*. Oklahoma City, 1977.

Holden, J. F. "The Story of an Adventure in Railroad Building." *Chronicles of Oklahoma* 11 (1933): 637-66.

Hudson, Charles. "The Cherokee Concept of Natural Balance." *The Indian Historian* 3 (1970): 51-54.

_____. *The Southeastern Indians*. Knoxville, Tenn., 1976.

_____. "Uktena: A Cherokee Anomalous Monster." *Journal of Cherokee Studies* 3 (1978): 62-75.

Johnson, Neil. *The Chickasaw Rancher*. Edited by Arrell M. Gibson. Stillwater, Okla., 1961.

Kappler, Charles J., ed. *Indian Affairs, Laws and Treaties*. 2 vols. Washington, D.C., 1904.

Katz, S. H.; Hediger M.L., and Valeroy, L.A., "Traditional Maize Processing Techniques in the New World." *Science* 184 (1974): 765-73.

Kensall, Lewis. "Reconstruction in the Choctaw Nation." *Chronicles of Oklahoma* 47 (1969): 138-53.

Kilpatrick, Jack Frederick, and Kilpatrick, Anna Gritts. *Run Toward the Nightland: Magic of the Oklahoma Cherokees*. Dallas, 1967.

_____. *Walk in Your Soul: Love Incantations of the Oklahoma Cherokees*. Dallas, 1965.

Lawson, John. *A New Voyage to Carolina*. Edited by Hugh R. Lefler. Chapel Hill, N.C., 1967.

Lewit, Robert. "Indian Missions and Antislavery Sentiments: A Conflict of Evangelical and Humanitarian Ideals." *Mississippi Valley Historical Review* 50 (1963-64): 39-55.

Littlefield, Daniel F., Jr. *Africans and Creeks: From the Colonial Period to the Civil War*. Westport, Conn., 1979.

_____. *Africans and Seminoles: From Removal to Emancipation*. Westport, Conn., 1976.

_____. *The Cherokee Freedmen: From Reconstruction to American Citizenship*. Westport, Conn., 1978.

_____. "Utopian Dreams of the Cherokee Fullbloods: 1890-1930." *Journal of the West* 10 (1971): 404-27.

_____, and Underhill, Lonnie W. "Timber Depredations and Cherokee Legislation, 1869-1881." *Journal of Forest History* 18 (1974): 4-13.

McCoy, Joseph G. *Cattle Trade of the West and Southwest*. Edited by Ralph P. Bieber. Glendale, Calif., 1940.

McKennon, C. G. *Iron Men: A Saga of the Deputy United States Marshals Who Rode the Indian Territory*. Garden City, N.J., 1967.

McLoughlin, William F. "Red Indians, Black Slavery, and White Racism: America's Slaveholding Indians." *American Quarterly* 26 (1974): 367-85.

McReynolds, Edwin C. *Oklahoma: A History of the Sooner State*. Norman, Okla., 1954.

_____. *The Seminoles*. Norman, Okla., 1957.

Mahon, John K. *History of the Second Seminole War, 1835-1842*. Gainesville, Fl., 1967.

Masterson, V. V. *The Katy Railroad and the Last Frontier*. Norman, Okla., 1953.

Maxwell, Amos D. *The Sequoyah Constitutional Convention*. Boston, 1953.

_____. "The Sequoyah Convention." *Chronicles of Oklahoma* 28 (1950): 161-92, 299-340.

Mayhall, Mildred P. *The Kiowas*. Norman, Okla., 1962.

Miner, H. Craig. *The Corporation and the Indian: Tribal Sovereignty and Industrial Civilization in Indian Territory, 1867-1907*. Columbia, Mo., 1976.

_____. "The Struggle for an East-West Railway into the Indian Territory." *Chronicles of Oklahoma* 47 (1969): 560-81.

Mooney, James. "The Cherokee Ball Play." *American Anthropologist* 3 (1890): 105-32.

_____. "Cherokee Theory and Practice of Medicine." *Journal of American Folklore* 3 (1880): 44-50.

_____. *Myths of the Cherokee*. Nineteenth Annual Report of the Bureau of American Ethnology. Washington, D.C., 1900.

_____. *The Sacred Formulas of the Cherokees*. Seventh Annual Report of the Bureau of American Ethnology. Washington, D.C., 1886.

_____, and Olbrechts, Frans M. *The Swimmer Manuscript: Cherokee Sacred Formulas and Medicinal Prescriptions*. Bureau of American Ethnology Bulletin, no. 99. Washington, D.C., 1932.

Morton, Ohland. "Reconstruction in the Creek Nation." *Chronicles of Oklahoma* 9 (1931): 171-79.

Moulton, Gary E. *John Ross, Cherokee Chief*. Athens, Ga., 1978.

Nesbitt, Paul. "J. J. McAlester." *Chronicles of Oklahoma* 11 (1933):758-64.

Nye, Wilbur Sturdevant. *Carbine and Lance: The Story of Old Fort Sill.* Norman, Okla., 1969.

O'Beirne, H. F. *Leaders and Leading Men of the Indian Territory.* Chicago, 1891.

Olbrechts, Frans. "Cherokee Belief and Practice with Regard to Childbirth." *Anthropos* 26 (1931): 17–24.

Peery, Dan W. "Captain David L. Payne." *Chronicles of Oklahoma* 13 (1935): 438–56.

——. "Colonel Crocker and the Boomer Movement." *Chronicles of Oklahoma* 13 (1935): 273–96.

Perdue, Theda. *Slavery and the Evolution of Cherokee Society, 1540–1866.* Knoxville, Tenn., 1979.

Prucha, Francis Paul. *American Indian Policy in the Formative Years: The Indian Trade and Intercourse Acts, 1790–1834.* Lincoln, Neb., 1962.

Rascoe, Burton. *Belle Starr, The Bandit Queen.* New York, 1941.

Rawick, George P., ed. *The American Slave: A Composite Autobiography.* Westport, Conn., 1972.

Reed, Mark. "Reflections on Cherokee Stickball." *Journal of Cherokee Studies* 2 (1977): 195–200.

Reid, John P. *A Law of Blood: The Primitive Law of the Cherokee Nation.* New York, 1970.

Ridings, Sam P. *The Chisholm Trail.* Guthrie, Okla, 1936.

Rister, Carl C. *Land Hunger: David L. Payne and the Boomers.* Norman, Okla., 1942.

——. *The Southwestern Frontier.* Cleveland, 1928.

Roosevelt, Theodore, and Remington, Frederick. *Ranch Life in the Far West.* 1888. Reprint. Flagstaff, 1973.

Rosa, Joseph G., and May, Robin. *Gun Law: A Study of Violence in the Wild West.* Chicago, 1977.

Ruth, Kent, comp. *Oklahoma: A Guide to the Sooner State.* Rev. ed. Norman, 1957.

Ryan, Frederick L. *The Rehabilitation of Oklahoma Coal Mining Communities.* Norman, Okla., 1935.

Savage, William W., Jr. *The Cherokee Strip Live Stock Association.* Columbia, Mo., 1973.

Smith, Geraldine. "The Mont Ballard Case." Master's thesis, University of Oklahoma, 1957.

Speck, Frank G., "The Creek Indians of Taskigi Town." *American Anthropological Association Memoirs* 2 (1907): 101–64.

——, and Broome Leonard, *Cherokee Dance and Drama.* Berkeley, 1951.

Spoehr, Alexander, *Changing Kinship Systems: A Study in the Acculturation of the Creeks, Cherokee, and Choctaw*. Chicago, 1947.

Steen, Carol T. "The Home for the Insane, Deaf, Dumb, and Blind of the Cherokee Nation." *Chronicles of Oklahoma* 21 (1943): 402–19.

Stone, Eric. *Medicine Among the American Indians*. Clio Medica: A Series of Primers on the History of Medicine, vol. 7. New York, 1932.

Strickland, Rennard. *Fire and the Spirits: Cherokee Law from Clan to Court*. Norman, Okla., 1975.

Swanton, John R. *The Indians of the Southeastern United States*. Washington, D.C., 1946.

_____. *Religious Beliefs and Medical Practices of the Creek Indians*. Forty-Second Annual Report of the Bureau of American Ethnology. Washington, D.C., 1928.

_____. *Social Organization and Social Usages of the Indians of the Creek Confederacy*. Forty-Second Annual Report of the Bureau of American Ethnology. Washington, D.C., 1928.

Taylor, Edith Wharton. *Money on the Hoof—Sometimes*. Fort Collins, Col., 1974.

Taylor, Lyda Averill. *Plants Used as Curatives by Certain Southeastern Tribes*. Cambridge, Mass., 1940.

Terrill, Tom W., and Hirsch, Jerold, eds. *Such As Us: Southern Voices of the Thirties*. Chapel Hill, N.C., 1978.

Thomas, Robert K. "The Redbird Smith Movement." In *Symposium on Cherokee and Iroquois Culture*. Edited by William N. Fenton and John Gulick. Bureau of American Ethnology Bulletin, no. 180. Washington, D.C., 1961.

Trachtman, Paul. *The Gunfighters*. New York, 1974.

Trenholm, Virginia Cole. *The Arapahoes, Our People*. Norman, Okla., 1970.

Ulmer, Mary, and Beck, Samuel E. *Cherokee Cooklore*. Cherokee, N.C., 1951.

Vogel, Virgil J. *American Indian Medicine*. Norman, Okla., 1970.

Wahrhaftig, Albert L. "The Tribal Cherokee Population of Oklahoma." *Current Anthropology* 9 (1968): 510–18.

Wallace, Ernest, and Hoebel, Adamson. *The Comanches : Lords of the South Plains*. Norman, Okla., 1952.

Wardell, Morris L. *A Political History of the Cherokee Nation, 1838–1907*. Norman, Okla., 1938.

The War of the Rebellion: A Compilation·of the Official Records of the Union and Confederate Armies. 70 vols. Washington, D.C., 1880–1901.

Warren, Hanna. "Reconstruction in the Cherokee Nation." *Chronicles of Oklahoma* 45 (1967): 180-89.

Washburn, Cephas. *Reminiscences of the Indians*. Richmond, Va., 1869.

Weslager, C. A. *Magic Medicines of the Indians*. Somerset, N.J., 1973.

Wiggenton, Eliot, ed. *The Foxfire Book*. New York, 1972.

Wilkins, Thurman. *Cherokee Tragedy: The Story of the Ridge Family and the Decimation of a People*. New York, 1970.

Williams, Samuel Cole, ed. *Adair's History of the American Indians*. Johnson City, Tenn., 1930.

_____. *Lieut. Henry Timberlake's Memoirs, 1756-1765*. Marietta, Ga., 1948.

Woodward, Grace. *The Cherokees*. Norman, Okla., 1963.

Wright, Muriel H. "American Indian Corn Dishes." *Chronicles of Oklahoma* 36 (1958): 155-66.

_____. "Colonel Cooper's Civil War Report on the Battle of Round Mountain, 1861." *Chronicles of Oklahoma* 27 (1949): 187-206.

Yetman, Norman, ed. *Life Under the Peculiar Institution: Selections from the Slave Narrative Collection*. New York, 1970.

Young, Mary E. *Redskins, Ruffleshirts, and Rednecks: Indian Allotments in Alabama and Mississippi*. Norman, Okla., 1961.

Index